Sir Nige

The Engineer a   *~ Family*

by
Geoffrey Hughes

THE OAKWOOD PRESS

British Library Cataloguing in Publication Data
A Record for this book is available from the British Library
ISBN 0 85361 579 9

Typeset by Oakwood Graphics.
Repro by Ford Graphics, Ringwood, Hants.
Printed by Cambrian Printers Ltd, Aberystwyth, Ceredigion.

Note on the Author

Geoffrey Hughes spent his career in the electrical industry, his work bringing him into contact with all branches of the engineering profession. On retirement, he was able to follow a full time interest in researching and writing about the the life and works of Sir Nigel Gresley and the operations of the London & North Eastern Railway. He is a Chartered Engineer, Fellow of the Institution of Electrical Engineers, and Member of the Chartered Institute of Transport; he was awarded a Doctorate at the London School of Economics for his thesis 'An Economic History of the LNER'. He is a Vice-President of the Gresley Society, President of the LNER Study Group, and member of a number of railway historical societies.

He has written several books and articles on his chosen subject, and lives on the South Coast with his wife, Rose Mary, who, he says 'Is always the last to read a draft, as she can spot the hidden errors better than I can'. They have family in the West Country and Australia.

Front cover, top: Portrait of Sir Nigel Gresley by William Brealey, commissioned by his family in 1936. *Tim Godfrey*

Front cover, bottom: A commercial postcard of Gresley Pacific No. 4472 *Flying Scotsman*. *John Alsop Collection*

Rear cover: Portrait of Sir Nigel Gresley by William Brealey, commissioned by the Institution of Mechanical Engineers in 1936. *Institution of Mechanical Engineers*

Title page: Several shots were taken by commercial photographers of the immaculate line-up of Pacifics heading trains out of King's Cross around 10 am on a summer weekday morning. Here are Nos. 4473 *Solario*, 2551 *Prince Palatine*, 2580 *Shotover* heading the 'Flying Scotsman', and a fourth unfortunately not identifiable. *F. Moore's Railway Photographs*

Published by The Oakwood Press (Usk), P.O. Box 13, Usk, Mon., NP15 1YS.
E-mail: oakwood-press@dial.pipex.com
Website: www.oakwood-press.dial.pipex.com

Contents

The Gresley Family at the time of their parents' Silver Wedding in 1926. Marjorie, Nigel, Roger and Violet are standing either side of their father, Herbert Nigel, with their mother, Ethel Frances, seated.
Tim Godfrey

Foreword

The book *Sir Nigel Gresley: the Engineer and his Family* tells the private story of a public man. Sir Herbert Nigel Gresley (1876-1941) was a railway mechanical engineer of the highest order. From the first, his career brought him into contact with the great railwaymen of his day, Francis Webb, John Aspinall and G.J.Churchward. As Chief Mechanical Engineer to the London & North Eastern Railway - the company was his home from 1923 - Gresley established himself as every inch the equal of the great names of the past.

Gresley's chief qualities, I believe, were his professional grasp and leadership. At the height of his powers, he commanded *hundreds of thousands* of items of rolling stock and yet personally approved design changes to this wide range of equipment. His outlook was international. The collaborative relationship he enjoyed with his great French contemporary, André Chapelon, led to radical improvements in locomotive power and efficiency.

Naturally, it is the locomotives that are the most eye-catching results of Gresley's ingenuity. The streamlined *Mallard* captured the world record for steam traction in 1938 and this Pacific-type machine can still be seen and enjoyed at the National Railway Museum, York. The 'Silver Jubilee' had introduced a regular 71 mph service to Darlington on the London-Newcastle route from the early Thirties; the average to Newcastle including the Darlington stop was 67 mph. It is typical of Gresley's more discrete shepherding of his design team, that LNER passengers could enjoy ride comfort as well as speed, and that all-electric restaurant cars would ensure a good breakfast as the scenery flashed by.

Being the former Board Member of British Rail responsible for engineering, I have had considerable involvement in seeing these activities transferred back to the private sector. There are many who have believed we are now entering a new golden age for railways. It would be wonderful if today's engineers could emulate some of the successes of Gresley, particularly in delivering safe and improved services to the customer.

My own Presidential Address for the Institution of Mechanical Engineers, follows in Sir Nigel's footsteps. His speeches before the Institution were magisterial, encompassing more than 30 years of railway development. These technical achievements are reviewed in the later chapters of this book. It may be supposed that Gresley's engineering is too well known to be recounted again. However, I am reminded that on his death, Sir Nigel Gresley did not merit an entry in our collected national memorial, *The Dictionary of National Biography*. The inexplicable omission has since been rectified, in keeping with Oliver Bulleid's assessment that 'He ranks with our greatest locomotive engineers'.

Dr Geoffrey Hughes' book also deals with the more personal aspects of Gresley's life and the great man's antecedents. It is the story of the making of an engineer whose character, while demanding of excellence, inspired great loyalty among his staff. This included Bulleid, quoted here, who was his long time personal assistant. That such affection survives the sixty years after Gresley's death is evidenced by the continued work of the Gresley Society. Like this volume, it is a fine tribute to Sir Nigel, and a measure of the man.

A.D. Roche BSc FREng CEng FIMechE
President, The Institution of Mechanical Engineers

Classic Gresley Pacific No. 4474 *Victor Wild* was a favourite on the Great Northern main line for much of the LNER period. Here seen at Potters Bar in July 1934 heading the 4 pm from King's Cross. This is Reg Batten's first railway photograph.   *R.E. Batten*

Introduction

'Everything in life from marriage to manslaughter turns on the speed and cost at which men, things and thoughts, can be shifted from one place to another.'

(Rudyard Kipling, quoted by Sir John Aspinall in the Thomas Hawksley Lecture at the Institution of Mechanical Engineers, 1925)

It was in 1928 when my interest was first aroused in the Gresley story. A friend had introduced me to the joys of locospotting, and we were sitting on the wooden fence near Oakleigh Park station when this beautiful green engine passed slowly by. *Grand Parade*, no less, proceeding gently up to Top Shed, King's Cross, brand new from Doncaster Plant. First impressions stick: if my parents had lived in Bushey, or Acton, or Woking, things might have turned out differently. But we lived in Barnet, within sound of the East Coast main line, and from this initial appreciation, acquaintance grew. I read Cecil J. Allen's articles in the *Meccano Magazine* - uncritical, as things were in those days - but as I learned about Nigel Gresley's part in the development of the steam locomotive, so my admiration blossomed into a determination to find out more about the man, his machines, and his family.

All this took many years. In the thirties I discovered other interests. I left school, started work, and for six years was a soldier. Then, the exigencies of earning a living in the electrical industry left me with little time to pursue the Gresley story, until lessening business pressure offered the opportunity to pick up the threads again. So, gradually, from reading, exploring research sources, and most importantly, acquaintance with railwaymen who had been close to the great man himself, as well as with his immediate family, the story began to be assembled. Moreover, since I learned that not only did a remote ancestor accompany Duke William on his invasion of England in 1066, and that another repaid the compliment by fighting the French at Agincourt, clearly there is more family history to be recounted than merely the facts of Nigel Gresley's own life. So, the narrative begins at Toesni, in Normandy, before the end of the first millennium, and continues through the next thousand years. It has not been concluded yet, despite the severe inroads which have been made into the Gresley family in the 20th century.

The quality and range of the Gresley locomotives have placed Sir Nigel as a leader among British engineers. Yet, with his predilection for building large engines, who knows what further masterpieces he might have produced, even though constrained by the limitations of the British loading gauge? So I have attempted not just to catalogue his achievements, but also with the benefit of hindsight offer a qualified assessment of his work - not, perhaps so much in technical detail as in broad principles. Fortunately, we have a substantial and active body of railwaymen and enthusiasts intent on keeping alive the Gresley tradition, a great deal of relevant literature, and several of his locomotives and coaches, painstakingly restored. Some are in working order, so that the smell of steam and hot oil, and the sound of the Gresley beat, will be with us for many years yet, for future generations to savour and admire. Locomotives bearing splendid names such as *Sir Nigel Gresley, Flying Scotsman, Mallard, Green Arrow* and *The Great Marquess,* as well a workaday suburban tank locomotive familiar to generations of King's Cross commuters, class 'N2' No. 4744, remain as a permanent memorial.

Several of my correspondents have adjured me to 'stick to the facts and ignore the mythology'. Well, I hope that I have provided a factual, as well as a full account, so far as is possible, although a fair amount of comment is necessarily included as well. A difficulty in some instances is deciding what is factual and what is not. Contemporary written material may not be entirely accurate, but if one does not have access to personal recollections, this - and other biographies - would be colourless indeed. Railwaymen are great raconteurs; to what extent do their memories play tricks, or are subject to omission or embroidery?

Such source material forms the contents of several books, and scores of articles, which have been written about the man and his achievements. Indeed, I have contributed to these myself, including *The Gresley Influence*, *LNER*, *LNER 4-6-0s at Work*, and editorship for several years of *The Gresley Observer*, the journal of the Gresley Society. Less has been written about the family, although the years down to the end of the 19th century are covered in masterly detail by Falconer Madan, in his epic chronology *The Gresleys of Drakelowe,* and in which our Sir Nigel earns a brief mention, at the very end. So I offer this study, albeit with some diffidence, but with the knowledge that it will break new ground, not only in the history of the unique family of Gresley, but also, following recent research, a fresh review of the outstanding contribution to mechanical engineering made by Sir Nigel Gresley.

More Faithful than Fortunate

In what old story far away,
In what great action is enshrined,
The sad sweet motto which today
Around the Gresley's name is twined?

Was it for country or for crown
They played a grand tho' tragic part?
Or did they lay their fortune down
To strive to win one careless heart?

We cannot tell: but this we know,
That they who chose in that dim past
Those noble words - come weal come woe -
Stood by them stedfast to the last.

And this we feel, when deep in dust
Lie earthly hopes and and wordly state,
In that fair land where all is just,
The *Faithful* will be *Fortunate.*

Florence Severne, 1889

The motto of the Gresleys is '*Meliore Fide quam Fortuna*', which translates as 'More Faithful than Fortunate'.

Chapter One

The Gresley Dynasty

In the years following William the Conqueror's invasion of England, many thousands of Normans came to England as settlers, but no more than 6,000 fighting men supported the Duke at his landing in Pevensey Bay on 28th September, 1066. Several families can trace their origins back to the later immigrants, but few can claim that their ancestors actually accompanied the Conqueror on the invasion. L.G. Pine, for many years the editor of *Burke's Peerage*, concluded that among those whose pedigree can be derived from this select band are the Gresleys, whose remote ancestors, Ralph and Robert de Toeni, were present on that eventful day. Today, the best known of this distinguished family is Sir Nigel Gresley, 1876-1941, Chief Mechanical Engineer (CME) of the London & North Eastern Railway (LNER) 1923-1941, and President of the Institution of Mechanical Engineers in 1936.

Sir Bernard Burke and Horace Round, the authorities on Norman genealogy, consider that the Gresley line can be traced back still further. The father of Ralph and Robert de Toeni was Roger, Baron of Toeni and Conches, whose ancestor was Hugh de Calvacamp, archbishop of Rouen in the 10th century. Hugh is said to have been descended from Malahultis, uncle of Rollo, a Viking, who obtained possession of the Duchy of Normandy in about 911. So there is the possibility of the Gresley pedigree reaching back to the mists of Norse mythology, through Ivar, Jarl of the Uplanders, to Fornjot, King of Finland.

The de Toenis derived their name from a village in Normandy, the present Tosny, which lies on the left bank of the Seine, about 25 miles south-east of Rouen. Conches is in the same area, not far from Evreux. The family were hereditary standard bearers to the Duke, but Ralph preferred to take part in the fighting, rather than carry the standard, and William agreed to his request. After the victory, the brothers were well rewarded for their services. Ralph was granted manors in Norfolk and became the forbear of the Clifford family, whilst Robert was presented with lordships in Derby, Leicester and Stafford, adopting the surname 'de Stafford'. He married Avice, daughter of the Earl of Clare, and his younger brother, or perhaps his son, Nigel is mentioned in the Domesday Book as holding, among others, the manor of Drakelowe in Derbyshire, from which the Anglo-Saxon Elric had been ousted. (In this context, a 'manor' relates to an extensive estate, rather than a house or a village.)

A generation later, Nigel's son William established himself at Gresley, five miles south-east of Burton on Trent, but still within the manor of Drakelowe. The de Staffords evidently were obligated to the Crown for their possessions, as Drakelowe was 'held of King John by an annual rent of a bow, a quiver, and twelve arrows'. They also built a motte-and-bailey castle at Gresley, but this appears to have been abandoned by the year 1250, although the mound of the castle still remains, and is known today as the Castle Knob. William also founded the Priory of St Mary and St George, about a mile east of the castle. This was to suffer severely at the hands of Henry VIII in his dissolution of the monasteries, after which it was left to decay, except for the priory church, which became the parish church of Castle Gresley. Three alternative derivations are suggested for the name 'Gresley'. In the old Norman-French, 'Gresle' was the name given to a person who suffered from a noticeably pockmarked face, while 'groesa' indicated a wood - or, in contradiction - a clearing. However, the simple English 'grassy lea' may offer the best explanation. So, the family took their name from the locality, and became known as 'de Gresley' in preference to 'de Stafford'.

Around the year 1090 Drakelowe suffered a 'visitation', in which the dead were said to have risen from their graves. This became known as the Devil of Drakelowe, and was probably a form of plague, from which the terror-stricken inhabitants fled. However, by the end of the following century the family had firmly established themselves at Drakelowe, and this was to be their principal seat for over 700 years, until, after suffering replacement and rebuilding, the mansion was sold, and finally demolished in 1936.

The first of the de Gresleys to be knighted was Sir Geoffrey, c.1245-1305, and others followed, as for example Sir Thomas de Gresley, who was member of Parliament for the county of Derby in the reigns of Henry IV and Henry V. Others were Sir George, knighted by Henry VIII at the coronation of Anne Boleyn, and Sir William, similarly honoured at the accession to the throne of Queen Mary. As another Royal favour, the second Sir Geoffrey was granted the right to erect a gallows at Drakelowe for the execution of felons. By the time of the Wars of the Roses, the family name had become simplified to 'Gresley'. They were resolute supporters of the Lancastrian cause, and provided troops for Henry V's adventures in France, the Sir Thomas of the time being among those fighting at Agincourt. His daughter Jane was appointed nurse to the infant Henry VI, and when she retired was awarded a pension of £40 a year. Her successor was given permission by the Privy Council to 'chastise the child from time to time as the case may be'. To have spanked the King without such permission would have been a treasonable offence.

It should be noted that there may be some confusion concerning descendants of Roger de Poitiers, who received lands 'between the Ribble and the Mersey'; later members of this family inherited the manor of Manchester. They bore the name Grelle, which was sometimes rendered Gresley. Roger de Grelle was one of the barons in attendance at the granting of Magna Carta at Runnymede in 1215; the barony became extinct a hundred years later. They were not however closely related to the Gresleys who were descendants of the de Toenis.

Most of the de Gresleys were shadowy figures, but enough has been written about them to provide evidence that they were a hot blooded lot, although perhaps no more so than many of their kind, in a turbulent age. For example, in 1293, a William de Gresley was outlawed for murder, a crime exceeded by a later Robert, who after four murders joined the army fighting the Scots. He performed so well that he received a free pardon. Joanna, widow of Sir Peter, was a doughty lady, and twice was charged for murder, on one occasion horsewhipping a man to death. She was acquitted on both charges. And, in a dispute over an inheritance, when John de Gresley was in residence at Drakelowe around the early 1400s, his grandson rode in with a band of armed men, and carried off a great deal of booty.

In 1611, James I created the order of baronets as we know it today, holders of the title being in a midway position between a peer and a knight. The title is hereditary, but a baronet does not sit in the House of Lords. The order was established to finance a scheme to encourage settlement in Ulster, by emigration from England and Scotland. It provided for the creation of 200 baronets, all to be from good families, in return for the obligation to meet the cost of 30 footmen for three years at a rate of eightpence a day; Sir George Gresley was the 28th baronet to be so created. He was one of the few of his kind who supported the Parliamentary cause in the Civil War, but despite this his family retained most of their possessions after the Restoration.

Once the baronetcy was established, the Gresleys appear in more detail, and they include some fascinating characters. A few emigrated to distant places, and the name is to be found in Australia, where a William Gresley was murdered in Bendigo, Victoria, in 1852. Canada, South Africa and the United States also have their Gresleys. Among the most common Christian names were Geoffrey, John, Richard, Robert and Roger, while Falconer Madan, in *The Gresleys of Drakelowe*, records 18 Nigels, from Nigel de Toeni, to Herbert Nigel, the subject of this book. Marriage introduced a number of surnames which became adopted as Christian names, such as Bowyer, Stukeley, and Walsingham. The most prolific Gresley was no doubt one William (not closely related to the main line), who lived in the late 18th and early 19th centuries, and who is commemorated in St Peter's Church in Marlborough. He was Master of a flourishing school situated on the south side of the High Street of that town, (not to be confused with Marlborough College). His pupils helped to cut the white horse on the side of nearby Granham Hill. William Gresley's wife was Mary Davis, daughter of a noncomformist minister, who surely deserves a mention in some book of records, as she presented her husband with no less than 28 children, eight of whom were named Nigel. Few of her family survived, and the grief of the parents can be imagined, as one child after another died in infancy. Following his wife's death, William married again, but this second marriage failed to bear fruit.

The first baronet to bear the name Nigel (1725-1787) was the sixth in the line, and on completion of his education took a commission in the Royal Navy. His most important duty was the capture of Flora Macdonald on her flight from Scotland to France after her association with Charles Stewart, the Young Pretender, and conveying her to London under guard. He must have treated her with the utmost correctitude, as she presented him with a miniature of herself, 'for his great courtesy to her'. Lieutenant Nigel Gresley also earns a mention in N.A.M. Rodgers' *The Wooden World: an Anatomy of the Georgian Navy*, in which he found himself in a tricky situation. He had a vote in the constituency of the Borough of Lichfield; should he exercise this in favour of his brother, or the candidate of Lord Anson, his sponsor in the Navy? His decision is not known, but he was unable to complete his Naval career, as in 1753 his elder brother, Sir Thomas, died from smallpox, and Nigel succeeded to the title.

This Sir Nigel was to leave a mark on the engineering of the period, becoming a patron of James Brindley, the pioneer in canal construction and builder of

Sir Nigel Bowyer Gresley, the Seventh Baronet.   *Tim Godfrey*

pumping engines. Together with his eldest son, who as Sir Nigel Bowyer Gresley succeeded to the title in 1787, Sir Nigel obtained Parliamentary powers to cut a canal linking the Gresley colliery at Apedale to a point near Newcastle-under-Lyme, so providing the inhabitants with coal at 5s. 6d. a ton. (An inn at nearby Alsagers Bank is called the 'Gresley Arms', presumably dating from those days.) The canal provided many years of useful service, but it passed out of Gresley ownership some 50 years after its construction. It became disused, and the bed was eventually sold off piecemeal. Sir Nigel is fulsomely remembered in the contemporary *Gentleman's Magazine*. 'He was a kind husband, a tender father, a zealous friend and a helpful neighbour. He is succeeded by his only son, and represented by numerous and beautiful offspring of lovely daughters.' Madan records several anecdotes about him; he was evidently very portly and could only enter his pew at Netherseale church by stepping sideways.

Sir Nigel Bowyer Gresley, the seventh in line, was educated at Manchester Grammar School, and followed his father's interests in industrial matters. These included iron and pottery works on the Drakelowe estate, while in 1795, a fine quality porcelain factory was established at Church Gresley, the product being known as 'Gresley China'. However, the enterprise proved unprofitable, and was sold in 1825. Surviving pieces have acquired antique status. Sir Nigel Bowyer Gresley is commemorated by a plaque in Bath Abbey, which mentions his descent from Rollo of Normandy, and pays tribute to his 'elegance of manners'. Incidentally, although there is no extensive history of the Gresleys in Freemasonry, Sir Nigel Bowyer is on record as having been Master of the Friendly Brothers Lodge at Newcastle-under-Lyme. There is also a plaque to his second wife, Dame Maria Eliza, in the Parish Church at Ledbury, Herefordshire

An interesting vignette of the period has survived in a letter from a Miss Anna Seward, who composed 13 couplets in an expression of regret that she was unable to accept an invitation to a masked ball at Drakelowe on 20th December, 1793. This includes the following unwitting prediction of a future Sir Nigel's railway prowess:

> Ah! Gresley, skill'd to deck the festal rite
> With Taste's coy art and Fancy's various light.
> Soon when those Powers shall lead the frolic *train*
> Beneath the splendo'r of their chosen Fane.*

The female Gresleys of the period were not without their personalities. One Dorothy, a daughter of Sir Thomas, the second baronet, was born at Drakelowe in 1655, and at the age of 16 fell in love with a servant, Thomas Ward. When her parents found out, Ward was instantly dismissed, whereupon Dorothy left home at 1 am, and was married to him at Tutbury the following morning. (Tutbury being 10 miles from Drakelowe, they must have made good progress along the dark roads through the night.) Her mother's will indicated that she never forgave her daughter, but nevertheless the marriage lasted until Dorothy was widowed in 1713, over 40 years later.

The mother of the eighth baronet, Sir Roger Gresley (although for some reason he adopted the spelling Greisley) was a formidable lady. Her son was

---

* The italics are mine. For those unacquainted with late eighteenth century verse, a 'fane' is a 'temple'.

only eight when he succeeded to the title, and he was made a Ward of Court. The trustees wanted to send him to Westminster for his schooling, but she insisted 'with much tartness and eccentricity' that he should be educated at home, and she got her way. Some years later, when Sir Roger fell in love with Lady Sophia Coventry, Lady Gresley was fiercely opposed to the marriage, and wrote to the girl's mother saying that 'as the parties are so young, intercourse between the families should be suspended until her son was better able to exercise his judgement'. Not surprisingly, Lady Coventry did not take kindly to this reflection on her daughter, and relations were broken off. The marriage eventually took place when Sir Roger became of age, but Lady Gresley chose not to be present. The couple's only child, a daughter, did not survive infancy.

Sir Roger lived extravagantly, and was a heavy gambler, such that he was forced to sell a large portion of his estates. This led to a well publicised lawsuit against his business manager, who appears to have swindled him out of much of his fortune. However, he was well regarded, as illustrated by Thomas Lilley's poem of 13 stanzas following Sir Roger's death at the age of 38; he had suffered fatal injuries after a fall from his horse.

> He's gone, the Scion of an Ancient House,
> Forever gone, regretted and esteemed,
> Struck to the earth in manhood's active prime
> Ere yet his fame its meridian beamed.

A surprising number of Gresleys took Holy Orders, including no fewer than five who were successive rectors of the parish of St Peter, Netherseale, some eight miles south of Drakelowe (*see page 20*). The locality was originally known as Seile, later to be divided into Overseale and Netherseale. 'Seale' (or 'Seile') is the Anglo-Saxon word for 'willow', hence Seale was the village of the willows. The current official spelling omits the final 'e', but both forms are in use. The Church dates back at least to the 13th century, and was restored in the Victorian fashion in the 1870s; the original rectory, now converted into two houses, is just across the road. The Seales are in farming country, but they lie on the South Derbyshire coalfield. Netherseale Colliery was sunk in 1855, and ceased production in 1947. Before the war, over 500 persons were employed there.

The first of this memorable quintet of rectors of Netherseale was the Revd Thomas Gresley, the incumbent from 1759 to 1785. He was followed by his son, the Revd William Gresley, who in turn was father of the Revd Sir William Nigel Gresley. He not only became the third Gresley rector, but succeeded to the baronetcy. Finally, the fourth and fifth of the sequence were the Revd John Morewood Gresley, younger son of the Revd William, followed by the second son of the Revd Sir William Nigel, the Revd Nigel, who was named after his father. He died in 1897, ending an uninterrupted period of 136 years of Gresley incumbency at Netherseale. He left a family of five, the youngest of whom was Herbert Nigel, the subject of this book.

The third of the five Netherseale rectors, the Revd Sir William Nigel, occupies an important position in the family tree. He was born in 1806 and ordained in 1830, in which year he followed his father as rector. He married a Norfolk lady, Georgina Reid, in Lichfield Cathedral in 1831, and succeeded to the title in 1837.

However, he suffered a breakdown in health and died in 1847, when he was 41. He managed to combine the duties of a parson with those of a country squire, who was devoted to his parishioners, but also enjoyed following the hunt. Madan tells of a man much beloved, 'of extremely high spirits'. He lived at Netherseale Hall, where all his nine children were born. After his death, his widow, Lady Georgina, moved to a house in Dunstall Road, Barton Under Needwood, which still stands; she lived into the new century, and died in 1904. The eldest son, Thomas, succeeded to the baronetcy, and there were five daughters, only one of whom married. Two other sons remained bachelors. One of them, William Lee Gresley, a member of the Free Foresters cricket club, and an officer in the militia, possessed an interest in science, but was epileptic. In a tragic accident in 1888 he fell into the fire in his workshop, suffering such severe burns to his hand that it had to be amputated, but the effects were so grave that he died soon afterwards.

A further Gresley cleric was yet another William, 1801-1876, who for a time was curate at St Chad's, Lichfield, and who was later at St Paul's, Brighton, and All Saints, Boyne Hill, near Maidenhead. An eminent High Churchman, he was a prolific author of tracts and longer works, with severely dogmatic themes running through them. He attracted the attention of the editor of *Punch*, who gave him a gentle ribbing in the issue of 4th September, 1858. It is a sad comment to observe that when Madan's history of the family was published at the end of the 19th century, the list of subscribers included six Gresleys who had taken the cloth, as well as two more who possessed 'Gresley' as a Christian name. Today's *Crockford's* lists none at all.

An intrinsic part of the Gresley story is the family seat of Drakelowe. The name was first recorded in 942, as Dracan Howe, the Dragon's Mound. The site had been occupied for many years before then, as evidenced by a jar dating from the sixth century having been found there. Details of its early history are vague, and like most great houses it was altered and enlarged according to the taste of individual owners. Parts are said to have been Elizabethan, and much was rebuilt by Sir William, the fourth baronet, in 1723, this date appearing on the lead rain pipe headers. Sir Roger, the eighth baronet, remodelled the West front, and in 1830 added a new wing, incorporating a billiard room, richly decorated with heraldic stained glass.

Although the house remained in the ownership of the family, there was a gap in occupation by the Gresleys after the death of Sir Roger in 1837. His widow, Lady Sophia, had a life tenancy, and married as her second husband Sir Henry des Voeux, who took up residence with her there. On her death in 1875, the title passed to Sir Robert, the 11th baronet, but as he was a minor, Drakelowe was let to John Gretton, of the well-known Burton brewing family; on Sir Robert's coming of age, the Gresleys resumed occupation. He made an important marriage, to Lady Frances Spencer Churchill, daughter of the Duke of Marlborough, and aunt of Sir Winston Churchill. In 1902, Sir Robert built the terraces, which still remain, but his lifestyle involved him in heavy financial losses, and he was forced to give up Drakelowe. In contrast to Sir Robert's profligacy, his father, Sir Thomas, the 10th baronet, was reputed to be a miser, and to have hidden large sums of gold and silver in the house. No doubt Sir Robert searched high and low, but nothing was found to restore his fortunes.

The Gresley Family

Abridged tree showing relationship between Sir Nigel, Knight, and Sir Nigel, 12th Baronet

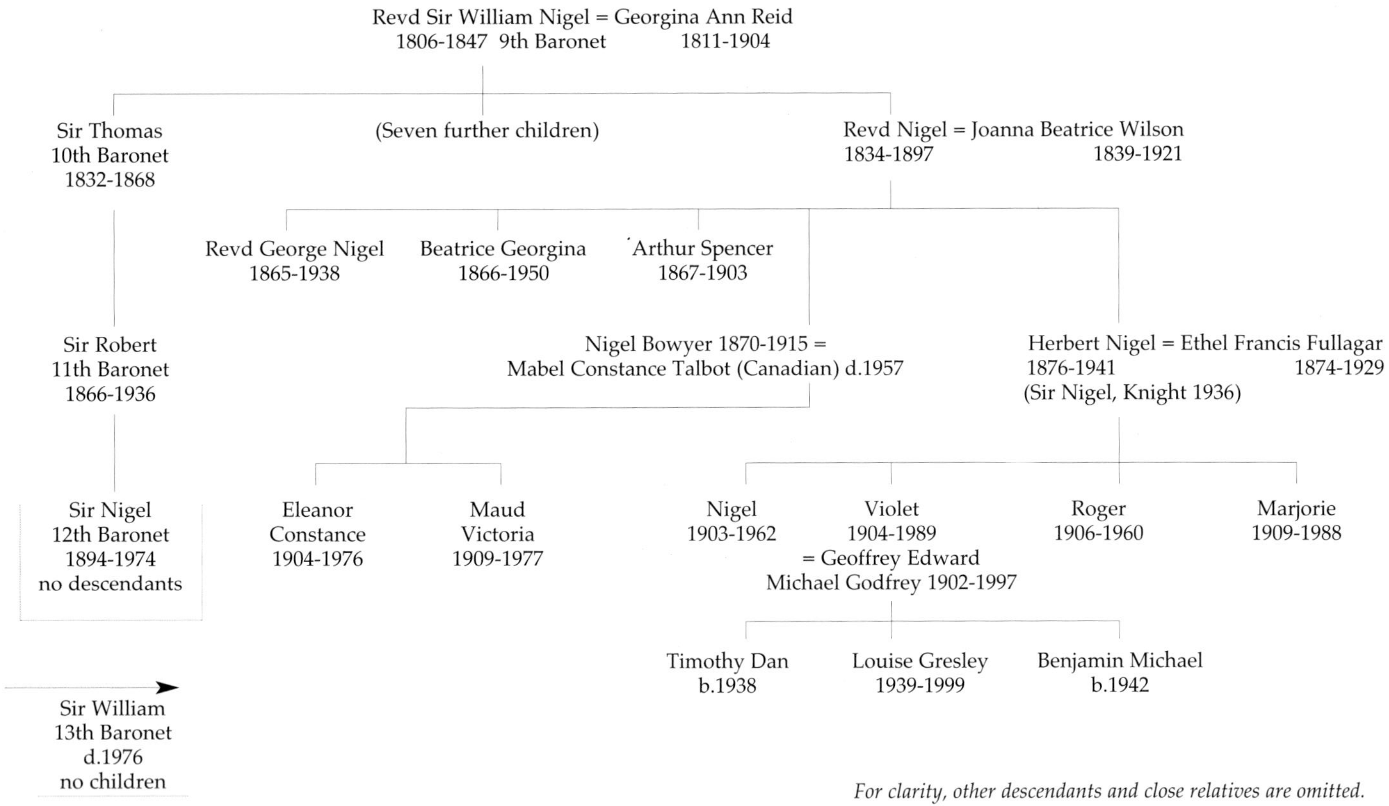

Revd Sir William Nigel = Georgina Ann Reid
1806-1847 9th Baronet   1811-1904

(Seven further children)

Revd Nigel = Joanna Beatrice Wilson
1834-1897   1839-1921

Sir Thomas
10th Baronet
1832-1868

Revd George Nigel
1865-1938

Beatrice Georgina
1866-1950

Arthur Spencer
1867-1903

Herbert Nigel = Ethel Francis Fullagar
1876-1941   1874-1929
(Sir Nigel, Knight 1936)

Sir Robert
11th Baronet
1866-1936

Nigel Bowyer 1870-1915 =
Mabel Constance Talbot (Canadian) d.1957

Eleanor
Constance
1904-1976

Maud
Victoria
1909-1977

Nigel
1903-1962

Violet
1904-1989
= Geoffrey Edward
Michael Godfrey 1902-1997

Roger
1906-1960

Marjorie
1909-1988

Sir Nigel
12th Baronet
1894-1974
no descendants

Timothy Dan
b.1938

Louise Gresley
1939-1999

Benjamin Michael
b.1942

Sir William
13th Baronet
d.1976
no children

For clarity, other descendants and close relatives are omitted.

Drakelowe Hall *c.*1900.   *Penelope Rigby-Hall*

The sale of the contents took place in 1933, and Christie's catalogue reveals a treasure trove of antiques. This included items of immense historical value, including portraits of the Gresleys from the 16th to the 19th century, and the Gresley Jewel, a 16th century pendant given by Queen Elizabeth I as a wedding present to Catherine Sutton, on her marriage to the Sir George of the time. In whose possession is this now, I wonder? And where, too, is the 'Bible at Drakelowe', a prime source of reference by Madan?

Attempts were made to convert the mansion into a country club, with a motor racing circuit, but the times were not propitious, and the house was demolished in 1936, the sale 'of the manor' being reported to have fetched £12,500. One of the features of the house was the painted dining room, the walls of which were decorated to create the illusion that the visitor was not inside a room but out in the countryside. A section of this was saved, and can be seen in the Victoria and Albert Museum, but the only other known relic of the house is a set of 17th century choir stalls in the parish church of St George and St Mary, Church Gresley. In 1948, Drakelowe's position on the bank of the River Trent led to the site being compulsorily purchased for a large coal-fired electricity power station, for which substantial water supplies are needed. It is now owned by an American company, Texas Utilities.

Finally, the Gresley name is not unknown in fiction. Mary Gresley is the heroine of a short story by Anthony Trollope, and Lord Alfred Gresley is a character in *Sir Harry Hotspur*, in which he is portrayed as a 'dull, rejected suitor' - unlike most of the real family, it would seem. Trollope took the name from his maternal grandmother, who was a Gresley, from Derbyshire.

Revd Nigel Gresley, with groom Joseph, donkey Jimmy, spaniel Sam *c.*1892.   *Tim Godfrey*

The Old Rectory, Netherseale in 1990.   *Gresley Society Trust*

Chapter Two

The Victorians

The Revd Nigel Gresley, the last of the five Gresley rectors of Netherseale, married Joanna Beatrice Wilson in 1864. She was the fourth and youngest daughter of John Wilson, gentleman, of Barton Under Needwood, near Burton on Trent, and his wife Catharine Ann. Joanna never knew her father, who died of 'apoplexy' the day before her birth, in 1839. Nevertheless, the family were comfortably off, and the household employed a number of servants, including a coachman for their brougham. Catharine Wilson lived in Barton until her death in 1872. Her house was close by that of the Dowager Lady (Georgina) Gresley, and it would be nice to think that Lady Gresley was instrumental in introducing the Revd Nigel to the Wilson family. Joanna, the mother of the man who was to become Sir Herbert Nigel, was an accomplished lady. She had ability as an artist, exhibiting at Nottingham in 1903, as well as an author, composing a very readable account of her home village, entitled *Netherseale Past and Present*. (It would have been appropriate to have reproduced a photograph of her, but one has not been traced, even among the family records.)

The Revd Nigel was educated at Rossall and Trinity College Cambridge, and his interests went beyond the spiritual, as he showed a considerable aptitude for science. Indeed, it has been said that he wrote studies of scientific topics, although no record can be found of these in the archives of local societies such as the Leicester Literary and Philosophical Society. His eyesight had been badly damaged as a result of a chemistry experiment which went wrong, and this disability was coupled with an increasing paralysis over a period of 20 years, although his mind remained alert. He took *The Times* and *Hansard*, which were read to him by a person from the village school, and he enjoyed playing the cornet and the flute. He kept up his parochial duties so far as he was able, visiting parishioners in a wheelchair drawn by a white donkey, accompanied by his groom Joseph and a pet spaniel named Sam. He is recalled as a gentle old man, with a white beard. In his later years, until his death in 1897, he was taken to church in a bathchair, the pastoral care being mainly in the hands of his curates, one of whom was a Revd Ernest Aspinall. (It is intriguing to think that he may have been related to Herbert Nigel's later chief, Sir John Aspinall.)

One of the Revd Nigel's lasting memorials is the Gresley Oak, growing in a plot of land used as a graveyard, just down the road from Netherseale Church. Here, in 1869 he planted a sapling (described on the plaque as a 'granddaughter') from the Boscobel Oak, in which Charles II was reputed to have hidden during the English Civil War. Possibly the connection with Boscabel arose from the portrait of Flora Macdonald, presented to Lieutenant Nigel Gresley, and later displayed at Drakelowe. The graveyard is also the resting place of the Revd Nigel and Joanna, as well as of their son, Sir Nigel, his wife Ethel, and other near relatives.

The Revd Nigel had five children. The eldest, born in 1865 and christened George Nigel, followed his father into the Church, and became vicar of Horsley Woodhouse, five miles north of Derby. The tradition at St Peter's Netherseale

Above: St Peter's Church, Netherseale *c.*1895, painted by Beatrice Gresley. *Gresley Society Trust*

Right: Desk in St Peter's Church, Netherseale, made by Nigel Gresley.
          Geoffrey Hughes, Gresley Society Trust

The Five Gresley Rectors of Seile (Netherseal(e))

Thomas Gresley 1734-1785
          Rector 1759-1785, second cousin of 5th and 6th Bts

William Gresley 1760-1829
     Rector 1785-1829, third cousin of 7th Bt, father of 9th Bt

Sir William Gresley 1806-1847
          Rector 1830-1847, 9th Bt, son of William above

John Morewood Gresley 1806-1866
          Curate at Seile 1841-1847 and 1860-1863,
                         Rector 1847-1860

Nigel Gresley 1834-1897
          Rector 1860-1897, father of Sir Herbert Nigel

had been one of High Church inclinations, and it is possible that this prompted the Revd George Nigel to have misgivings about his faith. Anyway, some time after his father's death, he resigned his living and went to stay with his mother, who had left the rectory in Netherseale for a house known as 'Green Bank', in the village of Turnditch, near Belper. Following the death of his mother in 1921, he spent some time in Rome, and was converted to Roman Catholicism. This period was said to have been the happiest of his life. Later he was appointed to the Parish of Halstead, in Essex, where he is still remembered with affection. On his death in 1937, he left instructions for a Requiem Mass to be said in his memory, and for a meal, with wine. This has been recalled as 'quite a party'.

The year after George's birth, the Netherseale rectory saw the arrival of the only girl of the marriage, Beatrice Georgina. From all accounts, she grew up to be a hearty lady who enjoyed country life, including fox hunting; after her father's death she joined her mother at Turnditch. She too was an accomplished artist, one of her paintings being a water colour of Netherseale Church, dated 1894, and as fresh today as when it was painted. Later she shared a house with her brother at Halstead, but never married. She died in 1950.

The next Gresley children were two further sons. The first, Arthur Spencer, was a partner in a Liverpool firm of cornbrokers, Gresley & Utermarck. He remained a bachelor, but suffered from tuberculosis. Despite taking sea voyages and spending time in Switzerland, he died in 1903. His brother, Nigel Bowyer, emigrated to Vancouver, where he joined the Bank of Canada. He married a local girl, Mabel Talbot, the couple having two daughters, Eleanor and Maud. One of the grandchildren was given 'Gresley' as a Christian name. However, Nigel Bowyer evidently had health problems as well, as he and Mabel returned to England. He died at Doncaster in 1915, after spending some time with his mother, Joanna, at Turnditch.

The four earliest children of the Revd Nigel and Joanna were all born at Netherseale, and had arrived at intervals of a year or two, as was frequently the case in those Victorian days. Joanna no doubt expected to have other children after Nigel Bowyer, who was born in 1870. However, difficulties may have ensued, as her fifth child was not born until six years later - and not in Netherseale rectory, but in Edinburgh. One can only speculate on the reason for this, but she may have been expecting problems with the birth. Indeed, Vi Godfrey's memoirs state that her father was a *sixth* child, so Joanna might have suffered a miscarriage or there may have been an infant who did not survive. The baptismal records of St Peter's Church do not show any corresponding entry, but a stillborn child would not have been baptised. Examination of the official registers discloses that two local girls bearing the name Gresley died in infancy in the early 1870s, but these were daughters of miners.

Edinburgh at that time was a leading centre for medical science, one of the specialist interests being obstetrics, since Sir James Simpson, professor of midwifery at Edinburgh, discovered the property of chloroformas an anaesthetic in 1847. The results were to be seen in a considerably reduced loss of life in childbirth. Vi Godfrey's memoirs go on to say that Joanna decided to go to Edinburgh to see a specialist, although she did not have the child in hospital, but at 14 Dublin Street, described at the time as a lodging house. In taking this decision she was no doubt

Left: Nigel Gresley's birthplace in Dublin Street Edinburgh, c.1977.

Ramsay Ferguson, Gresley Society Trust

Below: Nigel Gresley with Sam c.1890.   *Tim Godfrey*

influenced by a close relative, the Revd William Douglas, curate of the nearby St Paul's Church, who lived at number 18. Dublin Street was renumbered in 1967, following the incorporation of Duke Street, and the new number of what was 14 appears to be 32. This, then, is where Herbert Nigel Gresley, the future Sir Nigel, entered this world, on 19th June, 1876. He was named Herbert after one of his godfathers, and Nigel as a family name since Norman times.

Joanna's decision to make the rail journey to Edinburgh when heavily pregnant, and later to return with a small infant, must have been a difficult one. The likely starting point would have been Burton on Trent, on the Midland route from Birmingham to Derby. The Settle to Carlisle line had been opened a few years before, and she could have changed at Derby to catch a through train to Edinburgh via Carlisle, or she might have travelled from Burton to York, and thence to Edinburgh. In either case she would have caught the 8.51 from Burton, with an Edinburgh arrival at 8.30 in the evening via York and Newcastle, or 9.10 via Carlisle. To get to Burton, 10 miles from Netherseale, she would have taken a pony cart or carriage, driven by a groom, and probably stayed overnight in Burton. She does not appear to have been accompanied by her husband, but would almost certainly have taken a nursemaid with her, and she must have been very determined to have decided on such a long journey, in her condition. The possibility exists that Joanna decided that her child should be able to claim Scottish descent. Her maiden name was Wilson, a well-known Scottish name, although she was born in Derbyshire and it has not been possible to trace her ancestry further back, into the 18th century. Her uncle, the Revd William Douglas, was a Scot, and evidently influenced her. So, accompanying his mother on her journey back to Netherseale, the young Herbert Nigel experienced his first railway journey when only a few weeks old. But although he often visited Scotland on business, or for golf or shooting, Nigel Gresley is not on record as ever having claimed Scottish birth, even in jest.

The family were well looked after at the rectory, with living-in servants. At the 1881 census, these included a cook, housemaid, parlourmaid, a governess for the older children, and a Swiss nursemaid for the young Nigel, who taught him to say his prayers in French before he could say them in English. (Years afterwards, his daughter Vi recounted that her father claimed he had expressed a wish to become an engine driver, when he was only four years old.) Later, by the time he had departed for prep school, his father was registered as blind. Three servants then ministered to the needs of the household, but only two of the children remained in residence, Beatrice and Nigel Bowyer, who was then a banker's clerk, before he emigrated to Canada. An earlier servant was Mary Birch, in whose memory a plaque can be seen in the parish church, 'a faithful friend and servant of the Gresley family for 49 years'.

The Revd Nigel's clerical influence no doubt helped to decide the schooling of his youngest son. The prep school selected was Barham House, in St Leonards (now 15/16 Dane Road), the headmaster being the Revd Wright. In September 1890 the young Nigel went on to Marlborough College, where he was in B1 House. He came top of Modern Upper II in the Michaelmas Term 1892, when he was awarded the Form Prize. In his last term he won a Science Prize, having earlier distinguished himself in Chemistry and German. He left in July 1893, when he was 17, preferring to take up a practical training, rather than stay in the sixth form

Extract from the Crewe Register of Employees 1893.   *Public Record Office*

Webb 2-2-2-2 'Greater Britain' class locomotive No. 2054 *Queen Empress* painted white for Queen Victoria's Golden Jubilee, 1897.   *Gresley Society Trust*

and go up to university. He did not become a prefect, nor did he excel at sports. However, he has a permanent memorial in the college chapel, sharing a plaque with Sir Arthur Hill, a contemporary who became director of the Royal Botanic Gardens at Kew. Nigel's decision to pursue a career in engineering was possibly encouraged by his science-minded father, but it was undoubtedly fostered at Marlborough. During this period, his abilities at mechanical drawing can be seen in a tracing he made of a Stirling single-wheeler illustrated in *The Engineer* of 6th November, 1891. Also, he possessed skills in carpentry, exemplified by a desk he made, and which is a feature of Netherseale church.

One may wonder what lay behind Gresley's decision on where to undergo his practical training. He had been at college on the Great Western, and Swindon was not far from Marlborough. On the other hand, he had shown interest in Stirling's engines, so why not Doncaster? However, Crewe, under the autocratic Francis Webb, and with Henry Earl as Works Manager, had the highest reputation among the engineers of the day, and this was probably the reason for his choice. He was taken on as a premium apprentice on 17th October, 1893, his wages being four shillings a week, and on conclusion of his apprenticeship he progressed to a job as a fitter; by the time he left, on 25th March, 1898, he was getting 24 shillings. There is no record of his receiving favoured treatment, and in his parting reference, he was described as being of good character and good ability. (It may be noted that this was not the highest assessment, as 'very good' was sometimes awarded.)

Gresley has said nothing about the work on which he was engaged. Undoubtedly he would be given the tedious tasks suffered by an apprentice, such as cutting threads on bolts, but he could well have been employed during some of his time in the erecting shop assembling locomotives, in which his height - he was 6 ft 2 in. -and his strength would have been put to good use. The miners' strike of 1893/94 had led to a loss of work, and a four-day week, so he would have had the opportunity of observing labour relations during a period of stress. He was said to have been an enthusiastic supporter of the West Coast in the Anglo-Scottish Races of 1895, in which the London & North Western and Caledonian railways competed with the Great Northern, North Eastern and North British to see which could reach Aberdeen in the fastest time from London.

Remiscences of his years with the LNWR were given at the Crewe dinner in 1919, when he recalled that there was no lack of enterprise in those days. Not only were various methods of compounding tried, including a triple expansion version, but also what he described as a 'figure of eight' firebox, and boilers with water space beneath, and at the side of the ashpan. He was at Crewe when Webb's *Greater Britain* 2-2-2-2s were built, and it was considered that the limits of locomotive size and power had almost been reached. As for locomotive artistry, at the time of Queen Victoria's Diamond Jubilee, *Greater Britain* was painted red, and *Queen Empress* appeared in a shade of white, Gresley later describing this as 'a delicate hue, darkening like a well-behaved Meerschaum pipe'.

It was at this Crewe dinner, with Bowen Cooke, CME of the London & North Western Railway, in the chair, that Gresley and Aspinall sang in duet the celebrated Crewe Works song, composed by John Bowes, a onetime pupil of Webb's. To the tune of 'The Holy City', the first verse goes

Flange Couplings for Shafting

Cast Iron.

Proportions of Couplings.

D	A	T	B	C	E	Diam of bolts	No of Bolts.
			Inches.				
1	5	$\frac{3}{4}$	$2\frac{1}{4}$	2	$1\frac{3}{4}$	$\frac{1}{2}$	3
$1\frac{1}{2}$	$6\frac{1}{2}$	$\frac{7}{8}$	$3\frac{1}{4}$	$2\frac{1}{2}$	$2\frac{3}{8}$	$\frac{5}{8}$	3
2	8	$1\frac{1}{16}$	$4\frac{1}{4}$	3	3	$\frac{3}{4}$	4
$2\frac{1}{2}$	$9\frac{1}{2}$	$1\frac{3}{16}$	$5\frac{1}{4}$	$3\frac{1}{2}$	$3\frac{5}{8}$	$\frac{7}{8}$	4
3	11	$1\frac{3}{8}$	$6\frac{1}{4}$	4	$4\frac{1}{4}$	1	4
$3\frac{1}{2}$	$12\frac{1}{2}$	$1\frac{1}{2}$	$7\frac{1}{8}$	$4\frac{1}{2}$	$4\frac{7}{8}$	1	4
4	14	$1\frac{5}{8}$	8	5	$5\frac{1}{2}$	1	6
$4\frac{1}{2}$	$15\frac{1}{2}$	$1\frac{7}{8}$	$8\frac{7}{8}$	$5\frac{1}{2}$	$6\frac{1}{4}$	1	6
5	17	2	$9\frac{3}{4}$	6	$6\frac{3}{4}$	$1\frac{1}{8}$	6
6	20	$2\frac{1}{4}$	$11\frac{1}{2}$	7	8	$1\frac{3}{8}$	6

It is found better practise to make the flanges he & she than for the end of one shaft to enter the flange of the other shaft in order to keep the shafts in true allignement, as it is easier to disconnect them. The keys should be driven in from the inside & cut off flush. The face of the coupling should be turned up after being keyed on to shaft as driving in the key is apt to throw it out of truth.

Last night I lay a-sleeping
There came a dream to me -
I stood within a Steam Shed,
A marvellous Shed to see.
The walls were clean and spotless,
And smoke troughs white as snow,
And not a spot of grease was seen
Upon the pits below.
O Loco Men, O Loco Men,
Shout loud for well you may —
'Twas the Blessed Steam Shed of Paradise
We all shall see some day.

I believe that this is the authentic version, although Anthony Bulleid offers an alternative, composed for the 1894 Crewe dinner. To the tune 'In the Gloaming', the *seventh* verse went

In the firebox, Oh! my Foreman,
You may look in vain for me,
For I am inside the boiler,
And my feet you cannot see.
T'will be best to leave me there, Sir,
Best for you, and best for me.

By 1898 Gresley had decided that the time had come for him to move on from Crewe, and he obtained a pupillage under John Aspinall, Chief Mechanical Engineer of the Lancashire & Yorkshire Railway (L&Y), commencing work in the drawing office at Horwich. (The only recorded instance of him being known as 'Bert' occurred during his time here. To his family and his close friends, and only to them, he was 'Tim', shortened from 'Tiny Tim', on account of his height.) However, he seems to have become uncertain about his future, or maybe his mother decided to intervene - which seems strange as he was now 22 and well capable of making his own decisions. Perhaps Aspinall, after the initial interview, had been somewhat remote. Anyway, Joanna wrote to him in March 1899 enquiring about her son's prospects, and Aspinall replied in somewhat unclear terms saying:

I regret that it will not be possible for me to find work for your son at these works when he is out of his time, but if I find it possible to allow him to remain here for one month after his pupillage, I shall be willing to consider that question if your son sees me personally on the subject, but I cannot undertake that this period of one month should in any case be extended.

Following his mother's letter, Gresley wasted no time in getting noticed by Aspinall, who was obviously impressed by his ability, as at the end of his pupillage he was given a job in the materials testing laboratory. Although he spent little more than six months there, he gained experience which remained with him throughout his professional life.

At Horwich, Gresley became a close friend of H.E. O'Brien, an old Etonian, who, when with the London Midland & Scottish Railway in 1924, met with official displeasure by publicly advocating main line electrification, through

Left: Ethel and Nigel on their Wedding Day, 17th October, 1901.   *Tim Godfrey*

Below: Nigel and Ethel, probably at the christening of their firstborn, Nigel, 1903.

Tim Godfrey

papers given to the Institution of Electrical Engineers and other professional bodies. The pair struck up a friendship with the two elder Aspinall daughters, cycling and playing tennis together. Nigel was then described as a courteous rather than a gifted player, but there was to be no romance.

In 1899 Aspinall was promoted to become General Manager of the L&Y, being succeeded as CME by Henry Hoy. The following year, Gresley was moved from the quiet of the materials laboratory to the sound and fury of the locomotive department, being given the job of running shed foreman at Blackpool for the summer season. It was then that he met and fell in love with Ethel Frances Fullager, the occasion being one of the Bolton Assembly Balls; they became engaged in the autumn of 1900. He was 24, she was two years older, and obviously of a determined nature. An accomplished musician, she had spent a year in Germany studying the piano and violin. She was the daughter of Walter Palmer Fullagar, a well-known solicitor, who lived in St Anne's on the Sea, and who had a practice in Bolton. At the time, St Anne's was a seaside town with a population of some 7,000, possessing two hotels, and that symbol of Victorian seaside prosperity, a pier. It served not only as a watering place, but also as a dormitory for Manchester.

The young Ethel Fullagar clearly thought it was time she was married, although her father strongly opposed the match, no doubt on the grounds that his daughter could do better for herself than marry a mere engineer. Disagreement within the family reached a crisis when Ethel presented herself at Nigel's lodgings, saying that she had left home. By now, he was on sufficiently friendly terms with with his General Manager that he was able to persuade Mrs Aspinall to take Ethel in, so avoiding what might have been in those days a scandalous situation. However, love triumphed, with Mrs Aspinall helping the match along, telling Gresley that 'She is mad about you, and would marry you even if you lived in a coal shed'. Walter relented, and gave the couple a splendid wedding at St Anne's Parish Church, on 17th October, 1901; the ceremony was conducted by the groom's brother, the Revd George Nigel Gresley. The couple spent their honeymoon in Burnley, a strange choice except that it would have been handy for walking on the moors - unless the bridegroom spent his time observing operations at the nearby Rose Grove depot. They appear to have stayed at the Bridge Inn, now the Gannow Arms, where the landlord's daughter, a Miss Hartley, was a teacher of the violin. They commenced married life in Newton Heath, where Gresley had earlier been in digs with the family of the L&Y chief carriage & wagon draughtsman. Their first child, a son, named Nigel after his father, was born on 25th June, 1903, followed by Violet (universally known, at her request, as Vi) on 5th May, 1904. In that year they were living at Ely House, Newton Heath.

Like the Gresleys, the Fullagars can also trace their forbears back to medieval times, in their case the 11th century, although in the earliest years the line is more tenuous. The first recording of the name appears in Lincolnshire, in 1066, with a *Seualle filius Fulgeri*. Other related spellings which appear over the centuries include Fulcher, Fulgar, and a dozen others. The name as it was spelled by Walter Palmer's family was first recorded in Suffolk in 1167.

The Fullagars were strongly reinforced in the 14th and 15th centuries when numbers of Huguenot cloth workers and their families immigrated from Flanders. Many were said to have been of considerable wealth, and to have settled in the Weald of Kent, where there is still a strong concentration of Fullagars. Certainly, a firm line has been traced back to one Dominyche ffulagard, who died at Headcorn in 1538. There is a Fullagar archive in Maidstone County Library, and the family is also represented in Australia.

It is not possible to say with certainty to which source Gresley's father-in-law, Walter Palmer Fullagar, could have traced his ancestry. He was born in Leicester in 1842, where his father had been a surgeon; he was educated at the Collegiate School, and subsequently took up articles with a firm of solicitors. He moved to Liverpool, marrying Catherine Swainson at St Luke's, Liverpool, in 1868, the union producing five children. These were Emily, who remained unmarried until her death in 1949, Constance, and Ethel, born in 1874, who became Nigel Gresley's wife. There were also two sons, Francis, and Walter, the black sheep of the family, who was banished to Canada, where he died soon afterwards. Constance, universally known as Connie, was an outgoing character, fond of riding, who trained as a nurse before going to South Africa during the Boer War. Here she was taken prisoner, and brought before President Kruger, who was so captivated by her charms that he presented her with a unique bracelet of gold nuggets. In 1906 she married her second cousin, Richard Dixon, of Preston, and continued a close friendship with her sister Ethel, often staying with the Gresleys.

Walter Fullagar and his family settled in Lytham St Anne's, first at 'West Bank' Clifton Road, removing in 1900 to the sea front at 16 North Promenade. Sadly, his wife Catherine was latterly not in good health, and, accompanied by Emily, she decided to stay in Torquay. She spent her last few weeks at 'Hazlemere', a guest house on the corner of Torchurch Road, and died in November 1903. Later, to the disapproval of the family, Walter married his housekeeper, Marion Drew, she being the main beneficiary on his death in 1926, a few days before his 84th birthday. By now he was living at 6 Beach Road, St Anne's, just back from the sea front, a house which is still standing. He had been a prominent citizen, vicar's sidesman at the Parish Church, and a frequent contributor to the columns of the *St Anne's Express*. He was a leading member of the local Conservative party, and a friend of Dr Temple, sometime Bishop of Manchester, and later Archbishop of Canterbury.

At the end of the summer of 1900, Nigel Gresley was transferred to the Carriage & Wagon Department of the L&Y as an outdoor assistant, receiving a further promotion the following year, to Assistant Manager of the carriage & wagon works at Newton Heath. He succeeded J.P. Crouch, another young and ambitious engineer, who eventually, in 1910, decided to leave Britain to become CME of the Central Argentine Railway. Gresley was now on a salary of £200 a year, and gained a further rise, to £250, when on 1st April 1902 he became Works Manager, just over a year after being appointed Assistant. Two years later his income was almost doubled, on his promotion to Assistant Carriage & Wagon Superintendent, responsible to the Chief Mechanical Engineer, the job carrying a salary of £450. Whilst he was in the C&W Department, a large 12-wheeled dining car was completed at Newton Heath; one would like to think that Gresley had been instrumental in the design of this, as a forerunner of his future advanced coaching vehicles. However, this was not the case, as the vehicle undoubtedly had its origins in a visit to the United States in 1899 by Henry Hoy, the then CME, accompanied by George Hughes, who was to succeed Hoy in four years time. It was during this period that the young Gresley made what seems to have been a presumptuous intervention, at a meeting of the Liverpool Engineering Society. Oliver Winder, later to become Assistant CME and Works Manager at Horwich, read a paper extolling the virtues of an American method of bogie wagon frame design. Gresley challenged this, saying that it was not suitable for the side buffer type of construction used in Britain. Of course he had every right to contribute to the discussion, but he might have been thought indiscreet to criticise a more senior officer in public. The remarks don't appear to have done him any harm, however; probably he was right.

Gresley's rapid advancement must have given him the assurance that a chief mechanical engineer's position could be within his sights. However, early in 1904 Hoy moved to Beyer, Peacock as Managing Director, and George Hughes took his place on the Lancashire &Yorkshire, with another 20 years of service in front of him. Clearly, Gresley could not wait that long. He would, of course, have to fill a subordinate post on the way, and as it happened a vacancy occurred within his immediate grasp when Frank Howlden retired from the position of C&W Superintendent on the Great Northern Railway. The job was formally advertised, and six applicants were interviewed in November 1904, Crouch but not Gresley being among them. None was successful, and Aspinall, realising that Gresley would not stay with the L&Y indefinitely, no doubt spoke to Henry Ivatt, the GNR Locomotive Engineer, who was an old friend from Crewe days.

Evidently Gresley had a private interview with Ivatt, as the GNR Locomotive Committee Minutes for January 1905 record that Ivatt informed the committee that he had arranged for H.N. Gresley to take up the post of Carriage & Wagon Superintendent at a salary of £750, which was 'not to be considered final if his work justifies more'. So, after seven years with the L&Y, when he had advanced from pupil to assistant chief officer, Gresley joined the Great Northern at Doncaster, the date of his appointment being 20th February, 1905. As a parting gift, his colleagues presented him with a silver plated tea tray.

Another unsuccessful applicant for Howlden's job was Francis Wintour, who had earlier transferred from the L&Y to the Great Northern, and at the time was Locomotive Running Superintendent at King's Cross. Undoubtedly Gresley's greater experience in the C&W field was to his advantage, but as it happened, following the departure to Brighton of Douglas Earle Marsh, Works Manager at Doncaster, Wintour was appointed to succeed him. There seems to have been something of an internal disagreement about this appointment, however, which also carried the title of Assistant Locomotive Engineer. Ivatt is believed to have made the nomination of Richard Maunsell (both had been at Inchicore, with the Great Southern & Western Railway of Ireland) and indeed this was leaked to the press, but the GNR Board would not ratify it, preferring to promote one of their own staff. Maunsell would not have been pleased to have been embarrassed in this way, and moreover, if he had got the job, he and Gresley might have been elbowing each other for seniority. As it was, Ivatt declared that Gresley would not be subordinate to anyone at Doncaster, except the Locomotive Engineer (i.e. Ivatt himself), and, happily, Gresley and Wintour worked closely together for many years until Wintour's retirement in 1927.

Chapter Three

The Family in the Twentieth Century

Once Nigel Gresley had joined the Great Northern, he and Ethel moved to 'Milford', Thorne Road, Doncaster, accompanied by their two children, Nigel and Vi. Here, Roger was born on 15th July, 1906, and Marjorie on 15th September, 1908. The boys were given the names of earlier Gresleys, but not the girls; strangely, none of the children was given a second Christian name. Family life was relaxed and happy, in a Christian environment, with family prayers in the parents' bedroom and grace before meals, customs which endured until the children were grown up. On Sundays there would be morning service at the Parish Church, and prayers and hymns round the piano in the evening. Holidays would be taken in Scotland, where Gresley, an excellent shot, enjoyed the sport, or at seaside resorts such as Sheringham. Although Nigel and Ethel were both strong minded individuals, there was little collision of wills during this period whilst the children were young. Each respected the other, and often had their moments of fun. Vi recalled the occasion - she was only a little girl - when her father was given a rise to £1,000 a year. 'He thought this made him a rich man, and they chased each other all over the house'.

In 1910, while staying with his mother at Turnditch, Gresley suffered an injury which might well have proved fatal. Nigel Bowyer was over from Canada, and the two had been out shooting rooks, when Gresley got a blackthorn spike in his leg. His brother managed to remove it with a penknife, normally used to clean his pipe, but the wound became poisoned and phlebitis set in. The local doctor thought that the leg might have to be amputated, but when the Great Northern Chairman, Lord Allerton, heard of the matter, he arranged for a specialist to be sent down from London. The wound was cleansed by the application of leeches, and eventually healed, although Gresley was away from work for some time. The leg remained tender, and for several years afterwards he had a felt pad attached to his desk, to prevent any painful reminder of the incident. However, his sporting ability was unaffected, although he was conscious that when wearing plus fours, one leg appeared thinner than the other. A letter dated 22th January, 1911 indicates not only the interest which Lord Allerton had in the case, but especially the regard with which Gresley was held, bearing in mind that he was still only the Carriage & Wagon Superintendent.

Dear Mr Gresley,
I am glad to see that you report some progress - you will forgive my interference but . . . I don't believe in risks being taken . . .without any disrespect to your own doctor, I suggest for my own comfort that you should let Dr Braithwaite see you again . . . you may think me selfish, so I am, but I want you back at work as soon as you can be got fit. So please accede to my wish in this matter.
Yours very truly,
    Allerton

In a further letter, two months later, his Lordship said that he was 'glad to hear you are making good progress'. Clearly Gresley was away from his desk for several weeks, at a critical period, but this was not to prove any disadvantage to his promotion prospects. As will be recounted in the next Chapter, in the following October his career was to take a further major step forward when he succeeded Ivatt as Locomotive Engineer of the Great Northern.

After Ivatt's retirement, the Gresleys moved along Thorne Road to his chief's old residence at Avenue House, where family life continued its tranquil way, except that as the children grew older, they were sent away to school. Domestic affairs were well ordered, with a parlourmaid (who answered the door, laid table and cleaned the silver), housemaid and cook. Menus for the day were discussed in the morning, and then cook was left undisturbed until six o'clock, the children being forbidden to trouble her. Tea was taken in the upstairs nursery, with Fanny the Nanny, as Vi recalled her, who looked after the younger children, and later a governess, until the children were old enough for prep school. A gardener was employed, and, after Gresley had acquired a car, a chauffeur named Stubbs, whose wife bathed the children in a hip bath on nanny's day off. Ethel was extremely houseproud; the carriage & wagon foreman at Doncaster Plant came to Avenue House to French polish the furniture, an arrangement to which her husband was not a party. Musical evenings became a social feature, and the composer Wilfred Sanderson, who was organist and choirmaster at the Parish Church, and conductor for the Doncaster Musical Society, was a frequent visitor. His songs mostly had a West Country flavour, and one can almost hear the family in renditions of *Drake is Going West, Lad*, and *I'm just come up from Somerset*. Gresley himself, although not deeply interested in music, joined in the singing; he had a pleasant tenor voice.

Nigel Gresley was appointed CBE in 1920, and his engineering progress through the wartime years is described in later chapters, but he was to reach the peak of his career in 1923, when the Board of the newly formed London & North Eastern Railway made him their Chief Mechanical Engineer. Not long after he became CME, with his office at King's Cross, the family home was moved south, to Camlet House, Hadley Wood, a substantial property with two tennis courts and a billiard room, a few minutes walk from Hadley Wood station. He enjoyed golf, and for a time was captain of Hadley Wood Golf Club. He joined others of his profession in membership of Brooks's, and of the Junior Carlton Club.

It was here that Nigel and Ethel celebrated their silver wedding, but two years afterwards Ethel was taken ill with cancer. She had been in pain for some while, but kept this from her family. The time came when she could not continue, and a specialist, Sir Maurice Cassidy, was called in. Gresley's dressing room was converted into an operating theatre, and for a while she appeared to hold her own, expecting to recover; but her condition worsened, and she died on 5th August, 1929. Ethel had remained active until the onset of her illness, with hardly a grey hair; she was 54. Her body was taken to Netherseale, where she, and later her husband, were to lie side by side, the last of the family to be buried under the Boscabel Oak.

Gresley was devastated, and probably never recovered fully from her passing. He was advised to take a long holiday from work, and in the following month, accompanied by his daughter Vi, went on a trip which took them to the Canadian Rockies. During their stay, they were entertained by the Canadian Pacific Railway (CPR), and had their photographs taken on a giant CPR 2-10-4 locomotive. One would have thought that Gresley, having taken the trouble to cross the Atlantic, would have made the additional effort to visit the Altoona testing station of the Pennsylvania Railroad, but this was not the case; probably time was limited. On his return to Britain he contributed a short article on his CPR experience to the *Railway Gazette*, the only occasion on which he is known to have appeared in print, other than when his papers were published by the engineering journals (*see Appendix Three*).

After Ethel's death, Gresley could not bear to live at Camlet House, and for a year or so occupied a flat in Cadogan Square. Then, he took the lease of Salisbury Hall, a moated Elizabethan manor near St Albans, which has a history of visits by famous people. The story is told that the actress Nell Gwyn stayed there with King Charles II. She leaned out of an upstairs window, with a baby in her arms, and called to Charles to give the child a name or she would drop him. 'Don't kill the Duke of St Albans' was the King's response. In 1908, Winston Churchill became engaged to Clementine Hozier at Salisbury Hall, and, in later years, the house served as the design centre for the de Havilland Mosquito aircraft. Wild duck swam in the moat at Salisbury Hall, notably mallard, a species which was to give its name to one of the most famous of the Gresley Pacifics.

Vi acted as her father's hostess at Salisbury Hall, and for a period, his chauffeuse. Gradually they resumed entertaining, which he enjoyed. He was a kind and generous host, insisting on appropriate etiquette; dinner was a formal occasion, at which the men wore dinner jackets. Sunday lunch might include up to a dozen guests, relatives and business acquaintances, and sometimes there were tennis parties or musical evenings. Attendance at early service at North Mimms Parish Church was often a family occasion. During this period, Gresley continued his enthusiasm for sports. He played golf at Porters Park, Radlett, and took golfing holidays at North Berwick, as well as shooting in the Peak District and the Scottish Highlands. He was not overtly interested in horse racing, despite the provenance of the names of many of his Pacific locomotives. Once during the 1930s, Sir Charles Allom, who was the LNER's adviser on the internal decor of the 'Silver Jubilee' and other prestige trains, took the yacht *White Heather* for Cowes Week, and invited Gresley and Vi on board. And, as well as outdoor activities, there were family parties at Claridges and the Savoy, notably to celebrate the weddings of Nigel and Vi. Sir Nigel's richly deserved knighthood, bestowed in 1936, would surely have been the occasion for celebrations.

Sadly, Gresley's health began to decline towards the end of the 1930s, due to bronchial and heart problems. Nevertheless, it was a shock to his family and colleagues when he died at the home he then shared with his daughter Vi and her husband at Watton-at-Stone, Hertfordshire, on 5th April 1941, two months before his 65th birthday. He had never publicly spoken of his plans for retirement, but in all probability he was expecting to carry on in his job, at least until the end of the war. This certainly was the view of the LNER Board, as no plans had been made for his succession, the 'retire at 65' rule having been suspended during hostilities. Consequently the LNER Chairman, Sir Ronald Matthews, was to be seriously concerned over whom to appoint in Sir Nigel's place. The subsequent events are recounted in Chapter Eleven.

Gresley's four children all had family nicknames - Ni, Vi, Dodger and Boxie. The derivations are obvious, except for Marjorie's. As a child, she was not exactly slender, and her father somewhat unkindly said she was shaped like a box; so Boxie she became. The elder son, Nigel, was a good looking man with a fondness for the ladies. His mother adored him, but he had little interest in the family, or his father's achievements. He showed early brilliance as a scholar, and after prep school at Selwyn House, Broadstairs, followed his father to Marlborough. But he was to leave prematurely under a cloud, because of an infatuation with an actress. He was articled for a time to the GNR solicitor, presumably in the footsteps of his maternal grandfather, but he lacked the enthusiasm to concentrate on office work. He was engaged to be married three times, but none of these relationships achieved permanence. He was a sore trial to his father, who eventually arranged for him to take up work abroad, for many years in Mandalay, as an employee of the Bombay Burma Trading Corporation, from whom the LNER purchased teak panelling for its coaches. He was in other distant parts as well, becoming involved in the tea trade, and claimed to have knowledge of the Middle East, China, Australia and East Africa, where he learned to speak Swahili.

However, Nigel spent some of his time in Britain, and at last, when he was 33, he showed signs of settling down, and in January 1937 married Kathleen Lambe, whose father was a merchant in Shanghai, and where no doubt the couple met. The wedding, at All Souls, Langham Place, was a society affair, but the marriage only lasted a few months, Kitty returning to her parents' home in Shanghai. Nigel continued to live in the West End after the breakdown of his marriage, in Latymer Court, and, in 1939, Clanricarde Gardens. That April he followed the example of many of his generation, and enlisted as a gunner in 54 Anti-Aircraft Regiment, Royal Artillery, at the Territorial drill hall in nearby Putney. He realised the benefits of holding a commission, and tried to pull strings, hoping to be put on the Duke of Connaught's list, claiming that the colonel was an old friend of the family, and expressing a desire to join the Tower Hamlets Rifles. His application was successful in that he was selected for officer training at 168 OCTU at Heysham, Lancashire. Here he was reported to be a slow, but steady, worker, and on receiving his commission joined the Rifle Brigade at Tidworth. After a year in Britain, he was posted as Liaison Officer with HQ 2 Armoured Brigade, and proceeded to Egypt. However, he did not go with his unit to the desert - no doubt his age was against him - and found himself promoted to a staff captain's job in the GHQ Middle East Directorate of Works, located in the Semiramis Hotel in Cairo. (By an extraordinary coincidence, I was also stationed there at the same time, but our paths did not cross.)

Nigel was next posted to Iraq, where his knowledge of forestry was put to use. He does not appear to have been overstressed; a report he compiled on the local availability of timber - an important and scarce commodity in the Middle East - contains no specialised information on the subject. He would have been more usefully employed in Burma, where his knowledge of the country and its languages would have been invaluable to those in command of the Allied troops fighting the Japanese in that theatre. In fact, after two years in Iraq, this must have

Right: Major Nigel Gresley with his second wife, Natasha, Cairo 1945.
Tim Godfrey

Below: Violet Gresley, c.1928.
Tim Godfrey

been realised, as he was sent to Headquarters, Allied Land Forces South East Asia (ALFSEA), where he joined the Intelligence Branch with the rank of major. He gained the Burma Star, and one would like to think that he operated behind the lines with Force 136, the commander of which was an old Burma hand, but this was not the case and he remained a staff officer in Calcutta until he was due for home posting. In June 1945, he sailed from Bombay in the SS *Mooltan*. However, Nigel did not return straight home, but stopped over in Cairo, on two months' compassionate leave. He had earlier formed a liaison with a girl of White Russian parentage, Natasha Ishimpayeva, and they were married in the chapel at Kasr el Nil barracks in the July. She was a beauty, and together they made a handsome couple; at the expiry of his leave, they sailed for Liverpool on the *Georgic*, Nigel occupying a position on the ship's staff. He had no civilian job to go to in Britain, and obtained deferment of release from the army for two years, during which period he continued to act as an officer on troopships. He was unsuccessful in trying to obtain an appointment with the Allied Control Commission in Germany, and with no civilian prospects, was granted further deferment of his release.

Nigel Gresley stands at the side of the CPR 2-10-4, with his daughter Vi leaning from the cab, November 1929.   *The Railway Gazette*

His second marriage also ended in failure. After only a few months, Natasha returned to her home in Istanbul, and we find a pathetic exchange of letters in which each accuses the other of desertion. She wrote to Nigel's CO, saying that her allowance had been stopped, to which he replied by saying he was in temporary financial difficulties. During this period he occupied a staff job at the War Office, engaged at one time in the resettlement of Polish officers, until he was eventually demobilised in April 1952. In the meantime, he was married for the third time, to Betty Laird, at Kensington Register Office. It was said that she was able to exert some control over him, although both enjoyed their drink. They took over the management of an hotel near the Albert Hall, where Nigel died in 1962, followed soon after by his wife.

Roger, the second son, was educated at Uppingham, where he showed considerable interest in military affairs, becoming Company Sergeant Major in the Officer Training Corps. After leaving school he was apprenticed to the Trafford Park engineering firm of Taylor Brothers, who were major contractors to the railway companies. On completion of his apprenticeship he joined the Metropolitan Carriage and Wagon Company, who sent him to represent the company abroad, for three years. On his return, he was engaged in selling omnibus bodies. In 1935 he took up a position with the London firm of manufacturers' agents, George Stephenson and Company, and made a success of his job there, becoming a Director in 1939.

While in Manchester, he had maintained his army connections by joining the Territorials, and later received a commission in the Royal Artillery Reserve of Officers. His unit was embodied at the outbreak of hostilities and he went to France with 206 Battery, 52 (Manchester) Field Regiment, RA, as part of the British Expeditonary Force. After taking part in the rearguard action of May/June 1940, he was evacuated from the beach at Dunkirk. Back in England, because of his railway connections, he was posted to the Royal Engineers Railway Operating Division at Longmoor, but things did not work out, and he returned to the RA. Years before, he had suffered concussion and a broken arm in a motorcycle accident, and it was now discovered that he had an eyesight deficiency, resulting in an inability to observe the fall of shot accurately. This meant that he could not continue as a gunner officer, so he was transferred to the Royal Army Ordnance Corps (RAOC), and in August 1942 was posted to India. In the meantime, in July 1941, a few weeks after his father's death, he married Edna Neep ('Smudge') at Frinton Parish Church, but this was not to last, as separation led to a divorce in 1947. He was said to have been greatly affected by the break-up of his marriage.

Once in India, Roger's industrial experience was put to good use, and he was appointed to a staff job in Calcutta, in local procurement of engineering products. He lodged in Mrs Macdonald's house in Leroy Road, and is remembered as an active member of the army community during the time he was there. Since his period of service in Calcutta overlapped that of his elder brother, Nigel, one imagines that they would have spent leisure time there together. (There was a fair degree of affinity between the two brothers, each having been the other's best man.) The nature of Roger's work led to a transfer to the Royal Engineers, and he achieved the rank of major, before his return to

Britain in 1945. He rejoined Stephenson's, becoming Managing Director, and remained with them until his death in 1960, from broncho-pneumonia following a stroke, at the age of 53. During the 1950s he was a prominent member of the now defunct Transportation Club, and is still recalled as an outgoing personality, well suited to his position, in which maintaining influential contacts was essential.

Although the younger daughter, Marjorie had early ambitions to be a nurse, she showed an interest in acting. Her father tried hard to divert her from the stage, but she was determined. Her first engagement was a walking-on part (a different one in each act) at Drury Lane in the Ivor Novello musical *Glamorous Night*. Her father, Vi and Roger were in the audience on the opening night. She thought that her best part was opposite Laurence Olivier in *Caesar and Cleopatra*, although she was only an understudy. She had roles in several radio series, including *Mrs Dale's Diary*, and was often seen in films and television, including commercials. In her later years she was rather on the large side for romantic parts, but continued to appear in films, notably as a county lady in *Tony Draws a Horse*, and as an imperious matron in *The Life and Death of Colonel Blimp*. Her last engagement was at Roedean School, where for a spell she taught English as a foreign language. She was living in Lewes Crescent, Brighton, at the time, where she was known as the Duchess of Kemp Town. Evidently she retained her interest in her father's achievements, as Frank Brown quotes her comments in a letter to the *Daily Telegraph* of 27th September, 1962, in which she advocates aeroplane type seating for luxury carriages, 'With meals served to passengers at their seats by rail hostesses, to save that ghastly lurching trip to the dining car'.

Marjorie was remembered with affection by many stage folk, who paid tribute to her great sense of fun, and acceptance of the fact that she would never achieve stardom. Nevertheless, during most of her career, until arthritis overtook her, she was in constant demand for supporting parts. One of her friends described her as autocratic - especially with taxi-drivers. She died in 1988.

In these notes about Nigel Gresley's children, I have left Vi, the elder daughter, until last. She was the outstanding personality of the four, a steadfast Christian, and endowed with a strength of character which owed much to her parents. After the death of her mother, she acted as her father's companion during several years at Salisbury Hall. Vi's brother Roger was friendly with Geoffrey Godfrey, an engineer with Thornycroft's, and he introduced Geoffrey to Vi, with the result that they became engaged, and were married in March 1937, at St Ethelburga's Church in Bishopsgate. (The night before, Sir Nigel had hosted a fabulous party, with 90 guests, at a West End hotel.) This was within a few weeks of Nigel's first wedding, and until the failure of his son's marriage, Gresley must have been a very contented man, with two of his children apparently happily settled. Geoffrey was the youngest son of Sir Dan Godfrey, the eminent musician and founder of the Bournemouth Symphony Orchestra. *His* father had been bandmaster of the Grenadier Guards, and often played before Queen Victoria. When she discovered that he did not enjoy commissioned rank - no bandmaster did in those days - the Queen immediately

Right: Roger Gresley, *c.*1955.   *Tim Godfrey*

Below: Marjorie Gresley (*left*), with Cecil Parker in
the film *Tony Draws a Horse*, 1950.   *Carlton Films*

ordered that he should be made an officer, since when this has invariably been the case. Geoffrey Godfrey joined the Royal Army Ordnance Corps at the outset of war in 1939, later transferring to the Royal Electrical and Mechanical Engineers when that corps was established to take over the workshops activities of the RAOC. He attained the rank of major and was invested with the MBE. Vi was a close friend of William Stanier's daughter, Joan, and in later years she and Geoffrey would stay with the Staniers at their home near Rickmansworth. After a period in Swan Street in London's West End, the Godfreys set up home at Watton-at-Stone, where Sir Nigel joined them, not wishing to remain in Salisbury Hall on his own. It was at Watton that their three children, Timothy, Louise and Benjamin, were born. In their final years they lived in the village of Lockerley, near Romsey, in Hampshire. Vi passed away in 1989, and Geoffrey in 1997.

On public occasions, Gresley was only infrequently supported by his family. When in January 1930 his experimental locomotive No. 10000 was unveiled, he was photographed together with Vi and Marjorie, but there is no close photographic record of him and his sons together in public. In 1938 Roger was elected an Associate of the Institution of the Locomotive Engineers, and he accompanied his father when the Mechanicals had their summer meeting in Scotland in that year. Both Nigel and Roger were present at the Locomotive Engineers' Annual Dinner at the Trocadero in March 1939, when Gresley presided in the absence of William Stanier, who was ill at the time.

Two other Fullagars, distant cousins of Ethel, are of interest to the Gresley story. They were Hugh Francis, 1872-1916, and his brother, Leo Alfred, 1885-1964; both were mechanical engineers. Hugh, a bachelor, who lived in Newcastle-upon-Tyne, was responsible for developing a version of a gas/diesel engine, which bore his name. This was of a two-stroke vertical pattern, with claimed advantages of accessibility and almost perfect balance. Its first revenue earning applications came after his death, and seem to have been on ships, as in 1920 a small vessel named the *Fullagar* was built by Cammell Laird at Birkenhead. The idea was followed in the following year by the larger *Malia*, of 3,782 tons. Both ships had chequered careers, and were sold abroad and subsequently renamed within a few years of construction. However, the Fullagar design of engine was taken up for land use by English Electric at Rugby, and many were built for power stations and other purposes during the next 30 years, a number being exported. By the 1950s the Fullagar engine had been overtaken by more modern high-speed designs, and went out of fashion.

Hugh's brother Leo was a Member of the Institution of Locomotive Engineers, and also of the Stephenson Locomotive Society, having been proposed for membership by the well-known observer of Great Northern locomotive practice, Robert Weight. He was for a time a consulting engineer with McLellan and Partners, and contributed to technical discussions, notably on the occasion when Bert Spencer, Gresley's technical assistant for many years, gave his paper *The Development of LNER Locomotive Design* to the Locomotive Engineers in 1947. Leo was a firm supporter of Gresley practice, and family visits were paid to the Gresleys at their home in Hadley Wood, while Ethel was alive.

Some other offshoots of the Gresley tree also deserve mention. Charles Gresley, the younger brother of the Revd John Morewood Gresley, the fourth of the Netherseale rectors, had 10 children, and five of them, all unmarried, in their later years shared a house known as Burcher Court, Titley, in Herefordshire. These were Isobel, Eleanor, Rosamund and Augusta, and their brother Charles Vincent, all born between 1853 and 1865. Charles took Holy Orders, and among his appointments were curacies at Wincobank, Sheffield, and Newton upon Ouse, Yorkshire. The family became very well-known locally, and Nigel Gresley is recalled stepping off the train at Titley (at the time a GWR branch line station), and staying for a few days with his cousins.

Gresley's skills as a draughtsman have already been recorded, as have his mother's and sister's ability as painters. The ladies of Burcher Court are also known to have had artistic leanings, and Penelope Vavasour, wife of the Revd John Morewood Gresley, was a pen-and-ink artist of some distinction. Also, there is a line of Gresleys, distant from the mainstream of the family, who have an established reputation as painters in oils and water colours. They are father, son and grandson, James Stephen Gresley (1829 - 1908), Frank Gresley (1855-1936), and Harold Gresley (1892-1967). Their speciality was landscapes, mainly in the Midlands and Yorkshire, and they are well-known to collectors of paintings of their period.

Finally in this chapter we return to the Gresley baronets. The 11th in line, Sir Robert, died in 1936, soon after having sold Drakelowe. He left three sons, Nigel, (who succeeded him as 12th baronet), Laurence and Antony. Unfortunately, Nigel was epileptic, and unable to take part in family affairs, although he lived into his 80th year. He died in hospital in Basingstoke in 1974. Pine says that for part of his life he lived in Canada, but no more details are known. (It may be noted that from 1936 to 1941, there were *two* Sir Nigel Gresleys, the baronet and the knight.) None of the three brothers produced a male heir, and so the title passed to William Francis Gresley, a descendant of the second baronet. Sir William died in 1976, after only a brief enjoyment of the title, and was the 13th and last of the Gresley baronets, and he also left no heir. Although efforts were made to establish a claim on behalf of younger members of the family, the line was too tenuous, and, sadly, one of the most senior baronetcies in the country has become extinct.

So the Gresley family, from Robert de Toeni to Sir William, the 13th baronet, 'proved to be one of the very few to stand up to the serious investigations of the antiquarians, and come through unscathed'. There were some 30 generations in succession, and they owned Drakelowe for over seven centuries. Remarkably, although they included Members of Parliament and officers of their county, Derbyshire, none achieved eminence in national affairs. Today, there are no Gresleys in the current edition of *Who's Who* and in contrast to past years, the name is not often to be met, across the country. But enthusiasts at least will take comfort from the knowledge that at the time of writing the family connection with railways is continued in the person of Richard Gresley, a manager with a freight operating company on the West Coast main line.

Chapter Four

Carriage & Wagon Superintendent

When, in February 1905, Nigel Gresley joined the Great Northern Railway at Doncaster as Carriage & Wagon Superintendent, he was still a few months short of his 29th birthday. He was responsible to Henry Ivatt, the Locomotive Engineer, for the design and development of carriages and wagons, a task for which he had been well prepared by his training and experience at Crewe and Newton Heath. His predecessor, Frank Howlden, had had a distinguished career on the GNR, starting in the early days of the company as an apprentice under Archibald Sturrock and occupying the position of C&W Superintendent since January 1877. (Frank Brown has reminded us that when Howlden was appointed, his successor was a seven-month-old baby in the Rectory at Netherseale.) Coincidentally with Gresley's arrival, Alex Hastie was promoted to the position of chief C&W draughtsman, and he and Gresley began to work together, under Ivatt's general direction, to give further impetus to the development of GNR passenger and goods vehicles.

Howlden had left the Great Northern with a nucleus of solidly built bogie coaches, featuring a clerestory style roof imported from America, and typical of the period. In the later decades of his period in office, he introduced the side corridor, leading to a toilet compartment, and gangway connections between coaches. Riding was transformed by 4-wheeled, then 6-wheeled, bogies, whilst specialist vehicles such as restaurant and sleeping coaches were brought into service. Braking systems were improved, with continuous vacuum pipes along the train, and, as an outcome of Ivatt's visit to America in 1899, automatic couplers were fitted, first the Gould then the buckeye version being adopted as a future standard, associated with the type of vestibule connection favoured by the Pullman Car Company. But features which had been in vogue since the beginnings of the Great Northern were maintained, in that bodysides and ends were of teak panelling, highly varnished and with distinctive serifed lettering. Nevertheless, in 1905, a large proportion of passenger stock was still made up of short fixed-chassis vehicles, 4- and 6-wheeled, even a few 8-wheeled, characterised by a low roof profile.

Except for a limited number of coaches for special purposes, such as the LNER streamlined sets and tourist trains of the 1930s, Gresley's standard vestibuled coaches were to be distinguished by a high elliptical roof with sloping ends, stronger yet lighter than its clerestory predecessor, whilst maintaining the curved ends to the body and the traditional practice of teak panelled exteriors. This somewhat complex type of construction was more expensive than a straightforward rectangular body shape capped by a simple roof profile, but it saved money on the earlier clerestory, which by Gresley's time was coming to lose favour. The underframe was now to be all steel, whilst the buckeye coupler and Pullman vestibule connection were retained, the latter at a time when elsewhere in Britain a less commodious type was being standardised. This general style was undoubtedly Gresley's personal trademark and was adopted with enthusiasm by the Great Northern Board, and carried forward into LNER days until a simpler profile was introduced after his death. Also around this period, consideration was

Ivatt rail motor No. 1 on Edgware branch service at Finchley Church End in 1909.
Gresley Society Trust

Ivatt's compound Atlantic, GNR No. 1421, built at Doncaster in 1907. An early example of the use of Walschaerts valve gear in Britain.   *BR, Gresley Society Trust*

being given to improving bogie design, and Gresley's attention was drawn to a patent taken out in 1906 by Alex Spencer, of the firm of Spencer Moulton. This led to a joint design in which a compound bolster form of construction was employed, with pressed steel sides, forming a further distinctive feature of Gresley's coaches.

Little time was lost in putting his ideas into practice, and the first main line carriage to be built in the Gresley style, a corridor composite, was completed at Doncaster in December 1905. The bogies were of a 6-wheel pattern, as was the vogue at the time, although before long these were replaced by a 4-wheel version. This first Gresley coach was followed soon afterwards by small batches of open thirds and brake thirds. As an additional aid to safety and comfort, electric lighting was installed to a limited extent, a GNR Board minute of May 1905 authorising 'all future dining and sleeping cars to be fitted up with electric light, and all existing dining cars as opportunity offers'. But this did not extend to the generality of new construction, although the following month J. Stone & Co. of Deptford were awarded a contract to fit one suburban train with electric light for the sum of £763 10s. (Presumably this was a standard set of 4-wheelers.)

The Great Northern was of course not insular in its traffic routes. Services were provided to Scotland in collaboration with the North Eastern (NER) and North British (NBR) railways, using East Coast Joint Stock (ECJS), as well as to Newcastle, where the coaches were jointly owned by the GNR and NER. For a short time, NER influence had pervaded the ECJS to the extent that a small number of vehicles were constructed at York with matchboarded sides, not at all in keeping with the teak panelling otherwise employed. This style was not perpetuated after 1906, and from the following year construction was to Gresley design, built at Doncaster or York, except for half a dozen full brakes turned out in 1906 from the North British works at Cowlairs. None were built by contractors. The North Eastern chief C&W draughtsman, J.D. Twinberrow, on at least one occasion protested that in certain details NER practice was preferable to that of Doncaster, but firm instructions were issued that GNR practice should be followed. It was a tribute to the standards of the Great Northern, and as an example of East Coast harmony, when it was noted in 1907 that the new elliptical roof coaches were introduced on the joint recommendation of the three East Coast companies. Nevertheless as late as 1912 the established coupling and gangway arrangements were reinvestigated, but were confirmed at an ECJS meeting, authority being given for adaptors to be available should adjoining coaches be fitted with non-compatible gangways.

One of the innovations of the period was the 'rail motor', a diminutive locomotive coupled to a coach by a common bogie in a manner later to be known as 'articulation'. The assembly was capable of being driven from either end, and was thought to offer cost savings on lightly used services. The Lancashire & Yorkshire had introduced a couple of rail motors in 1905, which would have been under consideration during Nigel Gresley's time there, but there was little of the L&Y about them, the design being a straight copy of one originated by T. Hurry Riches for the Taff Vale Railway in South Wales. Ivatt was also looking at the idea, and obtained Board authority for six. Two were ordered from Kitson's of Leeds (Nos. 5 and 6), and two from the Avonside Engine Company (Nos. 7 and 8). They were delivered by the beginning of 1906, and were probably designed by the contractors, as there were considerable variations in detail, although with certain similarities to GNR practice, such as the cabs.

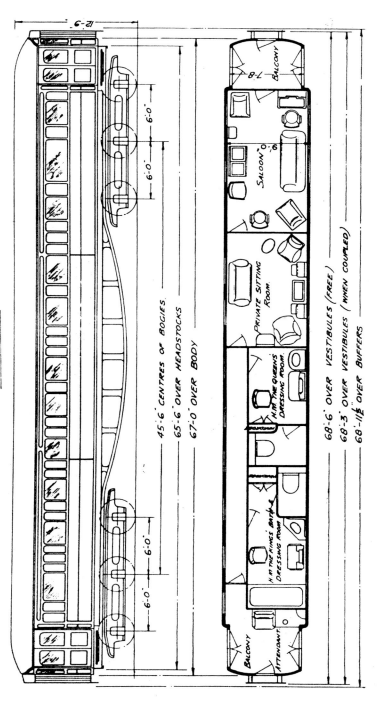

No 396
ROYAL SALOON
BUILT 1908

12-9

6-0

6-0

6-0

6-0

45-6 CENTRES OF BOGIES

65-6 OVER HEADSTOCKS

67-0 OVER BODY

7-8

BALCONY

SALOON 9-0

PRIVATE SITTING ROOM

H.M THE QUEEN'S DRESSING ROOM

H.M THE KING'S BATH & DRESSING ROOM

BALCONY

ATTENDANT

68-6 OVER VESTIBULES (FREE)

68-3 OVER VESTIBULES (WHEN COUPLED)

68-11½ OVER BUFFERS

Royal coach, originally Her Majesty's saloon, ECJS No. 396, built at York in 1908, as running in 1955 for use by HM Queen Elizabeth II and HRH the Duke of Edinburgh.

BR, Gresley Society Trust

Because of what Ivatt regarded as a high price for the four steam rail motors built outside, the remaining two, Nos. 1 and 2, were constructed at Doncaster. The engines differed in detail from those bought-in, and the coaches were given high, plain roofs, a novelty then for the GNR, and which probably could be attributed to Gresley. It is of interest that all six of the rail motor locomotives were fitted with Walschaerts valve gear, as were Ivatt's experimental compound Atlantics of the same period. Also in this period, as a further essay into small self-propelled passenger vehicles, the GNR purchased a Daimler petrol-driven railcar (No. 3), but this was not a success, lasting only until 1909.

An important project was initiated in 1906, when it was decided at an ECJS meeting that two new Royal carriages would be constructed, a saloon for the King, to be built at Doncaster, and a Queen's saloon, at York. These were most impressive vehicles, carried on 6-wheeled bogies. Splendidly finished externally and internally, the King's drawing room was fitted out in Louis XVI style, and the smoking room in Jacobean oak. The coaches bore no railway company or other insignia, except for a royal coat-of-arms on the centre panels on each side. In 1909, the King travelled to Ollerton in the Royal train, staying at Welbeck Abbey, for his annual visit to the St Leger meeting at Doncaster where he saw his Derby winner, Minoru, unexpectedly beaten by Bayardo. (Long after their racing days were over, these horses would be recalled in the names of two of Gresley's Pacific locomotives.)

The first new complete trains of Gresley coaches appeared in the latter half of 1906, well known as the 'Sheffield Stock', and working between King's Cross, Sheffield and Manchester. However, in the press announcement the credit for these was given to Ivatt, Gresley's name not being mentioned at the time. Also that year, six splendid restaurant cars, three first class and three third class, were built for general service. The first class coaches were still running 50 years later, having been converted to cafeteria cars. From 1907 complete trains of non-vestibule stock (although all compartments had access to lavatories) were built for semi-fast services to Cambridge, and even York and Grimsby. The coaches matched the new corridor stock in the teak panelled sides, but lacked the sloping roof ends.

Thus, the Gresley style was increasingly to be seen between King's Cross and York and on to Scotland. However, there was to be no wide-ranging replacement of existing stock, and new carriages were only designed and built to meet specific needs, or to replace coaches which had become outmoded and for which lesser work was found. Indeed, in the whole period from the time Gresley joined the Great Northern, up to the Grouping of 1923, only about 400 corridor coaches were built, for GN and the joint services, but to something like 40 different design diagrams. A main reason for this diversity in types of coach lay in the compartmental arrangements needed to suit differing requirements for through coaches. Two or three, or even single coaches were run to a variety of destinations, as part of a main line service. Provision had to be made for first and third class accommodation, smoking and non-smoking, luggage in varying amounts, and a guard's compartment for each section.

Throughout railway history - as, indeed, elsewhere - it has almost always been the case that the departmental head, or even the General Manager, took the public credit for developments for which he was nominally responsible, even although these may have been the work of a subordinate. This is fair enough; after all, the

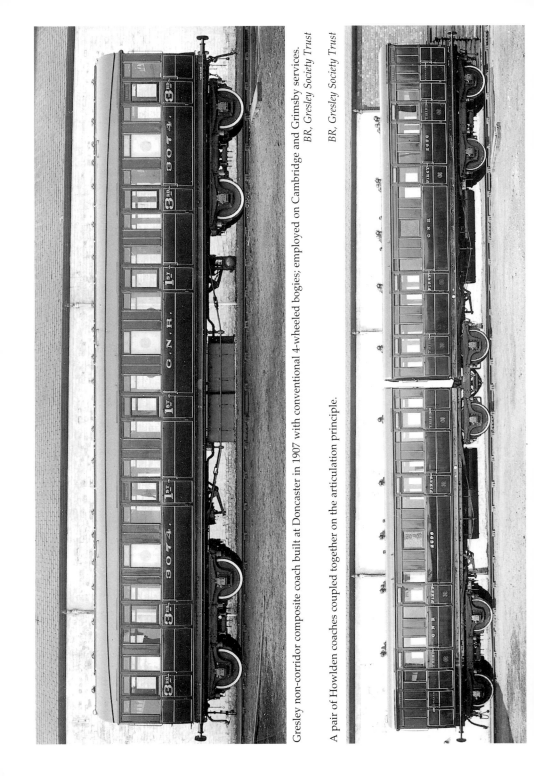

Gresley non-corridor composite coach built at Doncaster in 1907 with conventional 4-wheeled bogies; employed on Cambridge and Grimsby services.

BR, Gresley Society Trust

A pair of Howlden coaches coupled together on the articulation principle.

BR, Gresley Society Trust

chief had the responsibility, and would get the credit for successful projects - and the corresponding opprobrium if they failed. Indeed, it was unusual until more recent times for an assistant to have his name in the news at all, except perhaps on appointment or retirement. But in July 1906, a report in the *Railway Engineer* gave details of an experimental 35 ton bogie goods wagon built for the Great Northern Railway. This was provided with bogies designed to rotate, so easing the difficulty of turning such a long vehicle on an ordinary goods turntable. The credit for this innovation was given to H.N. Gresley, described in the press release as 'Assistant Superintendent of the Carriage and Wagon Department'. So, little more than a year after joining the Great Northern, Gresley was given the personal credit for work he had done. Another product of the period was a bogie well wagon, intended to carry heavy machinery, and which was photographed carrying a Stirling Single locomotive, to demonstrate its load potential. This was undoubtedly a Gresley design, but in this case he was not mentioned by name.

The slow transition from fixed wheelbase to bogie coaching stock had left the Great Northern with a substantial number of outdated, but otherwise sound, carriages, which gave passengers a hard ride. Lord Allerton, the Great Northern Chairman, put the point to Ivatt that perhaps they could be modified in some way to offer more comfort. This gave rise to the suggestion that rather than provide these short wheelbase coaches with a pair of bogies each, two coaches could be permanently coupled by sharing a single central bogie, with individual bogies attached at the outer ends, on the same principle as the rail motors. The first such pairing was completed in 1907, and immediately put to work on Anglo-Scottish services, on which it was favourably reported.

The technical press at the time were informed that the credit for these 'flexible twin carriages' was due to H.N. Gresley, 'the Manager of the Carriage & Wagon Department of the Great Northern Railway'. So, Gresley was now established in the public eye, and no longer an anonymous figure under Henry Ivatt. Moreover, he went to the trouble of taking out a patent on the principle, although it was not known at the time as 'articulation', the term not coming into general use until 15 years later. (Interestingly, 'articulation' - the word means 'jointed' - was first used in railway practice to describe a Mallett locomotive built in America.) Gresley is sometimes given the credit for introducing (or even inventing) articulation, but while he certainly pioneered its application to bogie coaching stock, the principle had been established for many years. Indeed, Hamilton Ellis mentions that a patent in the name of Claxton Fidler was taken out in the USA as long ago as 1869, involving 4-wheeled coaches connected by a frame with a single axle beneath. Eventually about 100 Howlden coaches were modernised by being grouped in articulated pairs, as well as smaller numbers in triplet and quadruplet sets. By the end of Gresley's term as C&W Superintendent, the articulation principle had been extended to new construction, an eight-coach train having been introduced for the London suburban service. This was made up of four twin sets, close-coupled to form a single unit. Gresley retained a partiality for the articulation principle throughout his career, and this will be discussed further, in Chapter Nine.

As an aside for the moment, it is interesting to contrast the town of Doncaster with other important railway manufacturing centres such as Crewe and Swindon, which were created by the railway. Doncaster was a focus of the coal mining industry long before it was chosen as the site of the Great Northern works, the Plant, as it was to become known. Also, for many years before the coming of the railway, the racecourse attracted the best in horse racing, especially after the Classic race, the St Leger, was held there. A good deal of passenger traffic was generated whenever a meeting was held, and of course movement of coal provided a major source of revenue for the GNR. But Doncaster also gained a very short lived fame in another form of transport, aeronautics, when in October 1909, no more than a few months after Blériot had made the first cross-channel flight, what was described as the first flying meeting in Britain took place on the Town Moor at Doncaster. Leading air aces of the time took part, including Col Cody, who was slightly injured when his aircraft was damaged whilst taxi-ing. Strangely, the Great Northern Railway offered a cup, valued at 50 guineas, for the aircraft achieving the highest speed, but this does not seem to have been awarded. One wonders what was the reaction of the hundreds of railwaymen based in the town, on watching the flimsy biplanes of the period taking the air. Also, around this period, Gresley addressed the Danum Social and Literary Society, on the subject of 'Aviation'. The text of his address has not survived, so his predictions for the future of this new form of transport have not been revealed. He is not known to have referred to the subject again.

In the 10 years from Gresley's appointment to the outbreak of the Great War, improvements in coaching stock were introduced gradually, changes being made in accommodation to meet passengers' demands for greater comfort and additional facilities. These are described in detail in the specialist books on Gresley's carriages mentioned in the Bibliography, but the continuation of his basic style can be appreciated by comparing Doncaster's products in 1905 and 1914. As well as structural improvements, there were subtle changes in livery and accessories, although the florid, heavily serifed, characters remained, gold shaded blue for GNR, shaded green for ECJS. Ventilators were more squat, evidently smaller, but probably the most noticeable feature was the general adoption of the Gresley/Spencer Moulton pattern of bogie, with its pressed steel sides.

Henry Ivatt, who had succeeded Patrick Stirling in 1896, made it known to the Great Northern Board that he intended to retire on his 60th birthday, on 16th September, 1911. There can be no doubt that he made his plans with the full knowledge that the succession was assured, and he would be followed as Locomotive Engineer by Nigel Gresley. The post was not advertised, and the note of anxiety in Lord Allerton's letters during Gresley's illness indicates the Chairman's concern in case his health prevented him from taking over the job. In fact, he made a full recovery, and assumed responsibility on 1st October, Ivatt postponing his retirement until the end of the year, to ease the changeover. As an aside, an interesting insight into GNR staff relations at the time took place when, to commemorate Ivatt's retirement, 200 officers and staff attended a farewell dinner and smoking concert at the Doncaster drill hall. The Works Manager, Francis Wintour, well-known for his forthrightness, and who had been Gresley's rival for the post of C&W Superintendent in 1905, presented Ivatt with his portrait - a 'speaking likeness' - and, in a reference to Gresley, promised the guests that their new chief would do all he could to help those who worked under him.

Chapter Five

Early Years as Locomotive Engineer

Nigel Gresley's appointment as Ivatt's successor was confirmed by the Great Northern Board at their meeting on 8th August, 1911, to be effective from the following 1st October. His title was that of Locomotive Engineer, the full extent of his duties being itemised in the Minutes, including the perquisite of being allowed to take on a small number of pupils. He had departmental responsibility for the development, construction and maintenance of all Great Northern rolling stock - locomotives, coaches and wagons - as well as for mechanical and electrical installations, including the workshops, docks machinery, and the miscellany of outdoor functions from power and water supplies to road vehicles and even down to the design of platform trolleys. As was usual at the time, he also had control of locomotive running, although this was to be made a separate department after the Grouping of the railways in 1923. (Civil engineering, and communications and signalling, were, of course, not his direct concern.) But, surprisingly, Gresley's extensive responsibilities were not to be recognised as such in his title. It is strange that the Great Northern did not accord him the title of Chief Mechanical Engineer, instead of merely Locomotive Engineer. Presumably he would have preferred the comprehensive title, as more fitting professionally, and being to the credit of the GNR. Even in those days, other major companies, and some lesser ones, recognised the point, and one wonders what internal opposition may have been voiced within the GNR Board. After all, he enjoyed the full support of Lord Allerton, the Chairman, who presumably would have been in sympathy with the more appropriate title. However, following Gresley's promotion, his salary was advanced to £1,800, to be further increased within a couple of years to £2,000. (For comparison, Charles Dent, the General Manager, was paid £3,500, W.J. Grinling, the Chief Traffic Manager, £2,300, and Charles Brown, the Civil Engineer, £1,800.)

Gresley soon strengthened his team with the appointment of Oliver Bulleid as personal technical assistant - a job description of sufficient breadth to allow its holder access to most matters within the chief's jurisdiction. Bulleid had joined the Great Northern in 1901 as a premium apprentice under Ivatt, subseqently becoming assistant to Webster, the Running Superintendent, and later to Wintour, the Doncaster Works Manager, before taking a job with Westinghouse in France at the end of 1907. Anthony Bulleid tells us that when his father left the GNR, Gresley told him, unprophetically, 'It is very easy to leave a railway, but very hard to get back on it'. But, four years later, his continental employment came to an end, and it was fortunate both for him and for Gresley that he was able to rejoin the Great Northern, and the two worked closely together until 1937, when Bulleid obtained the chief's position on the Southern Railway, in succession to Richard Maunsell. Also, Edward Thompson was recruited from the North Eastern Railway as Carriage & Wagon Superintendent, although of course Gresley still had the responsibility, and

Ivatt class 'N1' 0-6-2T LNER No. 4587, on empty coach working into King's Cross, 27th July, 1935. Built in 1912, after Gresley's appointment, this had a further 21 years of useful life in front of it. It was one of two requisitioned by the Government, and armour plated, for defence purposes.   *R.S. Carpenter Collection*

Gresley's first Mogul, here seen at King's Cross shed in GNR livery as No. 1630, soon after entering service.   *Gresley Society Trust*

maintained his close hold on this aspect of his department. The association between Gresley and Thompson was to last, with two brief intervals, until Gresley's death.

Ivatt had introduced his large Atlantics and 'Long Tom' 0-8-0 freight locomotives before Gresley's arrival at Doncaster. These continued to be built in batches through the first decade of the 1900s, coping respectively with the longer distance passenger and freight traffic of the period. After a few years, however, the need arose for more powerful locomotives for other duties, including a suburban tank engine, and a modernised design to cope with the growing number of goods services required to run at higher speeds. Although Gresley's position at the time did not specifically involve him with locomotives, one wonders to what extent he may have been drawn into discussions with Ivatt on these matters. Clearly, he was increasingly gaining his chief's confidence, and it would have been no surprise if Gresley had been consulted, in addition to Ivatt's usual contacts with his staff, particularly the Works Manager and the chief draughtsman, as well as, of course, Oliver Bury, the Chairman of the GNR Locomotive Committee. For the London suburban traffic, after an 0-8-2T design (LNER class 'R1') turned out to be unsuitable for these duties, a workmanlike and well-proportioned 5 ft 8 in. 0-6-2T (class 'N1') was evolved, first appearing in 1907. For fast goods and occasional passenger work, an improved design of 0-6-0 (class 'J1') with the same boiler and coupled wheels as the 'N1', emerged from Doncaster the following year. Indeed, these classes continued to be built after Ivatt had retired. They included 25 'N1s', followed by 10 further mixed traffic 0-6-0s ('J2'), an improved piston-valved version of those built earlier; all had entered traffic by the end of 1912, against orders placed in the preceding two years.

After his promotion, Gresley was not slow to bring in an entirely new locomotive concept, and in August 1912, concurrently with the batch of 'J2s', his first 2-6-0 appeared, a mixed traffic locomotive with 5 ft 8 in. driving wheels, later to become LNER class 'K1'. The speed with which the design was completed and the engine built leads one to question whether it had been on the drawing board even before Ivatt had retired. This wheel arrangement, popularly known as the 'Mogul', was not new to the GNR, as 20 of the type had been purchased in 1899 from the Baldwin Locomotive Works in America, to meet a motive power shortage. (The GNR were not alone in this; similar circumstances had forced other English railways to do the same.) However, these imported engines were primarily intended for everyday goods work, and although three of them worked for a time on London suburban trains, they were not standard in any way with Doncaster products and did not last long in service once the urgency had passed. Nevertheless, it is highly probable that Gresley took the idea for his Mogul from North America, and in this he followed the Great Western, where Harold Holcroft, a technical assistant to that railway's CME, the eminent engineer George Churchward, had convinced his chief of the merits of this type of locomotive for mixed traffic duties, resulting in the first of the GWR '43XX' class emerging from Swindon in June 1911.

Gresley went further than Churchward in providing his 2-6-0 with outside Walschaerts valve gear, the first time that this had been seen in Britain in a *class* of main line locomotives. The way was now opened for other engineers to do the same, although this was not to the liking of those who believed that the typically clean lines of British locomotives should not be cluttered by such machinery. It is of more than passing interest that not only had Ivatt employed this system on his experimental 4-cylinder compound Atlantics, and on the rail motors, but in 1907 Doncaster produced a drawing of a 2-6-2 design, with 5 ft 8 in. wheels and 200 lb./sq. in. boiler pressure. This would have been an advanced design for its day, a 4-cylinder compound, with Walschaerts valve gear driving the outside valves, and Stephenson gear those inside. Perhaps this had been found helpful by Gresley in the development of his first Mogul. Later, he was to justify his preference for outside cylinders and Walschaerts valve gear by stressing the greater accessibility of working parts. In his own words, 'With such an engine it is not necessary to put it over a pit before leaving the shed, and the essential parts can be examined in a good light, a very important consideration. You cannot see well underneath an engine in a shed, and light is a very great advantage'. Another novelty of the time was the swing link system for controlling the pony truck, adapted from the bogie pattern brought from Ireland by Ivatt. Gresley patented his 2-wheeled version in 1912. This new 2-6-0, a firm step into a new era of locomotive design, did not, however, signify a radical departure from the traditional Great Northern lines. The reverse curves of the running plate over the coupled wheels were retained, as well as the somewhat Spartan cab, whilst the boiler was recognisably a shortened version of that fitted to the Ivatt 0-8-0s.

The pioneer 'K1', GNR No. 1630, had not been long in service before a further nine appeared early in 1913, by which time it was appreciated that the boiler was undersized for sustained working at maximum power, and in future construction - to which the initial 10 were later converted - the boiler was increased in diameter from 4 ft 8 in. to 5 ft 6 in. This was the only occasion on which Gresley failed to observe Ivatt's dictum that an engine's performance depended on its capacity to boil water, but, unlike Stirling, whose cylinders on his final design of Singles were large in relation to boiler capacity, he was soon to rectify the matter. However, this may not have been an error. The new engines were badly needed, and using an existing boiler design saved the time involved in producing a new, enlarged one, which eventually appeared the following year. No. 1640 was the first of a class (LNER 'K2') which, after the first 10 had been reboilered to the later standard, totalled 75.

The 'K2s' were used to introduce improvements in design detail, which found their way into later Gresley classes. For example, in the final batches the live steam pipes were placed outside the smokebox. This might be regarded as another visual intrusion, but offered the advantage of a more direct steam flow to the steam chests, and was first seen on 'K2s' built by the North British Locomotive Co. in 1918. In these locomotives the steam pipes were concealed by covers of angled section, but Gresley's future outside cylinder designs featured rounded covers, which added a pleasing balance at the front end. The Mogul concept was also to be taken up by the South Eastern & Chatham (SE&CR) and London Brighton & South Coast (LB&SCR) railways, as well as, after Grouping, by the LMS, although none of these designs, nor that of Churchward, was to have the power capacity of the type as Gresley eventually developed it in his 'K3' of 1920.

The next major project for the Doncaster Drawing Office was a new class to deal with heavy freight traffic. This resulted in a 2-8-0, to be LNER class 'O1', possibly also inspired by a Churchward design introduced as far back as 1903, but again in advance of Great Western practice (although Churchward would have disputed this) by employing Walschaerts valve gear and a higher degree of superheat. Five were built in 1913/14, again recognisably in the GNR tradition, but with the longest stroke (28 in.) cylinders to be seen in a Gresley design. Boiler pressure, as on the 2-6-0s, was 170 lb./sq. in. Both classes were provided with Ramsbottom safety valves, later to be replaced by the Ross 'pop' type, which required less headroom and saved steam, but gave no warning of imminent blowing-off. Piston tail rod extensions were fitted, later to be omitted. Several engineers had specified this refinement, believing that this method of guiding the piston movement led to less wear to the cylinder walls. However, experience over a period of years convinced Gresley that the extensions caused more trouble than they saved.

These two classes, the 2-6-0 and the 2-8-0, were significantly in advance of earlier GN mixed traffic and freight engines, and sent a clear signal to the contemporary world of locomotive engineering that Nigel Gresley was a member of the profession who was not content with the past tradition of hiding connecting rods and valve gear between the frames, but, in the interest of operating efficiency and accessibility, unafraid of criticism on purely aesthetic grounds. However, at speed, they gave a lively ride, and following popular dance crazes of the period, the 2-8-0s were called 'Tangos', while the 2-6-0s were known as 'Ragtimers' - which term, affectionately abbreviated to 'Raggies', lasted until the engines were withdrawn, well into BR days.

The large-boilered Ivatt Atlantics, supported by the smaller version known as the 'Klondykes', and his 4-4-0s, dealt competently with the GNR passenger traffic of the period, so that in the first years of his administration Gresley was able to concentrate on meeting the increasing demands for greater power for goods traffic. This was also reflected in his further production of two traditional GNR types, the 5 ft 2 in. 0-6-0 for shorter distance goods traffic, and the 0-6-0 shunting tank. The first of these, LNER class 'J6', in fact differed little from an Ivatt design first seen in 1911, and they continued to be built in batches over the next 10 years, a total of 110 being turned out, all from Doncaster. However, a marked external change was seen in the 0-6-0Ts, in which the saddle tank dating from Patrick Stirling's early days was replaced by plain side tanks. These were extended forward to the front of the smokebox, to increase water capacity, but at the same time provided with a sloping front top, to give the driver a better view when buffering up during shunting operations. A cutout was provided in the tanks to allow access to the inside motion. The first 30 were provided with 4 ft 2 in. diameter boilers, subsequently increased to 4 ft 5 in., the originals eventually being rebuilt with the larger boiler. The LNER classification was 'J51' for the earlier version, 'J50' for the later standard. These small but powerful engines were first built for service in the West Riding, as a result of which they became known as the 'Ardsley tanks', several being stationed at that shed, but they were subsequently adopted as an LNER standard design, and were to be seen in many parts of the system. They

Gresley's first 3-cylinder 2-8-0, here seen as LNER No. 3461, heading an up coal train at Greenwood, when stationed at New England in the early 1930s. Note the inclination of the outside cylinders. *Photomatic*

The 2:1 motion bar in the final version of Gresley's conjugated valve gear, fitted to LNER class 'O2' 2-8-0 No. 3487. Note the bearings and linkages which needed regular lubrication.
BR, Gresley Society Trust

Ivatt class 'J6' 0-6-0 as GNR No. 522, fitted by Gresley with an experimental top-feed system in 1916.
BR, Gresley Society Trust

A later Gresley 'J6' 0-6-0, LNER No. 3584 hauling a down goods train at Crouch End on 29th August, 1925, with a 50-ton brick wagon immediately behind the engine.
Ken Nunn Collection, LCGB

The 'J50' 0-6-0T was not built in the same quantity as similar engines on the LMS and Great Western. For many years they were mainly to be seen in the West Riding, but here are two at work on the Great Central section. No. 3213 is in steam at Leicester GC shed on 16th July, 1939, oddly with an express train headcode.   *R.J. Buckley*

No. 3171 is presumably at Dukinfield with a locally made boiler beginning its journey.

Gresley Society Trust

appeared in batches up to 1939, by which time 102 had been built. All came from Doncaster, except for the last 14, which were turned out from the former Great Central works at Gorton in 1938/39. Originally provided with Ramsbottom safety valves, the Ross 'pop' type were fitted later.

In 1919, consideration was given to a 3-cylinder 0-8-0T as an enlargement of the 'J50', with outside cylinders, but this proposal was not pursued.

It is of interest that, unlike other standard 0-6-0Ts, such as the LMS 'Jinties', the Great Western pannier tanks, and certain of the Great Eastern 'J69s', although most of the 'J50s' were provided with the vacuum brake, they were never used regularly on passenger trains, apart from dealing with empty carriages. Probably the reason was that there were enough 5 ft 8 in. tank engines on the Great Northern specifically designed for passenger duties. Incidentally, after Gresley had been in office for 12 months, he pointed out that by painting goods and shunting engines dark grey, with white lettering, instead of passenger green, an annual saving of £1,000 would be achieved. The Board had no difficulty in agreeing with him.

By the time Gresley was appointed Locomotive Engineer of the GNR, two major improvements in the technology of the steam locomotive had gained wide acceptance. One was the use of piston valves for controlling the flow of steam to and from the cylinders, in place of slide valves, possibly encouraged by their development in connection with the internal combustion engine, and with Ricour, in France, in 1883, followed by W.M. Smith of the North Eastern Railway five years later, applying them to the steam locomotive. Improved control of valve events was obtained, and hence better use of steam, with less leakage, particularly after improvements in the quality of the steel from which the valve rings were made. Moreover, frictional losses were greatly reduced with piston valves.

The second major innovation, the superheater, followed the realisation that locomotive performance would be enhanced by raising the temperature of the steam entering the cylinders. This was associated with the employment of piston valves, slide valves being unsuitable for high steam temperatures. Essentially, the superheater carries boiler steam through a further set of element tubes, fitted into the large flue pipes, the superheated steam then entering a header from which it is led to the steam chests. Superheating brings improvements in that by increasing the steam temperature, moisture and the subsequent power losses due to condensation and water droplets are greatly reduced, whilst the higher volume due to more complete gasification results in greater power. The principles of superheating had been realised in the 1850s, but the first practical application resulted from collaboration between the Belgian engineer J.B. Flamme and the Prussian Dr Wilhelm Schmidt, and was seen in a 4-4-0 design of 1898. In the early years of the 20th century, British engineers began to incorporate it in their locomotives, led by George Churchward, and George Hughes of the Lancashire & Yorkshire, who contributed an article to *The Engineer* on the subject. It was to be found in practice that the superheater was of considerable benefit in power and economy to locomotives which needed to be worked hard for lengthy periods, but that its use on shunting engines was not normally worth while.

Superheating was one of the few major matters of steam practice to be debated by the Association of Railway Locomotive Engineers (ARLE), an informal group of which most chief locomotive engineers, and some carriage and wagon assistants, were members. Even so, the subject was not raised until 1911, when John McIntosh, of the Caledonian Railway, announced that he had incorporated a Schmidt type superheater in one of his engines, and that on a journey from Perth to Carlisle this had showed a saving of a quarter in coal and water costs. He was supported by James Holden, of the Great Eastern, and Douglas Earle Marsh, of the LB&SCR, whilst John Robinson, of the Great Central, who also had had experience with Schmidt superheaters, made the interesting suggestion that as a result, boiler steam pressure could be reduced, say from 180 to 150 lb./sq. in. An astonishing viewpoint was expressed by Wilson Worsdell, of the North Eastern Railway, who remarked that 'When the expense of the whole system, and the results obtained from the so-called saving of coal were considered, there wouldn't be much in the superheater'.

However, all this was rather late in the day, as by the time the ARLE had got round to discussing the topic, superheating was becoming established practice. Indeed, as far back as 1905, Ivatt had recommended that a superheater should be fitted to an express engine by way of a trial, and asked authority from the GNR Board to spend approximately £250 on buying one from the American Locomotive Company (Alco). This was agreed, but in the event the superheater purchased was of the Schmidt pattern, and fitted to one of Ivatt's 'Long Tom' 0-8-0s. The first GNR express engine to be superheated was a small Atlantic, in 1908, but the results were so convincing that when the final batch of 10 large Atlantics were built two years later, they were provided with Schmidt 18-element superheaters.

The next few years saw a very wide acceptance of the idea, marked by a disinclination to pay Schmidt the patent fees demanded, typically £50 per installation. Moreover, in the Schmidt system the element tubes were bolted to the header using copper joint rings, which tended to perish in time under the action of high temperature steam and smokebox gases. To take advantage of the situation, Robinson developed his own version, which was to become one of the most widely adopted in Britain. By expanding the elements directly into the superheater header, this had the advantage of avoiding the steam leakage to which the Schmidt system was prone. In 1913, Gresley designed and patented his own 'twin-tube' version, in which there were separate headers for saturated and superheated steam, but he employed the Robinson system in his larger locomotives.

Although Churchward was one of the first to appreciate the value of the superheater, he did not consider at the time that a high degree of superheat would be still more beneficial. He thought that if the steam temperature was high enough to ensure an absence of condensation in the cylinders, this would be sufficient, bearing in mind the problems of carbonisation when lubrication is affected by high temperatures. However, suitable oils were developed to cope with this difficulty. A further problem introduced by the superheater was the need to prevent overheating of the elements when steam was shut off during running. Ivatt's solution was to insert a 'snifting' valve on the inlet side of the superheater, to allow the ingress of cooling air. This was to be seen immediately behind the chimney, a distinctive twin thimble shape in Ivatt's day, while Gresley's version had the outline of a mushroom. Reference has already been made to the great improvement in the performance of Ivatt's large Atlantics by the addition of superheating, and Gresley was further to increase the power of these already capable machines by introducing a larger 32-element Robinson type superheater, in December 1918. Over the years, all the class were improved in this way.

Once he had made provision for meeting the Great Northern's need for larger freight and mixed traffic locomotives, Gresley turned his mind to passenger engines. Ivatt's 4-4-0s were not of great power, and it is possible that Gresley might have toyed with the idea of producing one of this type of his own, as in 1914 a wheelbase and weight diagram was drawn out at Doncaster, showing 20 tons on each of the driving axles, which indicated the possibility of something on the lines of Robinson's Great Central 'Director' class. However, nothing more has been found on the subject, and Gresley's eyes became focused on the next generation of front line express locomotives. He perceived that since the loading gauge imposed limitations on the size of outside cylinders, unless boiler pressure could be substantially increased (to which he was unwilling to agree, one reason being the greater incidence of formation of boiler scale in the days before effective chemical water treatment), a multi-cylinder configuration would be needed to provide the requisite power output. So, in 1913, Doncaster drew up plans for a 4-cylinder simple 4-4-2, with outside Walschaerts gear operating the inside piston valves by means of rocking shafts and pendulum levers, and two years later No. 279 was rebuilt in this form, for evaluation as a possible prototype. (It will be remembered that Ivatt's compounds had also had four cylinders, but were not too successful.)

Around this period Gresley was looking at Churchward's *The Great Bear* of 1908, and was keen to see how a Doncaster Pacific might appear. So, an outline of a Pacific was drawn out in 1915, following Ivatt's principles of large boiler and wide firebox. Although it was given the four 15 in. x 26 in. cylinders of the GWR 'Star' class, boiler pressure was still limited to 170 lb./sq. in. Also in his 'Stars', Churchward had provided a flat-topped Belpaire type firebox and was not afraid to adopt a working pressure of 225 lb./sq. in., but Gresley did not concur, at least for the time being. His Pacific's boiler was 20 ft long, three feet shorter than that of *The Great Bear*, and with the traditional windowless Great Northern cab, in appearance it was not unlike a 'stretched' Ivatt Atlantic. (In passing, it should not be thought that *The Great Bear* was a failure. It was in fact basically a 'Star', modified by the provision of a longer boiler and a wide firebox with 41 sq. ft grate area, but, due to weight restrictions, it was confined to the Paddington to Bristol line and did not have the opportunity to exploit the increased boiler capacity it undoubtedly possessed, on other more demanding routes of the GWR.)

However, Gresley does not seem to have been impressed by the results obtained from the rebuilt No. 279, and no doubt his thoughts went back to his days at Crewe, when Francis Webb, who believed in simplicity in driving mechanism, employed three cylinders in many of his compound locomotives.

For half a dozen years around 1930, modernised Ivatt Atlantics in a special link took a major part in the Pullman services from King's Cross. Twenty-three years after first entering traffic, and now with piston valves and 32-element superheater, No. 4411 heads the up 'Queen of Scots', passing Barkston on 10th August, 1929.   *F.G. Carrier, Gresley Society Trust*

Ivatt Atlantic No. 279 modified by Gresley to obtain experience with 4-cylinder drive.
          John Alsop Collection

A 4-cylinder drive possessed the benefit of offering a relatively simple direct rocking lever arrangement to drive the valves of the inside cylinders from the outside valve gears, but *prima facie*, three cylinders each required separate eccentrics and valve gear. However, apart from providing the necessary additional cylinder volume, three cylinders with cranks set at 120 degrees offered perceived advantages over a 2-cylinder drive, such as smoother torque and better balancing of reciprocating parts with consequently less hammer blow to the track. As well as locomotives intended for express passenger work, large freight and mixed traffic engines would also benefit from the advantages of 3-cylinder drive, which would be less cumbersome and less costly than four cylinders.

The concept of 3-cylinder drive had in fact been around for many years, first appearing in a drawing of a 'steam rail carriage' designed by Hick Hargreaves & Co. in 1833. There is also a record of a patent having been taken out as long ago as 1839, by one Isaac Dodds, for a 6-wheeled locomotive, although it is not known if it was built. Robert Stephenson & Co. are credited with the first to be put in service, two 4-2-0s being constructed for the York, Newcastle and Berwick Railway in 1846. These were followed by several examples on the Continent and in the United States. In Britain, following the work of Francis Webb in 1881 and W.M. Smith in 1898, on compound locomotives, John Robinson also tried compounding on four Atlantics built in 1905/06, employing 3-cylinder drive. Although these remained in their original condition until withdrawal 40 years later, he did not attempt any further compound designs, but in 1908 rebuilt one of his 2-cylinder simple Atlantics to 3-cylinder drive, but this was again rebuilt, to its original form, in 1922. His other 3-cylinder locomotives were four 0-8-4Ts turned out from Gorton in 1907 for hump shunting duties, the valves being actuated by individual Stephenson link motion between the frames. However, he did not extend 3-cylinder drive to his later locomotives, preferring a 4-cylinder arrangement in two of his final 4-6-0 designs, nor did he depart from his choice of Stephenson valve gear, also fitted internally. Another pioneer of 3-cylinder propulsion in Great Britain at that period was Wilson Worsdell, who in September 1909 had followed Robinson with his own heavy shunting tank, this time a 4-8-0T, also with three sets of internal Stephenson valve gear. In both these large tank locomotive designs, the use of three cylinders was justified by the more even torque, so desirable in avoiding wheelslip in shunting operations. Next, Worsdell produced a 3-cylinder 4-6-2T for short haul mineral traffic, and Vincent Raven continued Worsdell's philosophy with his notable class 'Z' (LNER class 'C7') Atlantic of 1911. These too were given separate Stephenson valve gear for all three cylinders, with six eccentrics, making for a congested layout between the frames. None of the other LNER constituents adopted 3-cylinder propulsion, except the Great Eastern, in James Holden's experimental 0-10-0T 'Decapod' of 1902.

Clearly, however, if a satisfactory indirect drive could be evolved for the valves of the inside cylinder, this would obviate the need for a third complete set of valve motion. Such a mechanism had been patented and built by David Joy in 1884, but for a triple expansion marine engine. Years later,

Nigel Gresley; a portrait taken *c*.1916. *Tim Godfrey*

Churchward's technical assistant Harold Holcroft studied the subject, and in 1909 patented a system by which the valves for the inside cylinder could be operated by motion derived from the action of the outside valves. Also, in 1913, the same principle but in a different form was incorporated in a 2-8-2T locomotive built by Henschel in Germany, this being applied eventually to some hundreds of engines altogether, including large numbers in France, and some in Spain. Gresley clearly visualised the benefits that this mechanism would add to a 3-cylinder drive, and drew out his own ideas for such a system. Holcroft's patent lapsed, no doubt because of the lack of interest displayed by his erstwhile chief, Churchward, and in 1915 Gresley decided to proceed with an application for a patent on two systems of his own, one somewhat complex, the other more straightforward, featuring a substantial motion bar, known as the '2 to 1' lever. It was this which was to become popularly known as his 'conjugated' valve gear.

The next step was to draw up a scheme to adapt the successful 2-8-0 to 3-cylinder drive with the first type of Gresley gear, and following this a prototype, GNR No. 461, was built at Doncaster, although due to wartime delays it was not completed until May 1918. This appeared to do all that had been hoped for, despite criticism of the complication of the mechanism, and what was regarded as the excessive inclination of the outside cylinders. The locomotive drive layout was the subject of comment in the correspondence columns of *The Engineer* by an anonymous mechanical engineer who was intent on criticising Gresley without revealing his own identity. He has since been identified as W.Rowland, chief draughtsman of the Great Central, and who in 1922 dealt severely with statements made by Cecil J. Allen in the discussion following a paper Allen gave to the Institution of Locomotive Engineers on the influence of design on locomotive performance.

Holcroft was now working for Richard Maunsell on the South Eastern & Chatham Railway, and had observed Gresley's new venture, and thought that he could assist in the layout of Gresley's simple version of the conjugated valve gear by employing horizontal actuating levers in place of the rotary cross shafts of the system applied to No. 461, mainly by inclining only the *middle* cylinder, and making a corresponding adjustment to the crank angle setting. He took the opportunity to present this in a major paper read at a meeting of the Locomotive Engineers in November 1918, opening by reminding his audience that 'It is fairly evident that successful design lies in producing from a given weight of material, maximum efficiency and power at a minimum first cost, combined with the greatest possible simplicity and least number of parts, so as to reduce upkeep'. (As a statement of objectivity in design, this would be hard to beat.) He went on to point out that the locomotive was only a part of the railway system, and the permanent way engineer must also have his say. Thus, while a large locomotive with two outside cylinders may be perceived to have advantages of simplicity from the locomotive engineer's point of view, engines that sway and hammer the track may cost the railway far more through the additional (and perhaps hidden) costs of track maintenance.

Holcroft went on to emphasise the fuel saving benefits of 3-cylinder drive, six exhaust beats per revolution being better than four heavier ones, so reducing

Gresley's two 2-8-0 designs. *Above:* GNR No. 456 was the first of his 2-cylinder version, built at Doncaster in December 1913. *Below:* No. 477, with three cylinders, was the first of the production series, built by the North British Locomotive Co. in 1921. Note the difference in the length of the connecting rods, the first (class 'O1') driving on to the third axle, the second (class 'O2') on to the second axle, also the contrast in slide bar design. *(Both) BR, Gresley Society Trust*

the tendency to throw sparks and 'pull' the fire. Moreover, whilst a 4-cylinder locomotive in which only two sets of valve gear were necessary had some advantages over a   3-cylinder one with three sets of gear, if two sets could effectively control the valve movements of three cylinders, then a still better arrangement would be achieved. He illustrated the value of this system to the railway, by quoting a 4-4-0, and claiming that a 3-cylinder version of this type could save costs over a 2-cylinder 4-6-0, with the same drawbar pull. Finally, he rounded up his case by presenting a mathematical model of a modified version of the 'simple' Gresley arrangement, and concluded by summarising the advantages gained by the use of three cylinders with cranks at 120 degrees.

The meeting attracted a wide-ranging discussion, which was opened by a Mr Sanderson, from the Baldwin Locomotive Works of the USA. Quoting from American practice, he questioned Holcroft's reasoning, concluding that 'Two-cylinder engines stay out on the road earning money when the four-cylinder engines are more frequently in the shop losing money, in consequence of the fact that they are laid up for repairs owing to the additional parts'. His attitude was clearly in favour of rugged simplicity in locomotive construction; other factors could take care of themselves. It is also true to say that the unequal turning effect of a 2-cylinder locomotive gave it a slightly greater peak tractive effort than the more equally balanced 3-cylinder type. This could be helpful in starting a heavy train at the limit of the locomotive's capacity. (But it contradicted the evidence of trials which Gresley had conducted between 2- and 3-cylinder 2-8-0s, the latter proving capable of starting heavier trains on gradients.) Sanderson was, however, probably expressing the view of a number of those responsible for locomotive running, as distinct from the design engineers (and in all probability, the civil engineers, too).

Nevertheless, Gresley obviously took note of what was being advocated by Holcroft, and the following January invited him to a meeting at King's Cross, when he so impressed Gresley that Maunsell was asked if he could be released, to join the Great Northern.   The answer was a firm 'No', Maunsell not unnaturally wishing to retain Holcroft's services for his own ultimate benefit. But by now, Gresley was sufficiently convinced that he had the answer to his search for an efficient 3-cylinder mechanism, and he was apply it to a number of important locomotive designs over the next few years. He reported on his experiences when he addressed the Mechanical Engineers in 1925, as mentioned in Chapter Seven.

Harold Holcroft deserves special mention at this point, in that he was one of those very able engineers who, whilst rarely reaching the limelight themselves, often provided the inspiration for their chiefs. Others who may be mentioned in this context from the companies which were to become constituents of the LNER included Fred V. Russell, of the Great Eastern, W.M. Smith, North Eastern, and W. Rowland, Great Central. Another, later to be particularly close to Gresley himself, and who was to present his own paper on LNER Locomotive Development to the Institution of Locomotive Engineers some years after Gresley's death, was Bert Spencer, who by coincidence had been welcomed as a graduate member of the Institution at the same meeting as that at which Holcroft gave his address. Norman Newsome, who served as Gresley's technical assistant for carriages and wagons, also gave a paper to the Locomotive Engineers after the war, summarising LNER developments in these aspects of rolling stock.

A number of senior railway engineers had been seconded to Government service in 1914-1918, Oliver Bulleid being one of these. As mentioned earlier, he had worked in France before the Great War, and returned there as an officer in the Service Corps (in later years, the RASC), as early as January 1915. Another was Edward Thompson, who in 1916 joined his former chief, Vincent Raven, at the Woolwich Arsenal, soon afterwards transferring to the Directorate of Transportation in France, in a position which carried the rank of lieutenant-colonel. Whilst Bulleid and Thompson were still away on military duties, Holcroft's assistance would have been invaluable to Gresley, but one wonders what personality difficulties might have arisen if he had been at Doncaster when they returned. Indeed, the post-war division of work between Gresley's two principal assistants is not clear. Bulleid was recognised as his senior technical assistant, presumably with a wide ranging area of consultancy, but without responsibility for any particular area of development. Thompson was effectively Carriage & Wagon Superintendent, which clearly defines his sphere of authority. Possibly there was some differences between the two, but if so it was soon resolved as in December 1920 Thompson left Doncaster and returned to his native North Eastern, as Carriage & Wagon Works Manager at York.

Although during his early years as Locomotive Engineer, Gresley concentrated on motive power, coaching stock was not neglected, although of course wartime did not permit any substantial development work. However, a notable event was the provision in 1914 of modern stock, some new and some refurbished, for the 'Flying Scotsman' trains. This prestige service had run since 1900 with Howlden clerestory coaches, and the fact that they had not been replaced earlier is a tribute to the quality of their design and construction. They may have become obsolescent but undoubtedly they were regarded as comfortable and even stylish by their regular patrons. Once again Great Northern practice was generally followed, new construction being shared between Doncaster and York, but there was an innovation in the provision of steel kitchen cars, intended as a protection against fire, as gas was used for cooking. (A number of serious accidents had occurred in previous years in which passengers had died as a result of fires due to the presence of gas.) The design of these kitchen cars is attributed to Vincent Raven, and although the outline followed the agreed Gresley profile, there were differences in detail. To match the teak finish of the rest of the coaches in the train, they were given a grained finish. Another notable vehicle was built in 1912 for the exclusive clientele who patronised the Harrogate service, when a conventional dining car was provided with individual oval mahogany dining tables, seating four people. However, this did not last, due to difficulties in providing waiter service of the quality required, in the confined spaces of the car.

Chapter Six

Evolution of the Gresley Style

A further important factor to influence Gresley's forward thinking was the publication in 1916, in the journal *Engineering*, of detailed drawings of the Pennsylvania Railroad class 'K4s' Pacific. (The 's' indicates that the locomotive was superheated. It is not to be confused with the Gresley 'K4' 2-6-0 of 1937.) The tapered boiler with a 19 ft barrel was pressed to 205 lb./sq. in., and possessed 5,189 sq. ft of heating surface, providing steam to two 27 in. x 28 in. cylinders. The wide firebox, with a grate area of 69.3 sq. ft, was of the flat-topped Belpaire type, featuring a substantial combustion chamber. Novelties to British eyes were the design of the slidebars and the use of lightweight nickel-chrome steel for the connecting and coupling rods. Gresley was said to have been very impressed by the overall concept, huge though it was by British standards, and made a serious mental note that here was something he could adapt for service on the Great Northern main line, when conditions returned to normal. But, whatever he may have learned from American practice, Gresley made no reference to the Pennsylvania Pacifics on any subsequent public occasion.

The 'K4s' itself had its own antecedents, the first of the lengthy series of Pennsylvania RR Pacifics being the class 'K28', No. 7067, built as a 'demonstrator' in 1907 by the American Locomotive Company. This was followed in 1910 by a further Alco Pacific, given the works number 50000, and which was claimed to be the first locomotive to have rationalised proportions of boiler, firebox, and cylinders. However, the prototype of the 'K4s' is regarded as the 'K29s' of 1911, despite its round-topped firebox, this also having been built by Alco, PRR No. 3395. The first of the 'K4s' class proper was No. 1737, built at the PRR works at Altoona in May 1914. Incredibly, the 'K4s' Pacifics were originally fired by hand, none of the class being fitted from new with a mechanical stoker, although these were provided later in the careers of the engines, no fewer than 425 of which were built up to 1928. In the course of their work prior to electrification, it is recorded that hand-fired 'K4s' locomotives hauled 17-car expresses totalling over 1,000 tons between New York and Washington, and that it was not unusual for them to be seen double- and even triple-heading trains over more heavily graded sectors of the system. At this point, it may also be of interest to recall how the Pacific type, and the name, originated. According to David Jackson's American sources, the pioneer 4-6-2 was built for the Lehigh Valley RR in 1886, the 'Pacific' appellation first being given to a 3 ft 6 in. gauge engine of this type, built by Baldwin for New Zealand in 1901. The following year saw the first standard gauge use of the name, applied to Alco 4-6-2s for the Missouri Pacific RR.

The origin of the flat-topped locomotive firebox goes back to 1862, and it has always been associated with the Belgian engineer, A.J. Belpaire. It was first used in Britain in 1891, by Thomas Parker, of the Manchester, Sheffield & Lincolnshire Railway, on an 0-6-2T, and remained a feature of that railway's engines, and those of its successor, the Great Central, under Harry Pollitt and

The Pennsylvania RR class 'K4s' Pacific is believed to have been studied carefully by Nigel Gresley, but major differences in design can be seen in the 2-cylinder drive and Belpaire firebox of the American locomotive. A total of 425 of the class were built between 1914 and 1928. No. 5451 was one of an order for 75 delivered by Baldwins in 1927.   *Rail Archive Stephenson*

Churchward's pioneer Pacific *The Great Bear* at Old Oak Common shed.   *G.W. Goslin Collection*

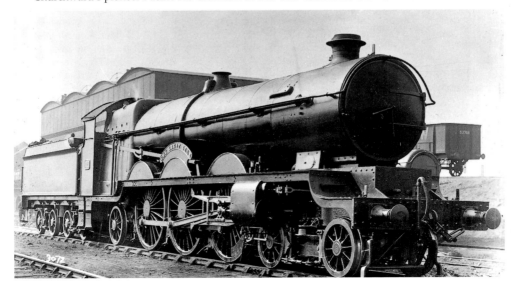

John Robinson, until the Grouping. The case for the Belpaire boiler was strongly argued by George Churchward, CME of the Great Western Railway, who more than any other British engineer brought the steam locomotive from its Victorian simplicity to comparative perfection in the early 20th century. He expounded his thinking on boiler design in a landmark paper entitled 'Large Locomotive Boilers' given to the Institution of Mechanical Engineers in February 1906, when he stated that the flat-topped firebox had the advantages of increasing the area of the water line at the hottest part of the boiler, and reducing foaming. Also, in conjunction with a tapered boiler, a flat-top firebox enabled the steam dome to be dispensed with, steam being taken by a pipe from the firebox casing. A tapered, rather than a wholly cylindrical, boiler, would improve water circulation and take fullest advantage of the hottest areas, at the top of the firebox and the firebox tubeplate. Churchward first adopted the flat-top firebox when he was responsible to William Dean for locomotive design, and this was continued by his successors on the Great Western, Charles B. Collett and F.W. Hawksworth. In addition, Churchward argued the case for the narrow against the wide firebox, which he considered to be more prone to leakage, and required greater skill on the part of the fireman.

In his 4-6-0 of 1903, Churchward kept the bottom line of the boiler barrel parallel with the track, whilst the top tapered from 5 ft 6 in. at the firebox to 4 ft 11 in. at the smokebox. An alternative, later to be favoured by Gresley and others, was to keep the *centre* line of the barrel parallel with the track, so providing more space beneath the front and giving better access to the machinery between the frames. This is more accurately termed a 'coned' boiler.

However, notwithstanding Churchward and the Pennsylvania 'K4s', Gresley would not be moved from his preference for the round-topped firebox. His response to Churchward's paper, although it may not have been intended as such, was given 12 years later, in May 1918, in what appears to have been the first public statement of certain of his basic principles of locomotive design. This was at the inaugural meeting of the Institution of Locomotive Engineers Leeds Centre, of which he was the first Chairman. In his address, he reiterated Ivatt's dictum that 'The power of an engine depends on its capacity to boil water, and is therefore without question its most important feature', and commented on 'The many engineers who compare the power of engines by their tractive force only, and ignore the boiler'. Without giving specific reasons, he expressed the view that 'Wide fireboxes last longer, and are more efficient than narrower ones'. He was dismissive of the Belpaire type. 'From a maintenance standpoint, the Belpaire boiler offers no advantages over the direct stayed round topped boiler, whilst undoubtedly its first cost is greater. This view is supported by the experience of American and Continental engineers, where the use of the direct stayed round topped boiler is most generally adopted for all new engines.'

It may be added that a circular firebox is theoretically better at resisting all-round pressure, hence one with a square top, such as the Belpaire, needs stronger staying. On the other hand, the Belpaire type, with its increased steam space, is claimed to offer greater help to the driver in preventing priming. In the last years of the LNER, Gresley's successor, Edward Thompson, differed

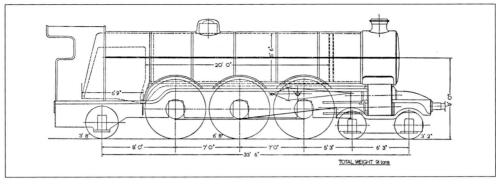

Nigel Gresley had set his sights on a Pacific design as early as 1915, as seen in this Doncaster drawing of the period.

A 1920 drawing, showing the transformation following Gresley's later thinking.

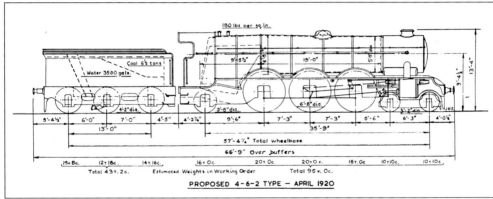

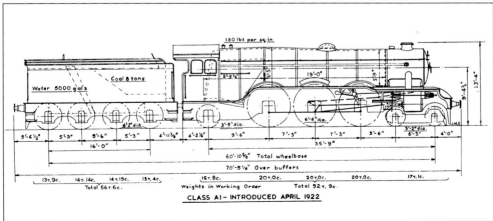

Class 'A1' as introduced in 1922.

from Sir Nigel over certain basic design features, but he certainly agreed with him on a preference for the round-topped firebox. However, all the British Railways' standard locomotives were provided with the Belpaire type, following the lead given by the Churchward-trained William Stanier when CME of the London Midland & Scottish Railway, and continued by R.A. (Robin) Riddles and Stewart Cox, but it is fair to conclude that no consensus has been reached on which type possesses the balance of advantage. Oddly, Bert Spencer, later to be Gresley's technical assistant, in a paper given to the Locomotive Engineers in 1923, dwelt on the advantages of the Belpaire boiler, saying that he was surprised that it was not used to a greater extent in this country - a statement quite opposed to Gresley's firmly held opinion. It is a fact that no Belpaire boilers were built at Doncaster until 1943, when the first of 30 Stanier '8F' 2-8-0s were constructed there to the order of the Ministry of War Transport. Edward Thompson is quoted as having said at the time that they cost 70 per cent more than the similar LNER standard boiler of diagram 100E.

Despite the restrictions imposed by wartime, Gresley's new passenger engine was slowly taking shape, and in 1918 consideration was given to alternative designs of 2-6-2, one with a wide, and one, surprisingly, with a narrow, firegrate. These led the way to further studies, and in 1920 a Pacific drawing emerged which is recognisable as outlining the version eventually to be built, the major external changes being a new side window cab, more commodious than the typical Great Northern cab with its cutouts, and a new design of rigid frame 8-wheeled tender replacing the GNR 6-wheeled version. Gresley was no doubt well pleased with the way his project was maturing. The design was to be finalised over the next few months, and early in 1921 an order was placed on Doncaster for construction of two of the new engines.

In the meantime, another interesting development was under way, when for once the Association of Railway Locomotive Engineers took on a job which went beyond its usual role of an unofficial forum, at which matters of detail - although often important - were discussed in a friendly fashion. In 1915, at the suggestion of the Government, the Association agreed to look into standardisation of design of 'metal coaches and wagons, and of locomotives'. No clear terms of reference were drawn up, but Churchward was asked to convene a group of locomotive engineers to see what might be done. Warning notes were soon sounded to the effect that standardisation would also have to be applied to rails and bridges, and, clearly, a common loading gauge would be a major problem, placing restrictions on rolling stock for those lines which had been built to tight clearances.

In addition to the original 'investigating' committee, a 'designing' committee was appointed, to consider two specific proposals for locomotives which could have a wide usage across most of the railways in Britain. These were a 2-6-0, for which Maunsell was to produce the drawings, and a 2-8-0, to be handled by Sir Henry Fowler of the Midland Railway. (This is interesting, as the Midland had for years been known as a 'small engine' railway, with its heavy mineral trains double-headed by a pair of 0-6-0s, due to limited bridge loadings. However, Derby had produced a workmanlike 2-8-0 for the Somerset & Dorset Joint Railway, in which the Midland was a partner and supplied the motive power.

Was Fowler hoping to use this ARLE project to influence his Board to change their locomotive policy?) Although early outlines of the two locomotives displayed characteristics of Ashford and Derby respectively, later drawings had more in common, and evidently both were prepared by James Clayton at Ashford.

Anyway, useful discussions took place, and Churchward was able to report to the ARLE's 1918 summer meeting that progress had been made with the proposed designs, and the outline drawings were submitted for consideration. Both followed principles not unlike those which were later developed for the British Railways' standard classes, incorporating two cylinders with outside Walschaerts valve gear, and Belpaire fireboxes. Gresley, however, was unimpressed. Any locomotive which had the appearance of a national standard, and which did not come from Doncaster, was not for him, and would only cramp his style. He had dealt with the subject of standardisation in his Leeds paper of May 1918, although admitting that he was touching on dangerous ground. He then stated clearly that he was a strong advocate of standardisation in principle, for example of components such as boilers, but not necessarily of standardised locomotives. In the event, the ARLE proposals came to nothing, beyond a series of 2-6-0s built over the next 13 years for the SE&CR, and later the Southern Railway.

Gresley now realised that a more powerful 2-6-0 than the 'K2' was needed, which he could use as a further step on the way to his Pacific. Peter Townend relates that he returned to Doncaster from an ARLE meeting and instructed Harold Broughton, the chief locomotive draughtsman, to put as large a boiler as possible on to the 'K2' chassis, and redesign it for 3-cylinder drive, with his improved 'simple' conjugated valve gear, but not to exceed a 20 ton axle load. This was done as a matter of urgency, with the result that the first of the new engines, LNER class 'K3', appeared in March 1920, being given the prestige GNR number 1000. Doncaster had taken their instructions literally, and the new locomotive was given a 6 ft diameter boiler, only leaving room for a squat chimney, this being further shortened when boiler mountings were cut down to meet the LNER loading gauge, which, because of the need to operate locomotives on other parts of the system, was more restrictive than that of the GNR. The design also took advantage of the lighter rods, slide bars and crossheads of the Pennsylvania 'K4s' Pacifics. Metallurgy had always held a fascination for Gresley, as evidenced by his time in the materials testing laboratory at Horwich at the conclusion of his pupillage. He gave the topic a brief airing in a paper given to the Locomotive Engineers in 1921, in Leeds, when he set out his views in detail. Nevertheless, the benefits of the light and elegant nickel-chrome steel rods were later to be discounted, as the original cost of manufacture was reckoned to be too high, the metal being difficult to machine, whilst the rods themselves, after a long period of service, were susceptible to embrittlement failures. On the other hand, Gresley persisted with the 'three bar' style of slidebar, which he had first used in his pioneer 3-cylinder 2-8-0 of 1918, and which was to remain a feature of all his subsequent outside cylinder locomotives. This has a broad bar as the upper guide, underneath which the crosshead travels between two narrower bars either side of a web projecting downwards, which provides the support for the gudgeon pin linking with the connecting rod. It has an additional advantage in that it does not obstruct access to the leading coupled crank pin, as may be the case with the conventional two bar pattern, in which the crosshead is larger, heavier and more cumbersome.

An early problem with the conjugated gear of the 'K3' 2-6-0s was over-travel of the centre valve, arising from lack of rigidity in the cross member carrying the main pivot of the mechanism. This caused damage to the covers of the centre steam chest, and was corrected by reducing the amount of valve travel. Eric Trask (later to rise to become Motive Power Superintendent of British Railways Eastern Region) has related how, when he was a technical assistant at King's Cross, on the first appearance of the 'K3s', the holding down bolts of the main pivot bearing of one of the class had sheared. He replaced them with ones of larger diameter, and when these also sheared, he replaced them by still larger bolts. The consequence was that the cross stay itself fractured, and this was brought to Gresley's attention. The enthusiastic Trask was suitably admonished, and the word came down to him: 'Never interfere with design'. In the end, a cast steel box type cross stay was provided.

The 'K3s' not only looked the part, but with 5 ft 8 in. driving wheels, three 18½ in. x 26 in. cylinders and 180 lb./sq. in. boiler pressure, on a tractive effort basis of 30,031 lb. they were at the time the most powerful 8-wheel engine running on a British railway. (In 1937, Gresley's new 'K4', with 5 ft 2 in. driving wheels, had a tractive effort of 36,600 lb.) The 'K3s' were to be seen at their best during the period of coal shortage arising from the miners' dispute of 1921, hauling what were prodigious passenger train loads for the period (600 tons has been quoted.) Like their predecessors, the 'K2' class, and many other powerful locomotives with a relatively short wheelbase, the 'K3s' could give a rough ride when run down, and their reputation as they 'danced' along the track earned them the title of 'Jazzers'. Why this should have been the case, and why Gresley appeared to do nothing about the problem, has never been explained. Possibly a serious investigation into the general springing arrangements, and the control of the pony truck, might have been of benefit. However, since there are records of drivers saying that 'K3s' new out of shops were steady riders, perhaps it was a matter of insufficient maintenance, to minimise play between axleboxes and hornblocks.

By 1920, the time had arrived for a further advance in design of the tank locomotives dealing with the Great Northern's increasing London suburban traffic. Ivatt's 0-6-2Ts, LNER class 'N1', were robust and powerful; Gresley investigated the case for a 2-6-2T, which was conceived with three cylinders, but concluded that a modernised 'N1' would be adequate for the task. In this, he was aware of the difficulty presented by the length limitations of the platforms at Moorgate station, where many of the inner suburban trains terminated. So, to the basic 'N1' he added his twin-tube superheater, increased the diameter of the cylinders from 18 in. to 19 in., and replaced the slide valves by piston valves. The consequence was that the centre line of the boiler was raised by seven inches, and this together with the necessity to cut down the boiler mountings and cab gave the engine a modernised appearance. The 'N2' proved to be faster

The Gresley Society Preservation Trust's 'N2', LNER No.4744, is seen at Loughborough, on the Great Central Railway. This was one of the order for 50 built by the North British Locomotive Company over a period of five months in 1920/21.   *W.R. Squires*

The Gresley 'N2' 0-6-2T and its eight-coach train of articulated coaches was a familiar part of the King's Cross suburban scene for over 40 years. No. 2669, built by Hawthorn, Leslie in 1928, is leaving Potters Bar for Hatfield on 28th May, 1946.   *Derrick Dant*

and more powerful than the 'N1', and hauled almost all the Great Northern inner suburban trains for 40 years, until the coming of the diesels in 1959. The design has been criticised because of the lack of leading wheels when running forwards, but it was the invariable practice to run chimney first out of King's Cross up the gradient to Potters Bar, returning to run downhill to the capital bunker first, with the trailing pony truck wheels leading and thus providing a steadying effect, as speeds of 60 mph or more were reached when passing New Southgate. The need for these engines must have been urgent, and full confidence placed in the design, as orders were given in 1920 for no fewer than sixty - 10 from Doncaster, and 50 from the North British Loco Co. in Glasgow. Perhaps, however, it was not only the need for new locomotives at King's Cross, but, lower down the line, Stirling tank engines were due for withdrawal, and the new 'N2s' enabled Ivatt 'N1s' and 'C12' 4-4-2Ts to be sent to the West Riding and the Lincolnshire branches in place of old 0-4-4Ts, in a process termed 'cascading'. Strangely, some enginemen at King's Cross and Hornsey are said to have preferred the older 'N1s', claiming that the lower centre of gravity gave a steadier ride.

Later, in LNER days, 'N2s' were allocated to Scotland, where they were not popular, and were said to be prone to derailment. On such evidence as has been established, this did occasionally take place, but the cause was inadequate permanent way rather than shortcomings with the engines, although in all probability the 'N2' wheel arrangement was not really suitable for some of the faster outer-suburban services in the local conditions. A later general cause for criticism concerned the twin-tube superheater, which was subject to leakage, and was replaced by a Robinson type. It is perhaps worth adding a comment on the condensing system fitted to the 'N1s' and 'N2s' used on the underground line to Moorgate. The intention was to use a flap valve in the blast pipe to divert the exhaust into the tanks, but this warmed the feed water, causing the injectors to fail, whilst the flap valve became overheated and if not regularly used would carbon up and not return to normal. So, although a few more disciplined drivers, with well maintained engines, did their best to keep the mechanism functioning, it became neglected, with the result that the tunnels became even more smoke filled, and it has been said that before the introduction of colour lights, firemen sometimes had to descend to the track to ascertain the position of signals.

In his address to the Locomotive Engineers in Leeds in 1918, Gresley referred to all forms of rolling stock. Not only did he expound his views on locomotive design, but he also referred to the scope for development in the carriage and wagon field, in which his attitude towards standardisation was radically different to his views on standard locomotives. 'It is very necessary that no time should be lost in producing a design of open and covered wagon which shall be standard for all the British railways.' As to coaching stock, he made some interesting comments on articulation, but without using the term as such.

I believe that there is a future in the use of multiple bogie coaches. A few coaches, 100 ft long, carried on three bogies, are now running on the Great Northern. The use of this system effects a reduction of about 10 per cent in the weight of a train, and the smooth running of coaches made on this system is admittedly superior to that of coaches carried on two bogies.

Although the generality of new coach construction after the war followed traditional bogie practice, the articulation principle was further taken up when two twin sets, providing a tea car service, were built in 1919. These were followed by a quintuple restaurant set, built specially for the morning Leeds service, returning in the evening.   This was unique in that its sectional dimensions were to the maximum of the GN load gauge, so that its employment elsewhere could not be permitted.   Indeed, there was no room for the conventional destination boards, and the legend "King's Cross & Leeds' was painted on the coach roofs in serifed gold letters, shaded red, The set continued in regular service on the Leeds run for over 30 years, throughout the LNER period, and into BR days.

To replace the rakes of close-coupled 4-wheeled coaches which had originated in Howlden's day, Gresley developed an 8-coach formation, consisting of two 4-coach articulated sets. These trains, holding 80 first class, 144 second class and 408 third class passengers, plus an 'N1' or an 'N2' locomotive, just fitted into the terminal platforms at Moorgate.   Similar 10-coach sets were provided for certain of the Liverpool Street suburban services. This was probably one of the most useful applications of articulation as applied to coaches, minimising the space between them. Fortunately, derailments were rare, as the job of rerailing up to five articulated coaches was not an easy matter.

The six-a-side third class accommodation was spartan, and popularly known as of a 'sit-up-and beg' quality. The second class was distinguished only by a different shade of upholstery, but offered the benefit of being nearest the buffers at the London end, so that passengers in this class got through the barrier before the exit queue built up. In contrast, the first class compartments were slightly wider, with spring backs to the seats, and blue upholstery. There were smoking compartments, originally unlabelled, only the 'non-smoking' and 'ladies only' compartments being designated as such. As a season ticket holder in the 1930s, I had plenty of experience of these trains, knowing for example where to go on a particular service to avoid having to stand. There was a well-known hazard at Finsbury Park, where three tracks had a platform on each side. Sitting, or even standing, in a third class compartment, a passenger would have his toes trodden on by commuters hurrying to catch a connection two platforms away from their original one.

Gresley held positive views on the use of electricity for on-train lighting and cooking, and these were simply stated in a discussion at the Institution of Electrical Engineers. Provision of adequate electrical power whilst on the move, however, was not straightforward. Batteries were used to supply energy to the cooking equipment, these being charged from trackside points at the terminals, and recharged from direct current generators, belt driven from the bogie axles, but capacity was limited, and insufficient for full cooking.   Consequently although provision was made for boiling and frying, large joints were pre-cooked, and reheated in the kitchen car. The additional weight of the electrical equipment was put at two tons, whilst some 15 horsepower was needed to drive the generator.

The period was not one in which much new work was done on the wagon stock. However, a notable introduction was a 50 ton bogie wagon for the

Fletton to Ferme Park brick traffic, with a carrying capacity of 20,000 bricks. The wagons were vacuum braked, and one would be marshalled next to the engine, leading a long rake of small 4-wheeled coal trucks. Twenty-five were built in 1921, and a further 25 under LNER auspices in 1930; they certainly justified their cost. Another unusual goods vehicle was an 8-wheeled brake van, with brakes on all the wheels, the intention being that this would provide greater braking power and better riding. In the event, however, it proved impossible to equalise the brake forces, and the wheels tended to pick up, so the standard brake van continued to be built on a 4-wheeled chassis.

An interesting series of trials took place in 1921, in which Gresley collaborated with Sir Henry Fowler. To judge the effectiveness of a new design of rapid acting valves when running long trains of vacuum fitted 4-wheeled box vans at a fairly high speed, trains of 63, 82 and 101 vans hauled by 'K2' No. 1646 were tested between Peterborough and Firsby. The Great Northern provided the box vans, and the Midland loaned three 6-wheeled vehicles to convey the measuring equipment. The trials demonstrated that it was feasible to work long trains of up to 100 vans, providing that suitably designed vacuum brakes were fitted throughout, and the results were presented to a meeting at the Institution of Civil Engineers in January 1922. A further trial took place between Peterborough and Boston in the following May, with 'K3' No. 1000, to demonstrate the improvement offered by six of the new 50 ton brick wagons, continuously braked, compared with the same load carried by thirty 10 ton wagons. The conclusions were reported to the Chartered Institute of Transport in February 1923. This question of the inefficiency of small low capacity wagons was a continuous source of concern to the railways, but no progress was made in efforts to replace them by larger ones, due to the high cost of converting terminal installations, which the coal owners in particular were unwilling to meet. Gresley was clear that the most important factor in general merchandise traffic was not tonnage capacity but cubic capacity, and if the standard 16 ft open wagon could be lengthened to 24 ft and built to the limit of the loading gauge, its capacity would be doubled. As for vans, he said that some were so small that he couldn't stand up in them.

The proportions of the second of Nigel Gresley's powerful 'K3' class 2-6-0s, GNR No. 1001, built in 1920, are seen at their best in this profile view. The Great Northern cab was later replaced by an LNER side window version.   *Gresley Society Trust*

The first Gresley Pacific to be built, No. 1470 *Great Northern*, in new condition in the locomotive yard at King's Cross, 1922.   *Duncan Adams Collection*

New from Doncaster Plant in April 1923, in early LNER livery before any renumbering or naming schemes had been adopted, No. 1475 was later to be named *Flying Fox*, after the winner of the 1899 Triple Crown.   *BR, Gresley Society Trust*

Finally in this Chapter, we come to the culmination of Nigel Gresley's 12 year period as Locomotive Engineer of the Great Northern Railway. In March 1922, the first of his two new Pacifics, No. 1470, was wheeled out from Doncaster Plant, and after local running-in, proceeded slowly up to King's Cross. The second, No. 1471, followed in June. The traffic objective of the new class was to haul 600 ton trains at an average speed of 50 mph, in the schedules of the day, and this they proved capable of achieving. Initial teething troubles seem to have been minor, although reports of hot bearings have been noted, and the two engines were soon at work hauling heavy expresses between King's Cross and Doncaster. The Pacifics must have been regarded as a success right from the start, as even before much experience had been gained, a further order, this time for 10, was authorised. Possibly the onset of the Grouping hastened this decision, with the Great Northern, and Gresley, wishing to impress the other constituent companies (and their engineers) that here was the locomotive of the future, capable of meeting the increasing traffic demands of the East Coast main line. To emphasise the origin of the design, and to ensure the memory of the railway that built it, the first was named *Great Northern*, even before it had left Doncaster Plant. The second was later given the name of the GNR Chairman, *Sir Frederick Banbury*. (Banbury was an implacable opponent of the Grouping. He was Conservative MP for the City of London, and openly quarrelled with members of his own party on the subject, including Sir Eric Geddes, the Minister who was piloting the Railways Bill through the Commons, and even the redoubtable Lady Astor.) However, the story of the subsequent development of the classic breed of Gresley Pacifics belongs more correctly to the post-Grouping period, and the London & North Eastern Railway. This will be discussed in the next Chapter.

No. 2545 *Diamond Jubilee* on the morning Leeds express passing the Western sidings, Finsbury Park. The leading coach is part of the quintuple articulated set built in 1921 and reserved for Leeds traffic. The destinations were painted on the roof, in gold shaded red lettering.   *A.B. Collins Collection*

An atmospheric study of one of the earliest of Gresley's Pacifics, believed to be *Great Northern*, standing at the buffers of King's Cross platform 1, early in 1923. Chimney and cab to GNR load gauge, right hand drive. The city gentleman observing proceedings is unidentified.

R. Greiffenhagen, Brian Wright Collection

Chapter Seven

The Classic Pacifics

Following the passing of the Railways Act in 1921, the companies which at first were known as the East Coast Group, later to become the London & North Eastern Railway, held meetings to decide on the organisational form the new company was to take, and who were to be appointed to the key positions on the Board and in management. It was decided that the attenuated railway system stretching from London to Inverness would best be run in a devolved manner, with three Areas (Southern, North Eastern, and Scottish), each under a Divisional General Manager responsible to a Chief General Manager in London. The North Eastern Railway, as the most important constituent company, was concerned that its position should not be eroded, but did not have an outstanding personage suitable for the office of Chairman. The solution was to elect William Whitelaw of the North British Railway to this position, whilst Ralph Wedgwood (shortly to be Sir Ralph), the General Manager of the NER, was appointed Chief General Manager. At first, it was considered that there would be no 'all-line' officers except for the Secretary and the Accountant; other functions, including engineering, would be managed separately in each of the Areas. However, second thoughts intervened, and it was finally decided that it would be more satisfactory for mechanical and electrical engineering to be managed at Head Office level, and a Chief Mechanical Engineer (there was no longer any difficulty about the title) appointed for the whole of the railway, and reporting to the Chief General Manager. Of those who held the post of CME or Locomotive Engineer of the constituent companies, Alfred Hill (Great Eastern), Walter Chalmers (North British) and Thomas Heywood (Great North of Scotland) either decided to retire, or were not considered for this important position. The choice lay between Nigel Gresley, who was then 46, Sir Vincent Raven (63) of the North Eastern, and John Robinson (66) of the Great Central.

The newly-formed LNER Board, carefully balanced in membership between the constituent companies, were anxious to retain a similar relationship in the appointment of officers. Since ex-North Eastern staff were in effect managing the railway - Wedgwood's senior people mainly came from the NER headquarters in York - it would have been difficult politically to appoint Raven as CME. Indeed, he simplified the problem when he realised the situation, and resigned, joining the Board of Metropolitan-Vickers. This left the choice between Gresley and Robinson, who was the senior in years of office, having been in charge of mechanical engineering on the Great Central since 1900, and responsible for a number of successful locomotive and coach designs. However, the LNER were to institute a staff retiring age of 65, and Robinson was already past this. In any case, faced with the massive job of integrating the varied stock (and the workshops) of the constituent companies, as well as meeting new challenges, an engineer was needed who had many more active years in front of him than Robinson. Gresley clearly filled these requirements, but Robinson appears to have had some support, notably from his former Chairman on the Great Central, Lord Faringdon, who had become the LNER Deputy Chairman.

To my mind, the situation was clear, but evidently the Board wanted to be seen to do the correct thing. Robinson, in a letter to the *Railway Gazette* just after Gresley's death in 1941, claimed to have been offered the CME's position, but declined it, and recommended Gresley for the post. Several years later Cecil J. Allen wrote that Robinson's memory was playing tricks, and he must have been mistaken. However, I think that the truth is that Robinson would have been interviewed by Whitelaw and Faringdon, and the point put gently to him that having regard to all the circumstances, would he not agree that Gresley was the best choice for the post? Robinson would have had no option but to fall in with this, and was rewarded by a year's appointment as a consultant to the LNER; Raven was treated similarly, and given a similar term as technical adviser. There is no record of any official task having been given to Robinson, but Raven chaired the LNER Technical Committee, on which Gresley sat as a member. This only concerned itself with proposals for electrification, and there was no question of the Technical Committee dealing with locomotive policy, otherwise a clash between Raven and Gresley would have been inevitable.

In addition, Raven, as technical adviser to the Board, was asked to submit two reports, on the best manner of utilising the workshops of the constituent companies, and on the management structure of the locomotive running department. This latter was an important organisational matter, affecting the day to day operations of the company's motive power. In most, but not all, of the pre-Grouping companies, locomotive running was included in the functions of the CME/ Locomotive Engineer, but in view of the considerable increase in the overall size of this operation following the Grouping, Raven recommended that a separate Locomotive Running Department should be established in each of the three Areas, although with the Running Superintendent responsible to the CME for standards of maintenance and repair. It might be thought, however, that removing locomotive operations from the direct control of the CME resulted in a lesser degree of supervision of this vital function.

Probably the best account of the outcome of events leading to Gresley's appointment comes from Eric Trask, when, in February 1923, as a technical assistant at King's Cross, he was involved with the return from the War Department of two 'N1' tank engines, Nos. 1587 and 1590, which had been requisitioned for defence purposes and armour plated. The accompanying Army form called for the signature of the CME, but Trask was told by the Chief General Manager's office that there was no one in that position, and to wait outside the Board Room. There he met Gresley, who told him that a final decision on the appointment was being taken at that moment. Soon, Robinson emerged and walked away, whereupon Gresley was called in. He came out shortly afterwards, grinning broadly. 'I can sign that form now' he told Trask.

So, Nigel Gresley became Chief Mechanical Engineer of the London & North Eastern Railway, a position he was to occupy with distinction for the next 18 years. The fact that the appointment was not confirmed until the Board meeting on 23rd February, 1923, seven weeks after the formation of the company, indicates that the matter was not decided in haste. First, the position itself had to be established as an all-line one, and then a decision taken on its occupant. Interestingly, Anthony Bulleid writes that his father, Oliver, was told by Gresley in October 1922 - over two months before the Grouping - that he was to be the new company's CME, and he would like Bulleid to continue as his assistant, as on the Great Northern. (But perhaps this was conditional on his actually getting the job.) In the event, that is what took place, and when the CME's office was set up at King's Cross, Bulleid became Gresley's *de facto* principal technical assistant, although evidently not enjoying any specific title.   No one was designated Carriage & Wagon Superintendent, but in all probability this role was filled by Bulleid. Gresley's salary was now £4,500, substantially more than he had received from the Great Northern.   This was approximately the level of the salaries of the other chief officers, and the Divisional General Managers, but contrasted with the £10,000 paid to the LNER Chief General Manager, Ralph Wedgwood, and the £7,000 of the company's Chief Legal Adviser, Sir Francis Dunnell - and at the other end of the management salary scale, £350 - £500 for the typical station master.

At the Grouping, Gresley's command extended to some 30,000 staff and a dozen workshops. The rolling stock included 7,400 locomotives, 21,000 coaches and 300,000 wagons, and there were utility supplies, road vehicles, and fixed stock such as plant and machinery, all of which had to be maintained and replaced as necessary.   At first, the financial outlook for the newly formed LNER appeared bright, but this was not to continue, and before many months had passed the company began to experience the kind of economic tribulations which were to beset it throughout the remainder of its existence.

Specialist technical assistance to the CME was provided by Bert Spencer, locomotives, and Frank Day, carriages & wagons, both promoted from the Doncaster drawing office.   Spencer claimed that he had come to Gresley's attention when of his own initiative but with the support of Harold Broughton, the chief draughtsman, he was drawing out a cab for the new Pacific, taken from measurements of the side-window cab which had been a feature of Great Eastern practice for the past 20 years. Evidently, Gresley, on one of his regular visits to the drawing office, saw what Spencer was doing, liked it and said 'Send it to the Plant and tell them to fit it'. Otherwise, No. 1470 might have appeared with the GN cab which was then on the drawings.

To represent the CME in the three Areas, appointments were made with the title of Mechanical Engineer, that at Darlington being filled by Arthur Stamer, for many years Raven's deputy, and who had stood in his place whilst Raven was away during the war as Chief Superintendent of the Woolwich Arsenal. Stamer was given the title of Chief Assistant Mechanical Engineer, later to be restyled Assistant Chief, a subtle alteration which may have clarified his relations with Bulleid. He retired in 1933.

For four of the constituent companies, the months just before and just after the formation of the LNER were a twilight period so far as mechanical engineering was concerned, with little in the way of new developments. The exceptions were the Great Northern and the North Eastern, both of which produced new Pacifics in the year before the Grouping, and it is of interest to compare the two designs. As we have seen, Nigel Gresley's version was the product of years of gradual evolution, introducing a completely new locomotive concept to Britain. It owed much to the Ivatt Atlantic, as well as to studies of the Pennsylvania RR 'K4s' Pacifics. But the overall concept was

Gresley's, the product of his inventive mind, and whilst the point may not have been realised at the time, the class was to be developed over a period of years, achieving some of the highest performance levels of the British steam locomotive, many years after its first introduction in 1922. Visually, Gresley's first Pacific was one of the most elegant of its kind, of any period. Its main components were well balanced, with a large tapered boiler affording 3,455 sq. ft of heating surface, a wide firebox with 41.25 sq. ft of grate area, three 20 in. x 26 in. cylinders with conjugated valve gear for the inside cylinder, and the traditional 6 ft 8 in. driving wheels.

The new locomotive had two initial limitations, which Gresley had considered but decided to leave for the time being, although they were established features of Churchward's engineering design. The piston valve diameter of nine inches was somewhat small in relation to the diameter of the cylinders, and the boiler pressure remained at 180 lb./sq. in., as in the 'K3' 2-6-0s. At the time it was widely held that that higher pressure resulted in increased scale formation, although Churchward had overcome this by using feed water filtration trays inside the boiler. The Pacifics' valve travel and steam lap were shorter than those used by Churchward, whilst problems of valve overtravel in the 'K3s', although under investigation, led to the necessity for longer cut-offs to be used at higher power outputs, with consequent less economical use of steam.

One particular design restriction of which Gresley had to be constantly aware was the limit of 20 tons axle loading. Had the boiler pressure been substantially higher, thicker and heavier plates would have been needed. To lessen the weight of the frames, these were constructed of 1⅛ in. steel plate instead of the more usual 1¼ in, and with lightening cut-outs in places where it was considered these would not lead to weakness. Further, following the 'K3s', the main rods were forged from lightweight alloy steel, and the result was that the Civil Engineer was satisfied. It was appreciated that engines with three cylinders were inherently better balanced than those with two, but this was not fully recognised by many civil engineers as a factor in permissible axle loadings until, after investigations by the Government-appointed Bridge Stress Committee, it was accepted that static weight was not the only factor in deciding the load-bearing capability of a bridge, but that balancing of reciprocating weights was also important. Indeed, an increase of 15 per cent in static axle weight could be accepted in the case of a multi-cylinder locomotive design, over an equivalent with two cylinders. However, for all their length (and girth) the new locomotives rode well, steamed well, and certainly demonstrated their ability to perform all that Gresley and the Great Northern expected. They had a fair appetite for coal, but this has to be considered in relation to the work done. By 1922 the weight of the heaviest Great Northern express trains was such that double-heading, usually with an Ivatt 4-4-0 or 'N2' tank engine assisting an Atlantic up the bank as far as Potters Bar, was becoming an increasing operational expense, which the new engines clearly would avoid.

On two occasions in their early life the Gresley Pacifics were subjected to comparative trials. Sir Vincent Raven had led expectations of main line electrification between York and Newcastle, but, after the trade recession and industrial disputes of 1921, the enthusiasm which had resulted in the construction of a prototype locomotive for this work was cooling. So, in the last months before

Raven Pacific No. 2400 (later to be named *City of Newcastle*) preparing to leave King's Cross in June 1923, on one of the trial runs to Doncaster. In contrast to the exchange trials of 1925, use was made of the dynamometer car. *Photomatic*

the Grouping, Darlington rushed out a design for a Pacific which relied more on past North Eastern practice than any new technology. Raven's instructions to the drawing office were simply to produce a Pacific based on the 'Z' class Atlantic, with a longer boiler and a wide firebox. The first of five to be built was turned out at the very end of 1922, in North Eastern livery, but did not commence running until January 1923, by which time the NER had become part of the London & North Eastern Railway. Clearly only one of the two Pacific designs could be adopted as the standard express passenger engine of the new group, and consequently a planned series of test runs took place on the Great Northern main line between King's Cross and Doncaster, using the NER dynamometer car. These have been described in detail by Oswald Nock, and by Peter Townend, and on the evidence from these limited trials, there was little to chose between the two locomotives so far as haulage capacity was concerned. The Gresley engine, No. 1472, was the first of a batch of 10 put in hand before the Grouping, and had entered traffic in February 1923. It had not yet been renumbered in the LNER sequence, but was later to become No. 4472 *Flying Scotsman*; the North Eastern Pacific was No. 2400, the first to be built. At the time of the trials, neither locomotive bore a name. No. 2400 was on strange territory, but was capably handled by a Gateshead crew, and responded with good results. However, with Gresley now in overall charge of LNER locomotive development, the Raven design would have to have been markedly superior for it to have any influence on locomotive policy, and it fell short on two counts: specific fuel consumption was rather higher, and the design itself had mechanical shortcomings. Although both locomotives had 3-cylinder drive, Raven persisted with his practice of concentrating the drive on the leading coupled axle, whose guiding function resulted in its being subjected to greater stresses than the second coupled axle, to which the drive was taken on the Gresley Pacifics. Also, Raven located three sets of Stephenson valve gear between the frames, which led to inadequate bearing surfaces for the driving axle, and presented serious difficulties of access for the fitters, while the length of the boiler led to cooler conditions at the front end. The Gresley design clearly had greater potential for development, whilst that of Raven was little more than a stretched version of his 'Z' Atlantic, capable locomotive though this was.

The GNR Board had had the courage to order a further 10 of Gresley's version of the Pacific, even before the Grouping had taken place, and following the outcome of the trial, 40 more were authorised in November 1923, 20 to be built at Doncaster and 20 by the North British Locomotive Co. in Glasgow. These were all in service by the middle of 1925, and allocated to sheds on the former Great Northern, North Eastern and North British railways. They were generally well received, as being of greater capability than any engines previously available, although on one well reported occasion Gresley himself attended a meeting of North Eastern enginemen who were having difficulty adapting to their new steeds. But such problems were short lived.

The second occasion on which the Gresley Pacifics underwent trial by comparison was the result of *Flying Scotsman* being exhibited on an adjacent stand to the Great Western *Caerphilly Castle*, at the British Empire Exhibition of 1924. This hugely successful event featured a Palace of Engineering, in which examples of the best British engineering practice were on view. The GWR 'Castle' bore a placard proclaiming it to be the most powerful locomotive in the British Isles. 'How could this be?' asked visitors, when it was clearly the smaller of the two. Well, it *was* more powerful, by 6 per cent, on the theoretical basis of starting tractive effort, but nothing was said about horsepower at the drawbar (dbhp), where power really mattered. The debate moved into the top echelons of the two railways, and early in 1925 arrangements were put in hand for representatives of the two classes to be compared in a series of trial runs on each other's main lines, King's Cross to Doncaster on the LNER, and the GWR's route from Paddington to Plymouth.

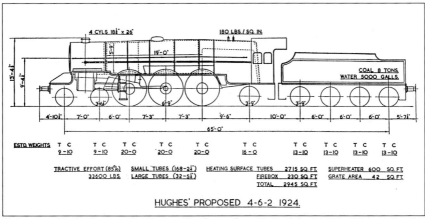

Following Gresley's example, George Hughes, when CME of the LMS in 1924, outlined a Pacific for West Coast main line expresses, but failed to get support for the project.

In view of the importance of the event it is surprising that nothing is known for certain how the trials originated. Of the General Managers and CMEs, only Sir Felix Pole of the Great Western wrote any memoirs, and he did not mention the trials. No one, not even Cecil J. Allen, nor the editors of the *Railway Gazette* or the *Railway Magazine*, seem to have made enquiries at the time, although the event turned into one of the most controversial of its kind ever to be held. Oliver Bulleid (who, one might think, would have known for certain) believed that Gresley 'incepted' the tests, and this theory is shared by others, in the belief that this would have been in keeping with his philosophy, which was to evaluate all developments of which he became aware, from whatever source. But on the other hand if Gresley had been responsible for inaugurating the trials, surely he would have insisted on a more scientific approach being taken, with accurate recording of the results through the employment of dynamometer cars (which both companies owned), for example to enable dbhp/speed curves to be derived and related to fuel consumption. But, as it was, only timings and fuel consumption were recorded. Further, he would have insisted on being consulted over the selection of locomotives and drivers, even although, unlike GN days, he no longer controlled locomotive running.

Edward Marsden, who in the 1930s was in the LNER Chief General Manager's office, and later became Secretary of the Railway Executive, in an effort to establish the truth, as late as 1965 decided to consult those who were still alive who might recall the event. He considered that

> It could have been Sir Felix Pole, who was nothing if not publicity minded. It could have been H.N. Gresley, in a moment of scientific curiosity, wanting to know how the GWR did it. It could have been Sir Ralph Wedgwood, with his puckish sense, seeking to establish the truth. Or it could have come from either company's Board of Directors as a practical experiment to show them they were getting value for money.

Marsden found that a majority of engineering opinion believed in fact that Gresley was the originator, as he was worried about the coal consumption of his Pacifics, and wanted to find out what could be done about it. He was said to have become increasingly depressed as the results of the trial unfolded.

However, this is contradicted by Bert Spencer, who was also one of those consulted by Marsden, and who believed that Gresley was *not* the initiator. By 1924, the coal consumption of the Pacifics was becoming the subject of discussion, and Spencer believed it was at least partly due to the practice employed by the drivers, brought up on the long cut-off and partially open regulator suited to the Ivatt Atlantics, resulting for example in the eight tons of coal in the tender being almost exhausted in a round trip hauling heavy trains from King's Cross to Doncaster and back. In his interview with Gresley which led to his being appointed to the CME's staff, Spencer said that Gresley talked for a long time about the Pacifics, and was very interested when Spencer mentioned he had looked into the possibility of modifying the valve gear. The topic was further discussed when he was installed at King's Cross in October 1924. The impression seems to be that by early 1925 Gresley was aware of the need to alter the extent of the valve movements, but with the engines still being built, this was not the moment to decide on an expensive modification.

Great Western 4-6-0 *Pendennis Castle* leaving King's Cross from platform 15, on a Sunday familiarisation trip in May 1925, before the trial runs commenced.   *Gresley Society Trust*

Gresley Pacific No. 4474 (later to be named *Victor Wild*) about to leave Paddington with the 10.30 am to Plymouth. Driver Albert Pibworth at the cab window.   *Gresley Society Trust*

Certainly, at that time, he would not willingly have wished his Pacifics to be subjected to a *public* trial.

Kenneth Cook, a Swindon-trained engineer who, following Nationalisation, had occupied the post of Mechanical & Electrical Engineer, Western Region, and was transferred to the equivalent position at Doncaster in 1951, was another to whom Marsden wrote. He replied to the effect that he had no doubt that the idea was floated by Pole, in discussion with Wedgwood at their club. This is supported by Oswald Nock, who does not, however, reveal his source. Eric Trask, who was nearer the action at the time, believes it resulted, perhaps at the same social occasion, from a challenge by the impetuous Alex Wilson, appointed in 1924 as the LNER's Southern Area Divisional General Manager, and proud of his newly acquired fleet of Pacifics. Cecil J. Allen also mentions the part played by Wilson, perhaps having heard this from Trask. But there is no corroborative evidence, and a straightforward decision based on a conversation between the two General Managers, seems to be the most likely starting point, with the CMEs, Gresley and Collett, instructed to proceed.

Once the trials had been agreed in principle, arrangements were hurriedly made for the exchange, which commenced in the last week of May 1925. The LNER got off to a bad start as the engine selected for the trials between King's Cross and Doncaster, the newly named *Flying Fox*, suffered an overheated bearing on the first day, whilst the substitute, No. 2545, at first had trouble with its sanders. The selected driver, Ben Glasgow, was reputed to be unenterprising, but as a senior King's Cross driver at the time, the shed foreman put him in charge. Glasgow probably did his best but having been brought up in the Atlantic tradition of driving, he was not economical on coal. The young Freddie Harrison accompanied him on the footplate as technical inspector, but according to Harrison's account, he was not welcome and was unable to play any part other than to observe events. Why nothing was done to change the situation remains a mystery; after all, the trials were spread over a fortnight, the first week being occupied by preliminary runs, to accustom the crews to the line, before the tests proper in the second week. Anyway, the Great Western's *Pendennis Castle* outperformed No. 2545, with appreciable gains on schedule and in the amount of coal used. On the GWR main line, the varied profile of which, particularly in South Devon, with grades of 1 in 36-42, was difficult for a visiting crew to master in a short time, the Gresley Pacific No. 4474, was in the hands of Driver Albert Pibworth. Here, the Pacific improved its performance and fuel consumption as the trials progressed, and the crew grew accustomed to the road, achieving a punctual arrival on each trip. They reported adversely on the quality of the track, lacking transitional introduction to the many reverse curves, which prevented their engine from achieving higher speeds on the downhill stretches, time having to be made up by faster running uphill, to the detriment of coal consumption. Indeed, some summit points were passed at higher speeds than previously known with GWR locomotives hauling equal loads.

The net result was that the Great Western proved to its own satisfaction that it had the superior locomotive, but despite the fact that a gentleman's agreement should have prevented any exploitation of the results, the GWR press department scored heavily with the media. This caused exasperation on the part of Sir Ralph Wedgwood, who wrote to Sir Felix Pole remonstrating on the tone of an article in the *GWR Magazine*, but Sir Felix responded by pointing out that as Cecil J. Allen had already broadcast the LNER version on the BBC, the Great Western had the right of reply. At Board level, the GWR Directors expressed their appreciation of the efforts of those involved, whilst Gresley submitted a report to his Board, but without complaining of the situation in which he had found himself. On reading this, there is nothing to convince the observer that this was written by the man who initiated the trials (*see Appendix One*). At this point, however, it should be added that Gresley respected Churchward's design practice, to which he later paid generous tribute when he responded to William Stanier's Presidential Address to the Locomotive Engineers in 1936.

In the long run, the LNER obtained considerable benefit from the trials, as important lessons were learned. The limited travel and relatively short lap of the Pacific's piston valves was due to Gresley's anxiety over the damage which had been caused by the over-running of the middle valves on the 'K3' 2-6-0s. From 1924, both Francis Wintour's staff at Doncaster, and Bert Spencer at King's Cross, had been working independently on long travel/long lap schemes which would improve matters without incurring substantial expenditure, but initially Gresley appeared slow to move, possibly wishing first to satisfy himself that provision of a more rigid cross member to carry the main pivot of the conjugated gear had overcome the over-travel problems of the 'K3s'.

To accompany *Flying Scotsman's* appearance at Wembley, the LNER issued a comprehensive brochure setting out the dimensions of the locomotive, but nothing providing similar detail was available from Great Western sources, which were very secretive on such matters. An account widely circulated in later years says that to make up for this lack of knowledge, one night, after the GWR team had left the shed in which *Pendennis Castle* was resting during the trials, a small team from Doncaster dismantled the valves and took detailed measurements of the assembly. The same story, with greater substance, was also heard after a similar opportunity offered itself later in the year, when two other members of the 'Castle' class, *Viscount Churchill* and *Windsor Castle*, took part in the Stockton & Darlington Centenary Parade. This seems a highly risky operation in view of the possible discovery by Great Western staff arriving on the scene earlier than expected. Had they found that their engine had been interfered with, more senior men than draughtsmen would have been in trouble. I have asked questions about the feasibility of this, and it appears that time would have permitted it, indeed Ronald Taylor, a senior Darlington draughtsman at the time, has stated that he took part in such an operation, on the second occasion the opportunity offered. But - at what level would the investigation have been authorised?

To coincide with the Stockton & Darlington Centenary in 1925, the summer meeting of the Mechanical Engineers was held at Newcastle in the July. It was very appropriate that Sir Vincent Raven was President at the time, whilst Nigel Gresley gave the keynote paper, entitled 'The Three Cylinder High Pressure Locomotive', which contained a detailed technical account of the development of the concept, including summaries of tests carried out between 2- and 3-cylinder versions of NER Atlantics, and between Gresley's 2-8-0s. It is worth quoting his conclusion:

> With the present type of locomotive boiler, it is neither practicable nor economical to make any considerable increase in boiler pressure, and owing to restrictions imposed by loading gauges the maximum allowable dimensions for outside cylinders have been reached; they already exceed the maximum which can be accommodated within the frames. Any further increase in power can, therefore, only be obtained by increasing the number of cylinders from two to three or four. A 3-cylinder engine is a cheaper engine to build and maintain than one with four cylinders, and moreover possesses certain characteristics in which it is superior. It will meet the requirements of the near future for increased power which, owing to physical limitations, cannot be met by the 2-cylinder arrangement. Undoubtedly a 4-cylinder engine can be designed, the power of which will exceed that of a 3-cylinder within the same gauge limits, but the construction of such an engine at the present moment would be premature, in the same way as the construction of 3-cylinder locomotives nearly 80 years ago was unneccessary for the requirements of the times.

The occasion was not, however, without controversy. In his paper, Gresley had not acknowledged the part played by Harold Holcroft in the application of his simple horizontal lever conjugated valve gear, and in the discussion this was pointed out by James Clayton, Holcroft's immediate chief at Ashford, to which Gresley's response could have been more generous. Also, Raven went as far as to emphasise their differing views on valve gear, saying that he always adhered to the Stephenson valve gear, as he believed in simplicity. He used three sets of valve gear, and if he went back to rail work today, he would do the same again.

Once the Centenary celebrations were over, the results of the interchange trials were studied. Following informed advocacy from his staff, especially Spencer, and after satisfying himself that the over-travel problem was solved, Gresley accepted the need for provision of longer travel and longer lap for the valves of the Pacifics. Although he was concerned that the expense might not be justified in engines which had been in service for such a short time, he agreed to experimental modifications which were applied to two of the class. These were No. 4477 *Gay Crusader*, which was fitted with the Doncaster version, and No. 2555 *Centenary*, to which Spencer's more complete redesign had been applied, and on which Gresley made a footplate trip. Test results favoured Spencer's modifications, comparisons with an original engine showing a reduction of over 20 per cent in coal consumption, which was enough to satisfy Gresley that the expense would be well justified. Consequently in 1927, two years after the exchange trials, authorisation was granted for all the class to be converted. The alterations resulted in a more powerful engine, capable of higher speeds with markedly lower coal consumption.

Improvements to the valve gear was not the only lesson to be learned from the performance of the 'Castles', and Gresley next reconsidered his attitude towards boiler pressure. Following the conclusions of the Bridge Stress Committee, the civil engineer was now prepared to accept an increase in axle loading from 20 to 22 tons, except on certain specified sections of the railway, notably most of the Great Eastern section, and the Calder Valley viaduct near

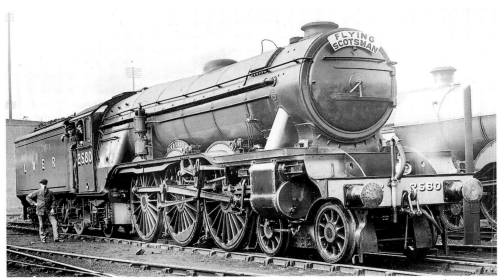

No. 2580 *Shotover*, recently rebuilt to class 'A3', at King's Cross shed on 1st May, 1928, having worked through from Waverley with the first up non-stop 'Flying Scotsman'. Fitted with Westinghouse brake equipment for use with North Eastern Area coaches.

F. Moore's Railway Photographs

A rear view of *Shotover* on the same occasion, illustrating the corridor tender.

F. Moore's Railway Photographs

Wakefield, which prohibited Pacifics from regularly entering Leeds Central for several years. As a result of the concession, trials were made with two engines reboilered at 220 lb./sq. in., and although the results were somewhat indeterminate, 10 new Pacifics were built at Doncaster in 1928/29 with the higher pressure, a further modification being to reduce the cylinder diameter from 20 in. to 19 in., to maintain the same ratio between maximum tractive effort and adhesive weight. A greater reserve of power was now available, which was to prove especially useful on the severely graded Waverley Route from Edinburgh to Carlisle, permitting an increase of train weight to 400 tons, unassisted, compared with 290 tons for the North British Atlantics. The new engines were class 'A3', the 1922 design being class 'A1', and the Raven version 'A2' (not to be confused with the later use of these classifications for post-Gresley designs).

The considerably reduced specific coal consumption of the Pacifics with long travel, long lap, valves led to the realisation that with the availability of water troughs *en route* ensuring an adequate water supply, the 8 ton capacity of their tenders would allow non-stop running between King's Cross and Edinburgh Waverley. (Indeed, it was found that with careful packing, nine tons or even more could be loaded.) However it was appreciated that this long run would be beyond the ability of a single driver and fireman, but to halt, however briefly, to change crews, would destroy any claim that the journey was performed 'non-stop'. The solution was to provide specially constructed tenders with a passageway, and gangway connection to the leading carriage of the train. This concept is thought to have originated in America, where Peter Townend has discovered evidence that trials were made there in 1907 of a tender vestibuled to the leading coach, in an effort to provide a more steady ride. When eventually the prospect of non-stop running from King's Cross to Edinburgh became a feasibility from the locomotive point of view, an informal discussion by a group of design engineers came up with the idea of modifying the tender interior to allow for a passageway, and this suggestion was conveyed to Oliver Bulleid. However, the need was clear, so that it is quite likely that the solution also occurred to Gresley himself. From then the accounts are widely known, that he arranged chairs and tables both in his office and at home, to simulate the arrangement, and decide on the dimensions of the corridor through which the crew would pass. A patent was issued in his name in August 1928.

For many years following the Races to the North in 1895, there had been an agreement between the East Coast and West Coast companies that the timing of their morning trains between King's Cross and Edinburgh, and Euston and Glasgow, respectively, should not be cut below 8¼ hours. So, in 1928, when the LNER introduced the non-stop 'Flying Scotsman' as its flagship service in the summer timetable, the train ran to the same overall schedule as in winter, which included stops at the principal stations. This resulted in a pedestrian average speed of little over 47 mph, and with their new Pacifics, the LNER thought that this should be reduced. Consequently, this restrictive agreement was eventually rescinded, although not until 1932, when the non-stop timing came down to 7½ hours. By 1937 the time had been further reduced to 7 hours.

In the summer of 1927, 'The Flying Scotsman' train is seen coming off the Royal Border Bridge at Berwick, headed by No. 2577 *Night Hawk* of Gateshead shed. Another Pacific, probably from Grantham, would take over at Newcastle. Photograph signed 'H.N. Gresley'.   *The Times*

The up 'Flying Scotsman' approaching Newcastle Central, *c.*1930. Ex-NER class 'D20' No. 2107 is seen behind Pacific No. 2573 *Harvester*, which was normally stationed at Gateshead. The arrangement whereby a pilot was coupled inside the train engine was often followed in LNER days, in this case perhaps to assist the Pacific up Cockburnspath. The pair would have been replaced at Newcastle.   *Photomatic*

South of Newcastle, it was very unusual for a Pacific to be assisted. Here, in July 1932, class 'K3'
No. 1397 is piloting a Gateshead 'A1' which may be ailing, or, possibly to avoid a light engine
working by the 2-6-0.   *Photomatic*

No. 4476 *Royal Lancer* was a favourite King's Cross Pacific during the 1930s, but was not
converted to 'A3' until 1946. Here seen *c.*1935 leaving the terminus with what is believed to be
a West Riding train.   *Photomatic*

No. 2796 *Spearmint* heading the Royal train at St Fort, on its way from Edinburgh to Ballater on 29th August, 1935. The Pacific would come off at Aberdeen. The train is probably not carrying the King and Queen, otherwise the Royal headcode of four headlamps would have been applied.   *LCGB, Ken Nunn Collection*

No. 2743 *Felstead* leaving York for King's Cross with the 'Scarborough Flier' on 27th July, 1937. Note the impressive array of signals, a characteristic of North Eastern practice.   *H.C. Doyle, Gresley Society Trust*

Two other modifications to the basic Pacific design deserve mention. Gresley was dissatisfied with the lower superheat temperatures of up to about 600°F in his Pacifics, compared with up to 800°F in the GN Atlantic, due to the greater cooling effect on the elements at the front end of the longer boiler of the Pacific. In an effort to achieve a higher degree of superheat, the Superheater Company offered its 'E' type, with 62 double elements housed in smaller diameter flue tubes, in theory raising the steam temperature by up to 100°F by doubling the superheater heating surface. One Pacific, No. 2562 *Isinglass*, was fitted with the 'E' type, in 1925, but the result was disappointing. The average temperature reached was only about 30°F higher than in the standard 'A1' Pacific with the 32 element superheater, and consequently the experiment was discontinued five years later. The locomotive was distinguished by a pair of snifting valves behind the chimney, in place of the usual one. Much more successful, following a study of the boiler design of the standard Pacifics of the German State Railways, was an increase in the number of superheater elements from 32 to 43. This took place concurrently with the introduction of the 220 lb./sq. in. boiler .

The need for ultra-short chimneys, brought about by larger boilers and the need to reduce the overall height of the Pacifics to conform with the restrictions of the LNER standard loading gauge, gave rise to a tendency for exhaust smoke and steam to cling around the boiler and obscure the driver's vision, especially when working at long cut-offs. The problem could not have been too acute in the locomotives' earlier days, or more positive steps would have been taken to counteract the difficulty, but following an accident involving an LMS 'Royal Scot' class engine, Gresley decided to see what might be done. First, in 1931, the top of the smokebox door of No. 2747 *Coronach* was cut away, and the smokebox top angled, with ducts which discharged at the rear of the chimney, but this experiment was not successful and after further modifications had been tried, the locomotive was restored to its original condition. The following year, No. 2751 *Humorist* was the subject of similar trials, later being provided with small deflector plates by the side of the chimney. In 1937 the same locomotive was chosen for trials of Kylchap double blast pipe and chimney arrangements, following construction of the 'P2' class described in Chapter Nine. But full acceptance of the need for smoke lifting arrangements on the non-streamlined Pacifics did not become acute until the late 1950s, following the general fitting of double Kylchap exhaust systems.

As a postcript to this chapter, it is of interest to note that most of Gresley's 'A1' and 'A3' Pacifics were given names of racehorses, all being winners on the flat, no hurdlers being commemmorated in this way. One of the earliest, No. 4479, was named *Robert the Devil*, after the winner of the 1880 St Leger. The horse itself recalled Robert le Diable, the seventh Duke of Normandy, the father of William the Conqueror, one of whose leaders at the battle of Hastings was Nigel Gresley's distant forebear, Robert de Toeni.

Among the first locomotives built to LNER order after the Grouping were 24 of the Robinson 'D11' 'Director' class. They were chosen as the most powerful of the pre-1923 4-4-0s, specifically for use in Scotland. Here is No. 6393 *The Fiery Cross*, passing through Princes Street Gardens. The Scottish Area had requested more of the NB 'Scott' class engines, but the 'D11s' proved popular, and they were given names selected from the works of Sir Walter Scott.   *Photomatic*

The first LNER designed 0-6-0s were the class 'J38', 35 of which were built at Darlington in 1926. They were intended for coal traffic on the North British system, and were rarely used on passenger trains. No. 1417 is seen in its early days; it was stationed at St Margaret's shed, Edinburgh, for practically all its life.   *BR, Gresley Society Trust*

Chapter Eight

New and Modernised Locomotives

The first decade of the LNER was marked by a general decline in profitability, arising from falling traffics due to economic depression and growing road competition. Consequently, after initial high hopes, the railway had to live with limited amounts of money to spend on capital projects, and a policy of scrap and replace was certainly not possible, so far as locomotives and carriages were concerned. As has been mentioned before, Nigel Gresley was not an advocate of rigid locomotive standardisation, apart from using standard boilers and other components where they were suitable for individual classes. Nevertheless, he did introduce a number of locomotive designs which, had the finance been available, would have been built in larger numbers than was the case, for general use throughout the system except where they were prohibited by structure gauge or weight restrictions.

However, in the early years of the LNER, it was imperative to provide new locomotives for certain services, and a choice had to be made from what was available, as time did not permit the development of new designs. An urgent request was made by the Scottish Area for a batch of NBR 'Scotts', a well-proportioned medium power 4-4-0 dating from 1909. Gresley had in mind an LNER locomotive of this wheel arrangement, but this had not yet been developed, so he decided on the most powerful 4-4-0 of the constituent companies, which happened to be the Robinson 'Director' class, and 24 of these were built by contractors in 1924. These were supplemented by the transfer to Scottish sheds of 20 ex-Great Northern 4-4-0s made surplus on their home ground following the introduction of the Pacifics. The Robinson engines earned the respect of the North British enginemen, but not so the less powerful Ivatts, which were regarded as rough riding and with insufficient comfort for the crews.

A further urgent need was for powerful 0-6-0s, the traditional general purpose locomotive of practically all the railways in Britain. Gresley at first put forward a 3-cylinder 5 ft 2 in. 2-6-0, a smaller wheeled variant of the 'K3', which had the virtues of multi-cylinder propulsion, giving more even torque and better riding, but their first cost was regarded by the LNER Board as too high. Moreover, a large number of Robinson 2-8-0s, which had been built to meet wartime demands overseas, became available from War Department disposal agencies, at knockdown prices offering excellent value for money to the LNER, which already possessed 131 of this class in use on the Great Central. Altogether, 273 were bought, many of which were new, although it was decided that wartime steel fireboxes should be replaced by copper ones. These engines, powerful and easy to maintain, obviated the need for an similar number of 0-6-0s and 3-cylinder class 'O2' 2-8-0s. Nevertheless a new LNER design of 0-6-0 was introduced in 1926, the first 35 being built with 4 ft 8 in. wheels, class 'J38', for work in the Scottish coalfields. After completion of this order, the wheel diameter was increased to 5 ft 2 in., resulting in a useful machine, class 'J39', which eventually

The 'J38' 0-6-0s were followed by 'J39s', with 6 in. larger driving wheels, making for a more versatile locomotive. They were used on all kinds of workings, as here on passenger duty, No. 2712 is hauling a Liverpool Street to Southend service, near Stratford, *c*.1935. The number is, unusually, on the left-hand side of the buffer beam.   *Gresley Society Trust*

'J39' No. 2738 of Eastfield shed hauling a down goods train on the West Highland line.
                                                                 University of Hull, W.B. Yeadon Collection

No. 1286 passing over the Durham Ox level crossing, Lincoln, with an excursion train *c.*1937.
E.R. Morten

'J39s' were in use on the GCR Woodhead line over the Pennines. In BR days No. 64748 is heading a mineral train in 1948. Construction of the overhead lines had not yet been resumed.
Eric Oldham

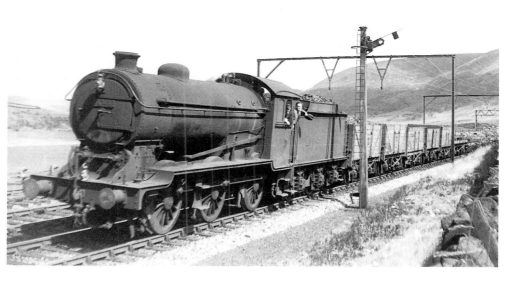

Above: Gresley's 2-8-0s were the mainstay of the New England to Ferme Park mineral trains for over 20 years. Here Class 'O2' No. 3482 takes the fast line through Hatfield in 1937, with mainly coal empties.   *Photomatic*

Right: H.N. Gresley in 1932. This is his passport photograph, unusually signed 'Herbert N. Gresley'.   *Tim Godfrey*

was to find its way to many parts of the system. The design was produced by the Darlington drawing office, and in appearance was distinguished by a generous side-window cab and quadrants at the ends of the footplating. The 'J39' was a handsome engine, free steaming and generally well-liked. Because of its ability it was often used on fast freight and excursion trains, but on such duties was sometimes in trouble with overheated axleboxes and even dropped motion. Some 289 of the class were built, the last as late as 1941.

It is sometimes said that the 'J38'/'J39' design was derived from the North Eastern 'P3' class, but this was not the case. The 'P3' (LNER 'J27') was intended for slow moving mineral trains, as was the 'J38', whilst within its limits the 'J39' was a truly mixed traffic engine. There was little in the new design to recall Darlington practice, indeed the valve motion arrangements were based on improvements made to the Robinson class 'A5' 4-6-2T design, a batch of which were built for service in the North East in 1925. Gresley's instructions to Darlington concerning the new 0-6-0s were to the effect that the design should be 'bold', and less 'rounded' than the 'P3s'. He caused amusement among the draughtsmen by adding that he wanted the tender to be a 'coal cart', not a 'hearse'. This was developed as an LNER group standard in two versions, the smaller with capacity for 3,500 gallons of water and 5½ tons of coal, the larger with 4,200 gallons and 7½ tons. The original design had stepped-out coping plates at the top of the side panels, but later the sides were flat. Both versions had an unequal wheelbase, 7 ft 3 in. between the leading and centre axles and 6 ft 3 in. between the centre and trailing axles.

The 'J39' was followed by a 3-cylinder 4-4-0, class 'D49', also from Darlington, with a boiler of similar dimensions, and which was intended to be a general replacement for Atlantics and older 4-4-0s, although its axle loading of 21 tons would have originally precluded it from much of the system, including the Great Eastern. However, the main need at the time was in the North Eastern and Scottish Areas, where all 76 of the class were to be stationed. All were built at Darlington between 1927 and 1935. The earliest batches were named after Shires, the first being No. 234 *Yorkshire*. Strangely, they were referred to in the minutes of the LNER Locomotive Committee as 'Improved Directors', although there was nothing of Robinson in their design. They were a blend of Darlington and Doncaster practice, with boilers and lineaments similar to those of the 'J39' 0-6-0s, and were of particular interest in that successive batches were given different valve mechanisms. The first 20 had piston valves and outside Walschaerts gear with the by now conventional Gresley conjugated mechanism driving the inside valves, but with the levers placed behind the cylinders, instead of in front as in the 'K3s' and Pacifics. This location eliminated the effects of expansion in the outside valve spindles and had the additional advantage that the gear was out of the way of smokebox ash. Gresley's preference for concentrated drive on the second axle was not possible in the 'D49' layout, and all three cylinders drove on to the leading axle.

The next batch of six 'D49s' was fitted with Lentz poppet valves driven by oscillating cams, but this arrangement was not wholly successful, and after being in service for 10 years and needing new cylinders, the engines were converted to conventional piston valve operation. However, the use of Lentz

One of a batch of eight 'Shires' built at Darlington in 1929. Despite its identity as England's smallest county, *Rutlandshire* spent all its working life in Scotland. Stationed at Carlisle (Canal) shed in the 1930s, its main concern would have been with secondary trains on the Waverley Route.   *F. Moore's Railway Photographs*

No. 365 *The Morpeth* was one of the last 4-4-0s to be built in Britain. In contrast to the typical Walschaerts valve gear of the 'Shires', the 'Hunts' were provided with Lentz rotary cam gear. This locomotive was to be rebuilt by Edward Thompson with two inside cylinders, in which form it was similar in some ways to the Robinson 'Director' class.   *LNER, Gresley Society Trust*

valves, but employing rotary cams actuated through cardan shaft drive, offered reduced valve gear maintenance costs, and no fewer than 42 were built in this form. There was little difference in the performance of the three versions, although some drivers at first took a dislike to those fitted with poppet valves, which initially had only five cut-off positions, later increased to seven, to provide greater flexibility in handling. To distinguish the poppet valve engines from those with piston valves, they were given the names of Hunts, the first being No. 201 *The Bramham Moor*.

There is a reference in Darlington records to two 'D49s' being proposed as compounds, possibly having in mind the first orthodox British 3-cylinder compound, Walter Smith's rebuilt NER 4-4-0 No. 1619 of 1898 (this had the high-pressure cylinder inside the frames, with two low-pressure cylinders outside - the reverse of Webb's arrangement). However, this idea came to nothing, as did a further proposal for a 6-cylinder power unit, utilising three Uniflow cylinders on each side of the smokebox, driving twin crankshafts and a bevel-geared final drive, the design for which presented insurmountable problems.

In 1926 the eminent French locomotive engineer André Chapelon was visiting Davey Paxman of Colchester, then the licensee in Western Europe for Dr Hugo Lentz's poppet valve gear patents, which Chapelon proposed to incorporate in a rebuilt Paris-Orléans Pacific. Paxman's technical director arranged for Chapelon to meet Nigel Gresley, which resulted in a fruitful association, and personal friendship between them. In 1925 Chapelon had patented his Kylchap draughting system, in which exhaust steam from the blastpipe passed successively through a highly efficient steam/gas mixing device invented by the Finnish engineer Kylälä, and a cylindrical petticoat before entering the chimney bell. This system, in which a much more even draught was achieved over the combustion gases leaving the boiler tubes, enabled steam production to be increased, as well as the blastpipe area, resulting in reduced power loss due to exhaust back pressure. In 1928/29 Gresley applied single chimney Kylchap exhaust arrangements to 'D49s' Nos. 251 *Derbyshire* and 322 *Huntingdonshire*, but unfortunately, as made at Darlington, the connecting links between the components partially obstructed the exhaust stream and the results were less good than they should have been, as Chapelon himself realised when travelling on the footplate of one of the locomotives concerned. He recommended modifications to the alignment of the components, but there were objections by maintenance staff, as the changes would have resulted in restricted access to the boiler tubes. In the absence of proved savings, this may have been the reason for the removal of the equipment after little more than a year; it had not been appreciated that the need for cleaning would be reduced. (The Kylälä system was to be reintroduced several years later, in double exhaust form, as described in Chapter Nine.) The last of the 'D49s' was built in 1935, and no more were contemplated.

The Great Eastern section had been provided with substantial numbers of well-designed 4-4-0s, the 'Claud Hamilton' class ('D15'/'D16'), and 4-6-0s of the '1500' ('B12') class, one of the most successful inside cylinder designs of its type in Britain, the more so since its maximum axle load was just under 16 tons. The bridges of the Great Eastern main lines had been constructed for relatively light loadings, but with the increasing weight of trains following the introduction of standard LNER coaches, more locomotives with greater power were needed. Matters reached a crisis in the summer of 1927, by which time the management had expected the CME to have found an answer to their problems, but although preliminary work had been undertaken at Doncaster, severe weight difficulties were being met in producing a satisfactory 3-cylinder design with concentrated drive complying with Gresley's principles, and yet with an axle loading sufficiently low to meet bridge limitations. As an interim measure a request was made for 20 of the now obsolescent 'B12' 4-6-0s, but the Board would not sanction this, and agreed to only ten.

Some years before, in 1919, the Great Eastern had ordered an earlier batch of these 4-6-0s from Wm Beardmore of Glasgow, but mismanagement of the contract led to delayed delivery and a dispute over the price. It is ironic that something similar should happen to this latest 10, which were built by Beyer, Peacock. In mid-contract, Gresley decided that these should be provided with Lentz poppet valves, trials with a 'J20' 0-6-0 and a 'B12' so fitted having shown considerable fuel economy. But this had not been made clear initially, and the manufacturers naturally regarded this amendment as an extra. This led to acrimonious exchanges between Beyer, Peacock and the LNER, in which court action was threatened. A letter from Sir Sam Fay, then Chairman of Peacock's to Gresley tells it all (*see Appendix Two*). Eventually, the matter was settled by compromise, the LNER paying £1,500, half the sum demanded by the manufacturers, who were probably happy at the outcome.

It has been suggested that after the 1925 exchange trials, Gresley might have wished to have shown that, like the Great Western, he too could produce a powerful 4-6-0, but this idea was refuted by Bert Spencer in the discussion following his paper to the Locomotive Engineers in 1947. Such a design would in any case run contrary to Gresley's conviction that a large firebox with a wide grate was preferable for a heavy main line locomotive, and this could not be achieved in a 4-6-0. However, the circumstances on the Great Eastern in 1927 were such that a Pacific was out of the question, and a modern 4-6-0 would have to meet the requirements. But Gresley's insistence on concentrated drive to the centre coupled axle involved an unacceptably high loading on this axle, and this alone ruled out the possibility of a heavy 3-cylinder 4-6-0, so far as the Liverpool Street services were concerned. Two outlines were drawn out by Doncaster, but one was too heavy for the bridges, and the other too long for the lay-byes at Liverpool Street, and for the turntables in East Anglia, most of which were only 50 ft. The Board appear to have lost patience, and the Deputy Chairman, Lord Faringdon, opened negotiations direct with Sir Hugh Reid, of the North British Locomotive Company, who had recently completed 50 'Royal Scots' for the LMS, and for which they had done much of the design work.

It is not entirely clear how the design was shared between the LNER and NBL, but it seems that the contractors were responsible for the general layout, in which the inside cylinder was moved further forward, so transferring weight to the bogie. This meant that Gresley's requirement for concentrated drive could not be met, but there were compensations in that the 2 to 1 conjugating levers could be located behind the cylinders, as in the 'Shires', and the all-important question of weight was resolved, maximum axle load being kept down to 18 tons. This was a 12½ per cent increase over the 'B12s', but was now acceptable due to the improved balancing of the 3-cylinder machine. The boiler was a shortened version of that of the 'O2' 2-8-0, and in its basic form was later to become the most widely used boiler on the LNER. Initial problems led to frame renewals soon after the new engines were placed in service, but after renewal and strengthening where necessary they settled down to hard work in East Anglia, where they proved economical on fuel and provided an appreciable increase in power over the 'B12s'. Despite the mixed origins of these new locomotives, Gresley seemed to take them to his heart, and in addition to the original 10, a further 38 were built in batches at Darlington up to 1935. As length remained a problem, they received Great Eastern pattern tenders, shorter than the LNER standard. These new 4-6-0s were classified 'B17', and were given the names of country houses, the first being *Sandringham*, after the Royal residence near King's Lynn. Twenty-five more followed in 1936/37, and were sent to the Great Central section, receiving group standard LNER tenders as length restrictions did not apply there. An anonymous member of the LNER staff made the suggestion that, as these engines would be used to haul football specials, they should be named after football clubs. This was done, the first being *Arsenal*, whose stadium is almost within sight of Finsbury Park station, whilst *Darlington* and *Doncaster Rovers* were also obvious choices. No doubt, after the effort the North British Locomotive Company had put into the original design, they expected repeat orders, but none came their way, indeed the final batch of 11 were contracted out to Robert Stephenson & Co.

In the first years of the LNER, locomotives were built to a number of other pre-Grouping designs, including 13 class 'A5' 4-6-2T, a successful Robinson product, improved by a new cylinder design and long travel, long lap, valves. These were required for shorter distance passenger work in the North East, where the equivalent was a Raven 4-4-4T, which had the disadvantage of the lower adhesion associated with this wheel arrangement (from 1931 they were improved by rebuilding as 4-6-2Ts). Also, proposals had been outlined in Great Northern days for a 2-6-2T design, principally for London suburban services, until it was realised that the 0-6-2T type was more generally useful, especially bearing in mind the short platforms at Moorgate station, where an 'N2' and an 8-coach suburban train could just be accommodated. However, the need for more powerful tank locomotives existed on other parts of the system, and in 1930 a nicely proportioned 3-cylinder 2-6-2T, class 'V1', No. 2900, emerged from Doncaster. 28 were built for services around Edinburgh and Glasgow, replacing North British 4-4-2Ts and Gresley 'N2s'. Subsequent batches were turned out for the North East and East Anglia, to a total of 82. Later, a further 10 were given 200 lb./sq. in. boilers instead of the original 180 lb./sq. in. version, to which standard most of the originals were converted (class 'V3'). An example of the original batch, No. 2911, was stationed at King's Cross for a few months when it was new, as was No. 2901 at Neasden, for evaluation purposes, but neither shed was to receive a permanent allocation.

The first 'B17', No. 2800 *Sandringham*. In ex-works condition, posing with the traditional Great Eastern discs to indicate the class of train. Because of turntable restrictions, a short GER pattern tender was provided.   *Ray Stephenson Collection*

Projected 4-6-0 of 1935. Larger than the 'Sandringham' class, but smaller than the GWR 'Castles'. The proposal was discarded in favour of the 'V2' 2-6-2.

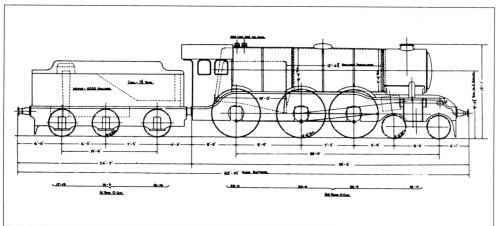

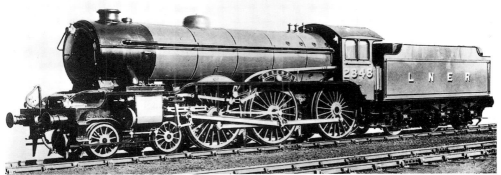

The first of the 'Footballers', No. 2848 *Arsenal*, was shedded at Leicester GC for three years after being turned out from Darlington in 1936. Note the green cylinder covers, typical of NER practice, conventional headlamps, and standard LNER 4,200 gallon tender. Print signed 'H.N. Gresley'.   *Gresley Society Trust*

The nameplate of No. 2856 *Leeds United*. The 'football' is flanked by white panels, matching the club's all-white strip. Although the LNER had adopted Gill Sans as a standard typeface several years before, this did not then apply to nameplates.   *Photomatic*

No. 2858 was originally named *Newcastle United*, but as it was to be stationed on the Great Eastern section, this was almost immediately changed to *The Essex Regiment*. Here seen near Ipswich in charge of a short train of mixed stock.   *Photomatic*

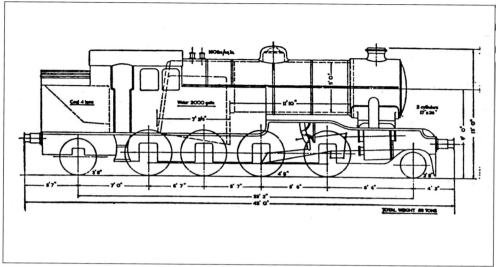

One of two proposed 2-8-2T designs, for the Nottinghamshire coal traffic. This would have become class 'P10'.

The unique LNER Garratt, class 'U1' built by Beyer, Peacock in 1925. It was featured in the Centenary procession.   *F. Moore's Railway Photographs*

More 'N2s' were built by contractors in the mid-1920s, and also Hill's Great Eastern 'N7' class, each being regarded as the better for local circumstances. A few 'N7s' were used on the Great Northern, gravitating to the Hertfordshire branch lines, but 'N2s' tried on the Great Eastern did not receive much of a welcome. Gresley evidently took a personal interest in the 'N7s', as they were selected for modification by the provision of round-topped fireboxes and longer travel valves. In 1927 Albert English of the Stratford drawing office was instructed to redesign the gear, although he protested that this would leave the mechanism more prone to failure. In the event this did happen occasionally, whilst the maintenance staff complained of the lack of space in which to work. But the locomotives' performance was greatly improved, such that Richard Hardy described them as 'brilliant'.

In addition to Gresley's own 'J50' class of shunting tanks, new locomotives with greater power were needed in early LNER days for the yards in the North Eastern Area and several years later for the new hump yard at Whitemoor, near March, Cambridgeshire. Here, Gresley convinced the Civil Engineer of the benefits of the German Frölich system of retarders, to control wagons descending from the hump to the sorting sidings. To avoid the expense of developing a new design, and to provide enginemen with locomotives with which they were already familiar, a further five of the Worsdell 3-cylinder 4-8-0T, class 'T1', were built at Darlington in 1925 for the North Eastern yards, whilst two of yet another Robinson type, his 0-8-4T class 'S1', came from Gorton in 1932, these being provided with steam booster engines driving the trailing bogie axles. At the other end of the scale, 10 diminutive Worsdell 0-6-0Ts, class 'J72', an 1898 design, came from Darlington, also in 1925. (This class must have had its unique uses, as a further 28 were also built at Darlington, under BR auspices, as late as 1951.) On two occasions Gresley attempted to introduce a heavy freight tank engine, scheming a 2-8-2T, known provisionally as the 'P10', as a replacement for the Ivatt 0-8-2Ts used on the Nottinghamshire coal trains. The class got as far as inclusion in the building programmes of 1930 and 1932, but in each case the authorisation was cancelled, the ready availability and greater range of the ex-War Department 'O4s' saving the need for capital expenditure on such locomotives during the years of economic depression.

However, Gresley was personally responsible for two of the largest British freight engine designs. One of these was the outstanding 2-8-0+0-8-2 Garratt, built for banking coal trains up the 1 in 40 Worsbrough incline, near Barnsley in Yorkshire. This had its origins in the close relationship which had developed between John Robinson and the firm of Beyer, Peacock, their works being on nearby sites at Gorton. The proposal was first mooted in pre-Great War days, Robinson having put it to Peacock's that two of the engine units of his then new 2-8-0s could be placed with cylinders facing outwards, on a substantial frame, and fed with steam from one large boiler, so virtually doubling the potential power output. The idea was not pursued at the time, but in response to pressure by the Great Central operators, Gresley reopened discussions with Peacock's, on the basis of two being required, having in mind the possibility of further use on the Mexborough to Immingham coal hauls.

The power of the Garratt is supplemented by an 'N2', No. 896, approaching Silkstone No. 2 tunnel in 1945/46. A number of these tank engines were stationed at Mexborough at the time, generally used on banking work up to Dunford Bridge. *E.R. Morten*

No. 2618 was one of the last order for 'N7s', built with round-topped boiler at Doncaster in 1928. The train is leaving Shenfield during the war, with a train consisting of a quintuple articulated set, plus four bogie coaches. *R.E. Batten*

Having obtained authority to proceed, Gresley then realised that it would be preferable to use a pair of his class 'O2' 2-8-0 3-cylinder engine units, providing 16 per cent more tractive effort, but Peacock's estimate was higher than expected, added to which Gresley's engine units cost more than those of Robinson, so only one Garratt was built, for the price of two Pacifics. In fact, it was never known to have been tried on the main line, and for many years the only times it was seen away from its immediate surroundings were on the odd occasion it was used for publicity, or sent to Doncaster for overhaul. The Garratt, No. 2395, performed the work of two Robinson 'O4s', the other source of banking power at Worsbrough, so saving the cost of a crew, and reducing running time by a third, but it was out of service for long periods, particularly when its unique boiler was under repair. An early problem was the highly corrosive local water supply, eventually corrected by the provision of a local water treatment facility. The locomotive was heavy on coal, much being burned just waiting for the next job. Eventually it became redundant following the electrification of the Worsbrough line in 1954, and what might have been a new lease of life commenced when it was transferred to Bromsgrove, for banking on the Lickey incline. It was said not to have been popular with its crews, due to the conditions whilst working through the tunnels, at least the Mexborough enginemen got on with the job. Bromsgrove crews are said on one occasion to have refused to work it, but that was in the more militant post-war days, and of course even after the Garratt had been converted to oil firing, it was a different proposition to the 'Big Bertha' 0-10-0 or the Fowler 'Jinties', to which they were accustomed.

At the same time as the Garratt was under construction by Beyer, Peacock, Doncaster was busy with Gresley's largest main line freight locomotive, a 2-8-2 Mikado, with 5 ft 2 in. wheels, a freight version of his Pacific, and intended for heavy mineral trains between the yards in New England, near Peterborough, and Ferme Park, Hornsey. Two were built, Nos. 2393 and 2394, class 'P1'. They were splendid locomotives, well proportioned and handsome: Oliver Bulleid is on record as saying he thought they were the best looking engines Gresley ever produced. But they could not be used regularly at their fullest capacity as the 100 wagon trains they were intended to haul were too long for general operation on the Great Northern main line, due to the inadequate length of most of the refuge loops. It had been hoped that high capacity bogie coal wagons would replace the 10 and 12 ton trucks of the period, but opposition by the coal owners to the expenditure which such a wholesale modernisation would incur was too great to be overcome. Probably, the authorisation for the construction of these engines had rested on the case that with higher capacity wagons marshalled in continuously braked trains, and track restrictions lessened, faster mineral transits would result. It may also be noted that one of the 'P1s' was originally given an 'E type' superheater, but this provided no greater increase in superheat than that fitted to one of the Pacifics. Also, as built, the Mikados were provided with a booster engine, driving on to the trailing wheels.

However, these operational problems should not distract the observer from appreciating the technical excellence of these three engines, the Garratt and the

Oliver Bulleid considered the two 'P1' Mikados to be Gresley's best looking engines. Certainly, they must have been among the most elegant British freight locomotives. No. 2393 is in pristine condition, prepared for the 1925 Centenary Parade.   *Duncan Adams Collection*

No. 2393 on its routine task of hauling coal trains between New England and Ferme Park, here seen passing Mutton Lane bridge, south of Potters Bar, on 4th August, 1936. Note the Westinghouse compressor for bringing the booster into operation, and the exhaust steam pipe below the cab. The booster was removed in 1938.   *LCGB, Ken Nunn Collection*

Mikados. Gresley was authorised to build the engines, and so he did. Perhaps a contributory reason was the forthcoming Railway Centenary parade, in which Nos. 2393 and 2395 took part, registering with the onlookers and the media of the day that the LNER was a railway which thought big, at least so far as its engines were concerned. Also, in his 'P1' design, Gresley was following the practice of the Pennsylvania RR, who had developed their 'L1s' Mikado as the freight equivalent of the 'K4s' Pacific.

As has been mentioned earlier, in efforts to get more power from existing locomotives at low speeds, Gresley was attracted to the 'booster', which had been pioneered by Harold Ingersoll of the New York Central RR in 1919. This consisted of a small auxiliary steam engine, generally driving the trailing uncoupled wheels of a locomotive, and which was supplied in Britain by J. Stone & Co. of Deptford. This had the effect of providing additional tractive effort and horsepower for a short period, at starting, or when climbing heavy gradients, so enhancing the locomotive's load hauling capability. The first trial was in July 1923, on an Ivatt Atlantic, LNER No. 4419, but it was found that even over relatively short periods the booster's need of additional steam was at the expense of boiler pressure, the condition being exacerbated for example when starting 'cold' from King's Cross. Other operating and maintenance problems were tackled, and several lessons were learned.

In a second application of the booster to passenger locomotives, in 1931 two of Vincent Raven's 'Z' class Atlantics (LNER 'C7') were virtually rebuilt, with longer firebox and higher boiler pressure. The locomotives were articulated to the tender, resulting in a 4-4-4-4 wheel arrangement, the booster driving on to the leading wheels of the bogie beneath the cab. For the purposes of classification, they were still regarded as Atlantics, and classed 'C9', Nos. 727 and 2171. The booster enabled them to restart heavy trains on severe gradients, such as the 1 in 96 Cockburnspath Bank and the 1 in 101 southbound from Durham, although a problem sometimes arose when starting a heavy train from rest on the curved platform lines at York or Newcastle. The driver would engage the booster and usually get a good start, but if the first attempt failed he would normally set back. However, the booster was not reversible, and opening the throttle in back gear would set the booster working against the main engine, so setting back could not be attempted until the steam in the cylinders of the booster engine had dissipated.

The booster was also applied to freight engines. The two 'P1s' were provided with boosters, which increased their maximum tractive effort by almost a quarter, which was useful for smooth starting of 1,000 ton trains, but the pipework connections were often the subject of mechanical failure on the sharp curves at New England yard. Another application was to the two new Robinson 'S1' hump shunting tanks built in 1932, in which the bogie wheels were coupled together, and booster driven. Stone's had offered five boosters at a reduced price, so Gresley took the lot, two being fitted to the 'C9s', and two to the new 'S1s', whilst the fifth was fitted to one of the older 'S1s'.

As the steam locomotive grew larger and more powerful, with a greater appetite for coal, the limitations of hand firing were being approached. The topic was raised at the International Railway Congress in London in 1925, when

Gresley's first experiment with the booster was on Ivatt Atlantic, LNER No. 4419. Here we see an unique view of the flyover at Wood Green, with the booster Atlantic No. 4419 heading a down express, 'N2' No. 4744 (now owned by the Gresley Society Trust) on a New Barnet train, and empty coaches passing overhead on their way to the Bounds Green carriage sidings.

A.B. Collins Collection

No. 2798, a Robinson class 'S1' shunting tank, built by the LNER at Gorton in 1932. Almost all its time was spent on hump shunting in the Mexborough yards. Note the pipe carrying the exhaust steam from the booster engine. *Gresley Society Trust*

A later application of the booster was to two Raven 'C7s', the renowned 'Z' class. This resulted in a 4-4-4-4 wheel arrangement, but they were still regarded as Atlantics and classified 'C9'. A larger capacity boiler was provided, but the Stephenson valve gear was retained. Here is a works photo of No. 727.   *Gresley Society Trust*

Another modification to the Raven class 'Z' Atlantic was in providing two of the class with Lentz rotary cam operated poppet valves, here seen on No. 732.   *Gresley Society Trust*

The original batch of 28 class 'V1' were all sent to Scotland, shared between Edinburgh and Glasgow districts. No. 2923 was shedded at Parkhead, and is here seen on 11th September, 1938 at Dumbarton, heading a Shettleston to Helensburgh service.

University of Hull, W.B.Yeadon Collection

In this panoramic view of the exit from Hull station, one of the final batch of Gresley 2-6-2T, built as class 'V3', BR No. 67686 (LNER No.395) heads a stopping train. An early dmu may also be seen.   *University of Hull, W.B. Yeadon Collection*

Gresley sought information as to the maximum in lb./hr which could be hand fired. Mr Crawford, who had pioneered mechanical stoking in the United States, gave a maximum of 7,000 lb., just over three tons, but with an average sustained rate nearer half that figure. Gresley decided to experiment with a small version of the mechanical stoker, on a shunting tank which spent much of its time waiting for the next job, in circumstances in which the wages of a fireman could be saved. As might have been expected, the idea was vigorously opposed by the footplatemen's union, and the engine concerned, and its controversial equipment, did not leave Doncaster Plant yard. Much later, in 1939/40, design work was commenced on a mechanical stoker for a projected 4-8-2 express locomotive, but wartime conditions caused this to be suspended. At the Crewe dinner in 1920, Gresley expressed the hope that one day they might see engines with an axle weight of 30 tons. Whether this was a serious statement, or said in jest, is not known, but the coal burning potential of such a locomotive would surely call for mechanical firing. As a practical example, on the 'Coronation' streamline trains, a fireman might expect to shovel an average of 2,500-3,000 lb./hr.

Gresley also investigated the possibilities of alternatives to the conventional form of steam locomotive. He was undoubtedly interested in a private venture known as the Kitson-Still, and built as a 2-6-2T in 1928. (Kitson's of Leeds were the builders, the patent rights being held by the Still Engine Co. of London.) This employed double-acting cylinders using steam on one side to start the engine, power when running normally being provided by diesel fuel acting by compression ignition on the other side, augmented by the steam cylinders when maximum power was required. The LNER offered support to the project insofar as it was allowed to run a number of short distance trials, but it was not a complete success, the power output being less than that of a 'J39' 0-6-0. However, it may have provided the idea for a Doncaster proposal made four years later in which an Ivatt 0-8-2T was to be converted to diesel/compressed air operation. A 400 hp diesel engine would drive a compressor, whilst steam would be produced by a boiler heated from the diesel exhaust. Nothing more was heard of this beyond the drawing board.

A more orthodox proposal had been made in 1928, when it was realised that the NER Bo-Bo electric locomotives introduced in 1914 for the Shildon to Newport mineral line, and made redundant when the need for them fell consequent on a severe reduction in coal traffic, could be re-utilised. It was thought that these machines could be converted to diesel-electrics, with the eventual possibility of their employment on the Ferme Park coal run. A 1,000 hp diesel engine would drive a generator, which would supply electricity to the traction motors. The project was developed in some detail, on paper, and English Electric and Beardmore were consulted. However, the manufacturers were not enthusiastic, and although Gresley did not agree with them, this idea was also dropped.

Unusually for a research project, this proposed conversion was reported in detail to the LNER Board, and one cannot help wondering if this was done to divert attention from a revolutionary steam locomotive known as the 'Hush-Hush', which was being built in secret at Darlington, and which was to be the best

British Railways No. 67638, this 'V3' 2-6-2T was originally LNER class 'V1', No. 481, but now rebuilt with a 200 lb./sq.in. boiler. Here seen at Botanic Gardens shed, Hull, on 10th July, 1956. These engines survived well into BR days, and were very popular with their crews.

P.H. Groom, Gresley Society Trust

Proposed conversion of the Shildon Bo-Bo electrics, with the Ferme Park mineral trains in mind, but the project did not get very far.

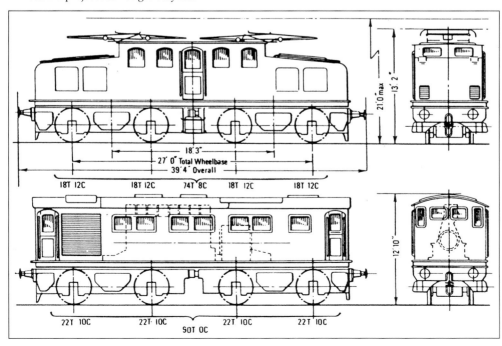

example of Gresley's efforts to improve on the usual form of steam locomotive. This employed a high pressure (450 lb./sq. in.) marine type water tube boiler to provide steam for a 4-cylinder compound driving system. Originally intended as a 4-6-2, it was later altered to 4-6-2-2, although generally regarded as a 4-6-4, class 'W1' No. 10000. The origin of this lay in the introduction by the Delaware & Hudson RR in 1924 of the first of its high pressure locomotives, with a 350 lb./sq. in. water tube firebox boiler, for which Yarrow & Co. of Glasgow had been the consultants to John E. Muhlfeld, the designer of the locomotive. A paper on water tube boiler construction had been read by Sir James Kemnal, of the boiler makers Babcock & Wilcox, to a meeting of the Institution of Mechanical Enginers in Glasgow, in 1923, the discussion being opened by Harold Yarrow. The following year, at Gresley's initiative, he met Yarrow to discuss the design of a suitable water tube boiler, derived from the Yarrow marine type, for locomotive applications. Gresley's intention was to use a much higher boiler pressure than normal, initially 350 but later 450 lb./sq. in., in conjunction with compound drive to achieve greater efficiency and fuel economy than in his existing Pacifics. Following three years of design studies the Gresley-Yarrow water tube boiler, with larger tubes dictated by the water scaling problems inherent in locomotive service, was patented, and the locomotive completed in 1929. At first, it had been intended to use a 3-cylinder compound drive, following discussions with the LMS engineer S.J. Symes, who had had wide experience of Midland compound locomotive design, but it was later decided to adopt 4-cylinder compound drive, possibly following Gresley's meeting with Chapelon. An ingenious mechanism patented by Gresley enabled the high pressure cut-offs to be adjusted independently of the low pressure, a desirable feature in a prototype compound locomotive.

In contrast to the proposed Bo-Bo conversion, no word of the 'Hush-Hush' reached the Board, at least officially, presumably because this new venture into unconventional locomotive steam generation was classified as 'research and development'. This would be considered as an expense against revenue account, and not charged to capital, which would have required Board approval. Also, Gresley was aware that Sir Henry Fowler and the London Midland and Scottish Railway were deeply involved in a high-pressure experiment of their own, and he wanted to keep his project out of the news until he was ready to unveil it. In fact, the locomotive's unconventional semi-streamlined outline and battleship grey finish generated a good deal of friendly publicity for the LNER. It remained nameless, although at one time the intention was to give it the name *British Enterprise*, for which plates were cast but not fitted.

No. 10000 was carefully nurtured, and employed in regular service from time to time, notably when after only six months it worked the summer 8¼ hr non-stop 'Flying Scotsman' from Edinburgh to King's Cross and return, the up train observed arriving on time. The following April it headed the train to its winter schedule, but for some reason arriving 25 minutes late. It had been employed on this train to work up to London as it was to take part in an exhibition at Norwich (the engine was often a star attraction at such events, held to benefit railwaymen's charities.) Later that year it completed three successive round trips on the 'Junior Scotsman', giving the Gateshead crew some anxious moments in their efforts, not always successful, to keep time.

The 'Hush-Hush' 4-6-4 No.10000 was often featured as an exhibit on Open Days, when the LNER showed off examples of its latest locomotives and coaching stock to the public, the proceeds going to railwaymen's charities. Here it is seen at Stratford on 1st May, 1931, *en route* to Norwich for exhibition. It was not used for revenue earning traffic in East Anglia.

Ken Nunn Collection, LCGB

In its original style with the experimental high pressure water-tube boiler, No. 10000 is seen at Leeds. Although a press photograph, this occasion in February 1931 was unlikely to have been a staged occasion, as the locomotive was undergoing trials at the time.   *Yorkshire Post*

Over the years, No. 10000 was the subject of several modifications, principally associated with indifferent steaming, which was finally overcome in 1935 by fitting a special double Kylchap exhaust and, at Chapelon's suggestion, a supplementary superheater to overcome condensation in the low pressure cylinders. The locomotive was frequently tested in conjunction with the dynamometer car, on one occasion developing 1,702 hp at 57 mph, which with a 35 sq. ft grate compares with 2,100 hp for the later *Cock o' the North*, with a 50 sq. ft grate (*see Chapter Nine*). However, although efforts were made to improve its reliability, it continued to give rise to problems, and with the new 'A4s' giving equal power and performance efficiency, as well as other new ventures claiming his attention, Gresley terminated the project. The locomotive was rebuilt in 1937, as a 3-cylinder simple on the lines of the 'A4' Pacifics, but retaining the 4-6-4 wheel arrangement, while the unique boiler was adapted for use *in situ* at Darlington Works. Had No. 10000 proved successful in its original form, perhaps the water-tube boiler would have been seen on other Gresley locomotives, as in 1931 attention was given to a design for a water-tube boiler version of the 'K3', retaining the 3-cylinder simple drive of the 2-6-0. But nothing was to come of this beyond a drawing office outline.

A point of particular interest in the Gresley story is that No. 10000 was a compound locomotive, the only example of this method of steam utilisation for which he was responsible. He held that this system only gave worthwhile economy with pressures of 250 lb./sq. in. or over, thus requiring a special type of boiler, as conventional stayed fireboxes were not considered suitable for higher pressures than this. He was well aware too that Francis Webb's last 4-cylinder compound 4-4-0s with modified valve gear, authorised by Webb just before his retirement in 1903, were extremely successful, and a great improvement on earlier 4-cylinder compounds. No doubt this, as well as the performance of the Nord super-Pacifics, was to influence his thinking. A year after the construction of No. 10000, Gresley described its conception and mechanical details in a classic technical paper presented to the Institution of Mechanical Engineers, when he was congratulated by several of those taking part in the discussion, on the relative simplicity of his locomotive compared with Continental designs with very complicated multi-pressure boilers. But no comprehensive account of the performance on the road of the 'Hush-Hush' has been published.

Reference was made in Chapter Four to the diminutive steam rail motors built by the Great Northern for service on lightly patronised services. Two firms which specialised in road locomotives, Sentinel and Clayton, came forward with designs of railcars with an integral steam unit, which offered a similar but more compact solution. These appealed to Gresley as offering good value, and he obtained the support of the Chief General Manager, Sir Ralph Wedgwood, in putting a case for the purchase of a number. In the event, no fewer than 80 of the Sentinels, of half a dozen different varieties, plus 11 Claytons, were purchased between 1925 and 1932. Whilst enabling operating costs to be roughly halved compared with an auto-train with a separate locomotive, the steam railcars' availability was variable and most did not have the capability to haul trailer cars to deal with the additional traffic which offered from time to time, such as on market days. Unfortunately Clayton's went into liquidation in 1929, after which their vehicles had to be withdrawn gradually because of lack of spares, but the Sentinels generally lasted

On 1st August, 1930, No. 10000 was in charge of the down non-stop 'Flying Scotsman'. Here it is seen going well up the 1 in 200 past Greenwood box.   *Ken Nunn Collection, LCGB*

No. 10000 had brought the up 'Scotsman' to King's Cross the previous day. Here the footplate crews are seen with the locomotive's designer soon after arriving in King's Cross platform 2. H.N. Gresley is with drivers J. Gascoigne and R. Eltringham, and firemen H.A. Brayson and J.W. Ritchie.   *Gresley Society Trust*

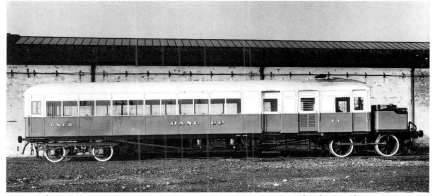

One of the Clayton railcars, *Bang Up*, numbered 44 in 1929. This had a short life of only nine years. In contrast to the Sentinels, the Claytons carried their coal and water externally, ahead of the coach section.   *Gresley Society Trust*

for 15 years or more. Within their limitations they were popular with the travelling public, and indeed with the staff (although the cramped firing arrangements were criticised), helped by their apple green and cream livery and choice of names, after stage coaches which ran on the early 19th century roads.

Sentinel also provided 56 small shunting engines, with power units similar to those of the railcars, and these achieved a respectable life span of 20-30 years. The design of this small but useful type had little to do with Nigel Gresley or Doncaster, but fuel consumption was relatively low and they saved the LNER money at a time when it was particularly short. The Sentinel shunter was in fact the subject of interest by all four of the main line companies, and joint discussions took place concerning details of the design. On the same theme, also in the 1930s, the LNER obtained three 250 hp diesel-electric railcars from Armstrong Whitworth, as well as a 95 hp railbus, but these early examples of their kind had poor availability and were withdrawn after a few years.

The LNER's net revenue (the difference between income and expenditure on the revenue account) in 1932 was barely half that of 1923, primarily as a result of the trade depression which was at its worst in the early 1930s. The effect on the railway's ability to invest is reflected in the fact that in relation to the then total stock of some 7,000, no more than 17 new locomotives were built in 1933. Probably more than any other statistic, this illustrates the difficulties in which the LNER found itself. However, new initiatives were already at work, and succeeding years were to see the culmination of Nigel Gresley's outstanding contribution to his profession. But according to Oswald Nock, things may have turned out differently had Gresley responded to overtures made by the LMS in 1932, when a successor to their then CME, Sir Henry Fowler, was needed. Sir Harold Hartley, the LMS Director of Scientific Research, was impressed by Gresley's papers to learned societies, and his forward-looking views, particularly as exhibited in No. 10000. As a result, Sir Harold advised Sir Josiah Stamp, the LMS President, that here was their man. Nock does not elaborate, but whatever the terms of the deal - and the LMS could have made Gresley an offer which in financial terms he might have had difficulty in refusing - nothing came of it. At all events, Gresley was later awarded a salary increase to £5,000. One can only surmise how events might have turned out had Nigel Gresley, instead of William Stanier, been appointed as CME of the LMS.

Chapter Nine

The Streamline Era

The acceleration of the non-stop 'Flying Scotsman' in 1932, from 8¼ to 7½ hrs, was an indication of changing railway management policy, with a greater emphasis on speed as an incentive to passenger travel, especially during a period of trade depression and increasing road competition. News from Germany in 1933 that an articulated two-car diesel-electric unit styled 'Die Fliegende Hamburger' ('The Flying Hamburger') was running the easily graded 178 miles between Berlin and Hamburg at an average speed of 77.4 mph, achieving up to 100 mph in the process, was received with interest in Britain. Nigel Gresley visited Germany and travelled on the service, but concluded that with a light train his Pacifics would be capable of similar performance. So, in the course of a trial run on 30th November, 1934, *Flying Scotsman*, since 1927 with long travel, longer lap valves, but still with its original 180 lb. boiler, in the capable hands of driver Sparshatt and fireman Webster, and hauling a four-coach train of 145 tons tare, including the dynamometer car and a restaurant car, covered the 186.8 miles between King's Cross and Leeds at an average speed of 73 mph. On the return journey, with two additional coaches, 100 mph was momentarily achieved down Stoke Bank, so approaching the Great Western's long cherished record of *City of Truro* in 1904, which had by then been questioned as to its accuracy. That the 'ton' could be exceeded with a train of this weight, was demonstrated the following March by No. 2750 *Papyrus*, an 'A3' engine built in 1928, which reached 108 mph down Stoke, whilst hauling 213 tons. This was in the course of a return journey between King's Cross and Newcastle, running to a four hour schedule, on which several minutes were saved in each direction, the net average speed being 70 mph. This proved to the satisfaction of Gresley and the LNER management that they could provide a high speed inter-city train between London and the North East with conventional type coaches offering greater comfort, as well as full restaurant car facilities, in contrast to the cold buffet of the 'Hamburger'. A study made for the LNER by the Germans concluded that a service similar to their diesel-electric would take 15 minutes longer than the four hours of the proposed steam-hauled train. It is interesting to note that the morning service from Hamburg to Berlin, and the evening return, with a six-coach train hauled by a 4-6-4 locomotive, averaged 72 mph, over a more easily graded route than the East Coast main line. (It may be asked why a longer diesel multiple unit, with intermediate power cars, could not have been developed for these services, but at the time the problems of control of such units operating in multiple had not been solved satisfactorily.)

These developments were taking place in a world slowly emerging from severe economic depression, in which design parameters generally were being relaxed. The popularity of Art Nouveau and what was to become known as the 'streamline' era were features of design everywhere, from buildings to domestic utensils. Indeed, streamline design for the sake of appearance was being used on otherwise functional products, and the LNER saw no reason why this should not also be applied to the steam locomotive and its train. It was also perceived that there would be an additional physical benefit in reducing a train's resistance to air flow, in terms of improved levels of performance for a given locomotive power output. They were no doubt also conscious that developments on these lines were already taking place on the Continent and the United States, even as far away as China. The LNER's initiative stemmed from Sir Ralph Wedgwood, the Chief General Manager, and led to discussions involving Gresley and Bulleid, with the enthusiastic support of operating and publicity departments. All this led to a determination that the LNER should set new standards which would raise the company to a leading position as innovators in high levels of speed and comfort in rail travel, so creating increased passenger traffic, and gaining them worldwide approbation. So, early in 1935, it was decided to provide a return service between Newcastle and King's Cross each weekday, arriving in the capital at 2.00 and departing at 5.30 pm. One stop would be made in each direction at Darlington, the overall time being 4 hours, at an average speed of 67 mph, with 70.4 mph between King's Cross and Darlington. This was heady stuff. At the time a few trains were scheduled at over 60 mph start to stop, with the Great Western 'Cheltenham Flyer' reaching Paddington from Swindon, 77.3 miles at 71.4 mph, and the LNER running the early morning up Leeds express from Grantham to King's Cross, 105.5 miles, in 100 minutes, at 63.3 mph. Three weeks before the new LNER train entered service, the Great Western accelerated the 'Bristolian', Paddington to Bristol, to cover the 117.8 miles at just over 67 mph, but no regular high speed service over as long a distance as 268 miles had been seen in Britain before.

A further step forward in the development of the Gresley Pacifics had already been taken by the building at Doncaster in 1934/35 of a new series of nine 'A3' Pacifics, with enlarged internal steampipes, and distinguished externally by an elongated steam collector in place of the conventional dome. The last of these was No. 2508 *Brown Jack*, and it was followed only seven months later by the first of a batch of four, No. 2509, bearing the name *Silver Link*, with further internal design improvements, and quite unlike its predecessor in looks. These new engines were to be the class 'A4', 35 being built between 1935 and 1938. Boiler pressure was raised to 250 lb./sq. in., Gresley's original hesitation finally having been overcome with the introduction of effective chemical water treatment to minimise scaling. The boiler tubes were shortened by a foot with a corresponding increase in the length of the combustion chamber, and a Churchward-type jumper top blast pipe was provided to reduce exhaust back pressure when working hard. Cylinder diameter was reduced to 18½ in., and valve diameter increased to nine inches to improve freedom of steam flow, which was also helped by smoothing the steam passages from the superheater to the cylinders. This in fact was internal streamlining, the principles of which had been pioneered as far back as Crampton's locomotives, and later developed in France by du Bousquet and Chapelon, although the term 'streamlining' had not then come into use. Indeed, relatively little was published at the time about this important development, possibly because its effect was not fully appreciated, although tests were to show that when driven with full regulator, locomotives with a well designed steam circuit had practically no drop in steam pressure between the regulator valve and the steam chests. The importance of this is illustrated by the statement made some time later by Gresley to the son of Andrew McCosh, the chairman of the LNER Locomotive Committee. To the question, 'What is the most important improvement you have made to the steam locomotive?' the answer was 'Internal streamlining'.

In the 'A4s', the familiar Pacific outline was replaced by a smooth overall steel casing, resulting in a surface offering considerably less air resistance than the conventional steam locomotive. Gresley had travelled on one of the railcars running in France between Paris and le Havre, and Paris and Deauville, the outline for which had been prepared by the automobile engineer Ettore Bugatti. Gresley was particularly impressed by the wedge-shaped front end, which lifted exhaust steam and smoke from passing steam trains clear of the railcar. The eventual Pacific design was the result of wind tunnel experiments at the City and Guilds Engineering College, and this, and a minor modification to the shape of the casing behind the chimney, had the additional benefit of lifting the exhaust away from the front cab windows. This was an essential requirement, as in certain wind conditions the softer exhaust of the 'A3' Pacifics sometimes led to the driver's view being obscured. A further minor but important improvement was the adoption of a wedge-shaped front to the cab, first seen in 1895 on the PLM Railway in France, where it was introduced to reduce air resistance particularly when running against strong Mistral winds. This followed the streamline form, and incidentally gave the crew a better forward lookout, preventing reflections.

Tests at the National Physical Laboratory between ½ scale models of Pacifics in streamlined and non-streamlined form led to the conclusion that streamlining reduced the effort required to overcome air resistance from 97 to 56 hp at a speed of 60 mph, and from 451 to 261 hp at 100 mph. However, air resistance depends on the direction as well as the force of the wind, and Bugatti is said to have mistrusted wind tunnel tests, conducting his own experiments with alternative body shapes fitted to fast road vehicles. The perception that air resistance was a form of vehicle skin friction which ought to be tackled was nothing new, however, the topic also having been given intermittent attention ever since the early days of railways. For example, a discussion on 'train resistance' took place in November 1901 at the Institution of Civil Engineers, at which two leading engineers of the day, John Aspinall and Francis Webb, took part. Another contributor was T. Hurry Riches, who despite his comparative obscurity with the Taff Vale Railway, nevertheless took a leading part in national committees. The *dragging* effect of air resistance on a train was emphasised, and it was suggested that a cone form at the end of the train would be preferable to one at the front. The discussion was wide ranging but somewhat discursive, not surprisingly in view of the lack of precise data on the subject. No practical trials are known to have taken place in the UK following the meeting, but there was a detailed analysis of the Berlin-Zossen high speed tests in 1903, when an electric railcar attained 133 mph.

The traditional form of steam locomotive, with its external asperities, clearly would benefit by a reduction in resistance to airflow, particularly at high speeds, and embryonic attempts to achieve this had been seen on the Continent many years before, initially by Ricour on an Etat 2-4-0 in 1883. These were described in 1935, when Dr Wagner of the German Railways gave a paper to the Locomotive Engineers in which he recommended 'fitting a petticoat over the locomotive's motion arrangements'. Understandably, however, any attempt to disguise the classic lines of the locomotive, or to reduce its accessibility, was not always looked on favourably by those concerned with maintenance. Wagner went on, more fundamentally, to emphasise the stresses set up in a steam locomotive running at 100 mph '. . . It should be laid out for at least 110 mph to stand up for everything coming [sic - he meant 'for all stresses']'.

The new LNER Tyneside service was introduced on 30th September, 1935, and to commemorate the Silver Jubilee of King George V and Queen Mary, the train was given the title 'Silver Jubilee'. The streamlining of the locomotive was carried through to the coaches, the body sides of which were covered in rexine, and provided with fairings below the underframes and covering the gaps between the vehicles, so contributing to the reduction in windage resistance. Finished in silver grey livery with stainless steel letters, the 'Silver Jubilee' at first consisted of seven coaches, with articulated twins flanking a restaurant triplet, and weighing 220 tons. Its popularity was such that an additional coach was added early in 1938, by converting one of the twin units into a triplet. A more comprehensive contrast to the traditional green locomotives and teak coaches would be difficult to imagine. The design and construction of the engine and carriages was a formidable challenge to the CME's Department, and was met successfully, no more than six months elapsing from the presentation of the first detailed proposals, to the completion of the train, just a fortnight before it was to go into service.

Before the 'Silver Jubilee' took up its regular duties, a trial run was organised for 27th September, 1935 from King's Cross to Grantham and back, the most remarkable achievement being the maintenance of a minimum of 100 mph over 24 miles between Hitchin and Offord, with maxima of 112½ at Arlesey and Sandy. Rather than keeping this proving run to themselves - after all, they were venturing well into the unknown - the LNER management allowed the press to make the most of the opportunities offered by this record breaking excursion, although it was not without mid-journey trepidation on the part of some passengers, notably when rounding the Offord curves, which were normally subject to a speed restriction of 70 mph, but taken at 85 mph. Silver Link rode well, but it was clear that the coach suspension required further tuning. Also, work was put in hand to improve the transitioning of entries to curved track. It was just as well that news had not leaked out of a near miss which had occurred only days before, when, at Northallerton, the driver of the 5.30 pm King's Cross to Newcastle train was approaching the junction of the line from Ripon when he misread the colour light signals ahead, and narrowly missed a sidelong collision with the 'West Riding Pullman', which at that period was timed to terminate at Newcastle 14 minutes before the 5.30 down, and consequently was normally given precedence. The signals were sighted for left-hand driving, but the Pacific concerned was one of the earlier examples which had not been converted from right-hand drive. The driver was presumably disciplined, but

The last of the initial batch of four class 'A4' streamlined Pacifics, No. 2512 *Silver Fox*, in silver grey livery, with the name painted on the boiler cladding. When later the engine was painted blue, a conventional nameplate was fitted. The fox emblem was provided by Samuel Fox & Co., suppliers of steel to the LNER.

BR, Gresley Society Trust

In the early days of the 'Silver Jubilee', one of the new 'A4s' is running alongside 'A1' No. 2582 *Sir Hugo*, with the 10 am Liverpool train, via Sunderland, on the King Edward Bridge, Newcastle. Normally smoke of this density would not be seen on such a prestige train, but this was probably by special arrangement with the photographer, W.Bryce Greenfield, MBE.

John Richardson Collection

nothing was ever admitted about the occurrence, by official sources. Perhaps, however, there may have been extenuating circumstances, such as adverse weather or a signal malfunction.

The 'Silver Jubilee' was a success from the start, financially and operationally. In its earliest days, *Silver Link* hauled the train exclusively for 13 successive return trips. This was not without its moments of anxiety, as on more than one occasion during the overnight stay at Gateshead the brick arch needed partial rebuilding but time did not allow the firebox to cool. This meant that repairs were carried out in a temperature which was excessive for the workman concerned, although the practice of working inside hot fireboxes was common on US railroads, with locomotives on high utilisation rosters. The cause was soon diagnosed and corrected, and no ill effects were reported, although Gresley, when told about it, said that 'A green engine should have been substituted'. As well as *Silver Link*, the other three engines built to run the 'Silver Jubilee' were appropriately named *Quicksilver, Silver King,* and *Silver Fox*. *Silver King* was the standby engine at Gateshead, the others being stationed at King's Cross and sharing the working between them. The 'Silver Jubilee' was an excellent timekeeper, and the selected link of drivers handled their engines so that they ran well within their capacity, and in fact rarely had to exceed the normal maximum of 90 mph to maintain schedule. Occasionally, a 'green' engine did substitute for the 'A4', as on 19th November, 1935, when No. 2503 *Firdaussi* kept time on a round trip to see how one of the final 'A3s' could handle the train, and to compare fuel consumption, but no figures were made public. On two occasions in 1936 the rostered 'A4' failed - on 4th September, when driver Samwells was forced to take one of the poppet-valved Raven Atlantics, No. 732, from York to Doncaster, finishing the journey to King's Cross with an Ivatt Atlantic, No. 4452, and on 14th October driver Sparshatt took over No. 4477 *Gay Crusader* at Doncaster, *Quicksilve*r coming off the down train on each occasion. Sparshatt had been one of the regular drivers in this link since the inauguration of the *Silver Jubilee* the previous year; this was to be his last week on this duty before his retirement.

Some years before the introduction of the 'A4s', Gresley was at work on another major project, the consequence of the decision in 1928 to provide third class sleeping carriages for the Edinburgh and Aberdeen overnight trains. In the summer these could load well beyond the capability of the North British Atlantics, and even the Pacifics stationed at Haymarket. Double heading was necessary, with an NB Atlantic plus a 4-4-0, the piloting of Pacifics being prohibited as the result of bridge limitations. Gresley regarded this practice as uneconomical, and met the request of the operating department by providing a locomotive which would undertake haulage of the trains single-handed. This was a powerful 2-8-2 Mikado type engine, an enlargement of the basic Pacific, with 6 ft 2 in. wheels, an 'A3' boiler barrel with an enlarged firebox of 50 sq. ft, heating surface of 3490.5 sq. ft, and three cylinders 21 in. x 26 in. In addition, the influence of Gresley's friend André Chapelon was seen in the provision of the Kylchap exhaust system, as tried earlier on two 'D49s', but now with twin blastpipes and a double chimney, to maximise steam production capacity and to reduce exhaust back pressure. Other refinements lay in the provision of an

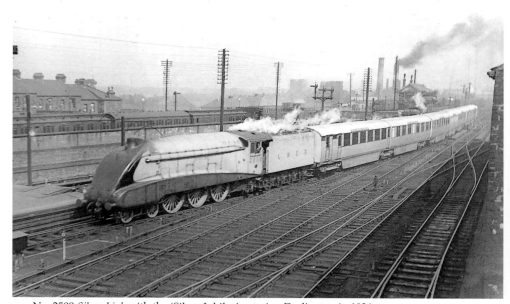

No. 2509 *Silver Link* with the 'Silver Jubilee' entering Darlington in 1936.

John Richardson Collection

Here we see *Silver Link* with the 'Silver Jubilee' on Durham viaduct, overlooking Durham City, with the cathedral in the distance.   *Durham County Advertiser, Gresley Society Trust*

In 1939, No. 4489 *Dominion of Canada* took a few turns on the 'Silver Jubilee', and is seen here picking up water at Werrington troughs, on 25th July. Note the bell, presented the previous year by the Canadian Pacific Railway. Little more than a month later, war broke out and the streamlined trains ceased to run. *H.C. Doyle, Gresley Society Trust*

The down 'Silver Jubilee' passing Welwyn Garden City on 25th July, 1938. No. 4465 *Guillemot*, being a Gateshead engine at the time, only made a couple of appearances on the 'Jubilee'. On this occasion it was standing in for No. 2510 *Quicksilver,* which had been stopped for a minor repair. *R.E. Batten*

No. 2001 *Cock o' the North* as originally built in 1935, with Lentz poppet valve gear; the outline may be compared with the rather larger Belgian 4-6-2 type 1 of 1935.

An early photograph of *Cock o' the North* at platform 6, King's Cross, whilst on trial. Bert Spencer is seen, wearing a felt hat, in the centre of the group of three. It is believed that the figure by the tender, with his back to the camera, is Nigel Gresley.   *Photomatic*

ACFI feedwater heater and Lentz rotary cam poppet valves, originally operated by continuous cams but later, because of excessive profile wear, by stepped cams offering six choices of cut-off. A determined attempt was made to prevent interference to the driver's vision caused by the exhaust beating down on the cab, by provision of deflector plates as a forward extension at the sides of the smokebox, the top of which was flat and angled as in No. 10000.   The locomotive was evocatively, even arrogantly, given the name *Cock o' the North*, transferred from an NB Atlantic, but if ever an engine's name was appropriate, this was the one. It was classed 'P2', and given the number 2001, in succession to the pioneer NER passenger 4-6-0 which had borne that number until withdrawal in 1931. The rostered maximum loading permitted over the severe gradients of the Aberdeen line was increased from 420 tons southbound and 480 tons northbound for the 'A3' Pacifics to 530 tons for the new Mikados.

During the summer of 1934 No. 2001 ran trials from King's Cross, and in Scotland, in both areas being recorded as hauling substantial loads at speeds reaching the seventies.   However, before being put to regular service, in November the locomotive was sent to France for appraisal at the testing plant at Vitry-sur-Seine, opened the year before, the main purpose being to determine the optimum blast pipe dimensions. Here, a good deal was also learned about the engine and its performance. Oliver Bulleid was in attendance for much of its time at Vitry, whilst Gresley visited on more than one occasion. Trouble was experienced with overheated axlebox bearings, due to the solid mounting of the rollers on which the locomotive wheels rotated, the resultant vibration breaking up the oil film in the bearings. Later, the rollers were provided with resilient mountings. Bulleid is on record as having said that its performance under controlled conditions showed that it was an economical machine, having regard to its power, although on a measured output basis, Chapelon's compound Pacific and 4-8-0 were considerably more powerful, due to their more economical use of steam. The 'P2' was in France for 10 weeks and as well as occupying the test facility and undergoing repairs to its axleboxes, several test runs with brake locomotives took place on the main line between Orléans and Tours, a maximum dbhp of 1,910 being sustained at 68 mph, with all bearings cool. (It would be interesting to learn what payment was made by the LNER for these extensive service facilities, which were not available in Britain.)

A second 'P2', No. 2002 *Earl Marischal*, left Doncaster Plant in October 1934, and was deliberately more conventional, with Walschaerts gear in place of the Lentz poppet valve gear. Also, it was concluded that the additional expense, not least the maintenance costs, of the ACFI feedwater heater, was not warranted by the fuel savings, as an appreciable (although lower) increase in the temperature of the feed water could be obtained by the use of the conventional Davies & Metcalfe exhaust steam injector. In the same fashion as No. 2001, the boiler cladding plates of No. 2002 were extended forward in an effort to improve smoke lifting, but due to the softer exhaust of the piston valve engine, these were now unsatisfactory, and a further pair of deflector plates was fitted outside the originals. Experience having proved that the second 'P2' was the more economical machine, due to its smaller cylinder clearance volumes and more flexible cut-off control, Gresley later decided to rebuild *Cock o' the North* in

Cock o' the North passing Greenwood box, with indicating shelter and dynamometer car, and judging by the coach destination boards evidently hauling an important train.

Richard Tarpey Collection

Cock o' the North in regular service, leaving Waverley station with the 9.55 am to Aberdeen in August 1935.

J.F. Clay, Gresley Society Trust

this manner, with Walschaerts valve gear. However, 1935 saw the introduction of the streamlined 'A4s', and he was sufficiently impressed by the smoke lifting results of their wedge-shaped front end that he decided to apply this to four further 'P2s', and convert No. 2001 in similar fashion. The new engines were all turned into traffic by the end of 1936, one of them, No. 2004 *Mons Meg*, working for a month between Doncaster and King's Cross before being sent north for final posting. It would be seen on heavier express trains, which it mastered effectively. Its appetite for coal was reported to be high, but not excessively so, but, like others of the class, it had to be handled carefully in the locomotive yards, where its long wheelbase was sometimes the cause of derailments. Detail differences were made to the last two to be built, No. 2005 being given a single exhaust system, and No. 2006 a longer combustion chamber.

The 'P2s' of course were not meant for the main line in England, and such running as was carried out there was for the purpose of running-in and evaluation, Doncaster being closer to the CME's office than Edinburgh. But by the end of 1936 all were in Scotland, where their welcome was mixed. In the hands of competent enginemen they could 'haul anything you hooked on behind them', but not all drivers, certainly not all firemen, took to them. At first they ran through on trains between Waverley and Aberdeen, 261 miles return, but saving a second crew by employing a larger engine was not favoured by the trades unions in those days of high unemployment, so that instead of making the most effective use of the engines, before long the six were shared between three depots, Dundee, as well as Haymarket and Aberdeen getting an allocation, and the routine was adopted of changing men, and often engines, at Dundee. Moreover, there was not always work available to justify such large locomotives. The 'Aberdonian' in each direction, certainly, often duplicated at the height of the summer, and heavy meat and fish trains, but this traffic was seasonal and one wonders if as many as six 'P2s' were needed - except that their reliability was not of the highest order, although this could not have been foreseen when the decision was made to build the engines. (Additional traffic arose in the war years, through the need to transport large numbers of servicemen.) The long rigid wheelbase did not take kindly to the sharp curves on the Aberdeen road, with consequent rapid end wear of the side rod bushes, which needed frequent renewal. This was dealt with at the sheds, but more serious was the flexing of the frames which occasionally led to fractures and steam blows as tubes became loose in tube plates, needing out of course visits to works for repairs. (General repairs were mainly carried out at Doncaster, Cowlairs being responsible for light repairs until the war years, when more work was undertaken there.) Middle big end failures were not unknown, and on more than one occasion, a crank axle fractured. To alleviate stresses induced by the curving nature of the track, the flanges of the second and third pair of coupled wheels were thinned, but a proposal that a knuckle joint should be designed to reduce the stresses in the side rod joints was not adopted.

A further suggestion was that improved guiding control could be achieved by replacing the swing links of the long arm Bissel truck, with spring control. A more fundamental idea was a redesign on the lines of the Krauss-Helmholtz truck, introduced in Germany in 1888, with the pony wheel and leading coupled wheel

No. 2002 *Earl Marischal* was built on more conventional lines, with Gresley's conjugated valve gear, Kylchap double exhaust, and additional smoke deflecting plates.

BR, Gresley Society Trust

No. 2006 *Wolf of Badenoch*, the last 'P2' to be built, was given the streamlined front end of the 'A4s', in which form all six of the class eventually appeared. Named after the Earl of Buchan, who terrorised the population of north-east Scotland six hundred years ago.

BR, Gresley Society Trust

sets carried in a single truck, and pivoted from the main frame structure. Chapelon himself, when *Cock o' the North* was running on the Paris-Orléans main line, had remarked that the similar Italian Zara-Bissel bogie type truck would allow more lateral flexibility to the leading coupled wheels, so improving the negotiation of curves. Gresley became aware of the problems of the 'P2s', but considered that the introduction of further new design features was undesirable in a small class of six engines allocated to three depots. He felt that the engines had enough in them which was new, and if drivers resisted the temptation to run fast downhill - the 'P2s' were very free running - the problems could be contained.

In everyday service in Scotland, the overall fuel consumption of the 'P2s' was relatively high, but there were good reasons for this. 'Toram Beg' (Norman McKillop), a well-known Haymarket engineman of the period, wrote that they had the most voracious appetite in his experience '. . . They could burn a hundredweight of coal to the mile'. Having fired, and driven, the 'P2s', he should know. Stories have been told of 'P2s' running out of coal by Inverkeithing, and having to burn the signal box stock of coal and even, on one occasion, the wooden steps. (These may be enginemen's yarns, although none the worse for the telling.) However, it is true that on one early occasion, when on a test run through from Aberdeen in the face of a south-westerly gale, *Cock o' the North* ran out of coal by Dalmeny (it is surmised that this would have been on the return leg of a trip from Waverley to Aberdeen and back, the tender not being refilled at Ferryhill.) In contrast to these vernacular reports, the LNER produced figures of average coal consumption on a ton-mile basis for each locomotive class, in the respective Areas and, in considering the reported excessive appetite of the 'P2s' for coal, it is worth noting that over the period 1936-39 the statistics showed that they averaged 73 lb./mile. This may be regarded as not unsatisfactory in all the circumstances, having regard to their standby losses, with the fire still burning in the large firebox whilst awaiting their next turn. Moreover, for a given firing rate, coal consumption per mile increases in proportion at lower speeds, and the average overall speed of the Edinburgh - Aberdeen trains was only around 40 mph. Comparative coal consumption figures may be quoted for the Scottish based 'A3s' at 59 lb./mile, and 67 lb./mile for the Reid Atlantics. As a final comment on this subject, Bulleid contrasted the fuel efficiency results obtained from the tests at Vitry, and those from everyday service, where 'Most of the coal was burnt by misuse in shunting and standing, rather than in working trains'.

A factor often overlooked in comparing locomotive coal consumption on the basis of pounds of coal per mile, is the calorific value of the coal. For example, much Scottish coal possessed only some 85 to 90 per cent of the calorific value of the coal from Yorkshire pits used by locomotives in the LNER's Southern Area. (There was some compensation in that the Scottish coal cost less.) Thus, Pacifics based at Haymarket returned markedly higher fuel consumption figures than those based at King's Cross. Further, as a consequence, more ash was generated per ton of coal burned, so adding to disposal problems at the end of a journey. Where the tender capacity was limited in relation to the length of the journey and average power output, as with the 'Coronation', higher calorific value coal was specially made available at Haymarket, so that the maximum heat could be extracted from each ton carried.

The sumptious interior of a 'Coronation' first class compartment. Gresley wanted it to be 'One better than the Pullmans'.

Bedford Lemere , Gresley Society Trust

The 'P2' was in many ways an admirable design to meet difficult operating conditions, but it should be noted that in addition to the problems imposed by the hilly and curving route, another impediment to the smooth working of long trains was the need for drawing up at the smaller intermediate stations. It has been said that in wartime the class would have been better employed on the extremely heavy trains south of Edinburgh on the East Coast main line, but the Pacifics were generally capable of handling these, and no strong representations were made for the 'P2s' to be transferred south, although they were certainly used between Waverley and Newcastle, so avoiding piloting over Cockburnspath bank. The problems associated with the 'P2s' were to be addressed after Gresley's death, when as mentioned in Chapter Eleven, under Edward Thompson's direction they were rebuilt as Pacifics, but this was not well thought out, and still did not result in a wholly satisfactory locomotive for the Aberdeen road. Incidentally, the names of the later 'P2s' were the subject of a competition in which Boy Scouts were invited to suggest appropriate names. Two thousand entries were received, the winners being awarded a guinea and a trip round Doncaster Plant. One name which received a prize but was subsequently rejected was *Maid of Glamis*, evidently not being thought appropriate for such a masculine looking locomotive.

Returning now to the East Coast main line, the 'Silver Jubilee' ran successfully and profitably throughout 1936, and Leslie Burley's records show the three King's Cross 'A4s' performing extremely creditably. On 27th August the dynamometer car was attached in both directions, and impressive results were obtained. The reserve Gateshead engine was hardly ever called into 'Silver Jubilee' service, normally working ordinary expresses to York and Edinburgh. Indeed, the success of the 'Silver Jubilee' led the LNER management to extend the scope of their streamlined services, and in 1937 two more were introduced. These were the internationally famous 'Coronation', with two stops northbound and one southbound, between King's Cross and Edinburgh, in July, and the more prosaically named 'West Riding Limited', between King's Cross, Leeds and Bradford, in September. To work these new trains and to provide more power for regular trains such as the 'Flying Scotsman', 31 more 'A4s' were built at Doncaster. The first six of these appeared in apple green and in accordance with Gresley's wishes were named after wild birds, then the next five were painted garter blue and named after countries of the British Empire, to be identified with the 'Coronation', as a symbol of British pride, in George VI's coronation year. Then, until the war brought an overall unlined black, all were painted garter blue, but were to be subjected to other changes of livery in their later years.

The 'Coronation' was a harder locomotive proposition than the 'Silver Jubilee'. It ran a further 124.4 miles, and with nine coaches in a two-tone blue livery weighed 312 tons tare, an increase of 40 per cent over the original 'Jubilee' formation in the summer months, when a beaver-tailed observation coach was included. (This was removed in the winter, so reducing the load to 278 tons.) Unlike the 'Silver Jubilee', which ran an out-and-home service in the one day, two sets were provided for the 'Coronation', so providing an entirely new late

The up 'Coronation' at Low Fell, July 1939, with the observation car, hauled by No. 4492 *Dominion of New Zealand*. This engine was not a regular performer on the train, only making a small number of return journeys. *W.B. Greenfield, Gresley Society Trust*

Before entering regular service, a press trip was made by the 'Coronation' train to Barkston and back on 30th June, 1937, when a speed of just over 109 mph was recorded down Stoke bank. Probably for the benefit of the photographers, a final polish is given to the observation car.
Fox Photos, Gresley Society Trust

afternoon service between London and Edinburgh in each direction. The 'Coronation' commenced running on 5th July, 1937, the down train leaving King's Cross at 4 pm and arriving at Waverley six hours later and the up train leaving at 4.30 pm, taking the same time to the capital. The overall speed over the 392.7 miles was 65.5 mph, the down train averaging 71.9 mph between King's Cross and York. Compared with the 'Silver Jubilee', the 'A4s' hauling the 'Coronation' had less margin to recover from out-of-course delays, although considering the difficulties sometimes experienced from operating problems, and the weather, the punctuality record was good.

On a number of occasions the engine had to be changed, or assistance provided, sometimes with unexpected results. Although the relief engines were generally 'A1' or 'A3' Pacifics, a number of Atlantics stood in, while a 'K3', an Ivatt 4-4-0, a 'J6' 0-6-0 and even a North Eastern 0-4-4T made appearances on the 'Coronation'. The worst example of lateness was on 29th October, 1937, when in addition to a half-hour delay near Belford, the train was diverted via Lincoln because of a derailment at Newark, resulting in a two hours late arrival at King's Cross. Nevertheless these adverse occurrences were exceptional, and it is to the credit of the locomotives and their dedicated crews, and the attention given by the shed staff, that over the entire period when the 'Coronation' ran, until the outbreak of war, a punctuality record of 81 per cent was achieved, within a maximum lateness of 5 minutes. Indeed, on many successive occasions the train was recorded as having arrived at King's Cross right time, or even a couple of minutes early.

The third of the LNER streamline trains, the 'West Riding Limited', began running at the commencement of the 1937 Winter Timetable, on a schedule of 163/164 minutes between Leeds and King's Cross and vice versa. Two suitably named 'A4s', Nos. 4495 *Golden Fleece* and 4496 *Golden Shuttle* were nominated for the train, which ran up to reach King's Cross at 2.15 pm, returning at 7.15 pm. This had a good record of punctuality, with very few delays attributed to the locomotive.

No. 4496 *Golden Shuttle* was one of the pair of 'A4s' allocated to haul the 'West Riding Limited'. The other was *Golden Fleece*, and it was unusual for another engine to be substituted on this train.   *BR, Gresley Society Trust*

Mallard at Peterborough after achieving 126 mph. At left, fireman T. Bray, driver J. Duddington, inspector Sam Jenkins.
                                        H.M. Hoather, Gresley Society Trust

Two official photographs were taken of Sir Nigel Gresley standing proudly alongside the 'A4' which bore his name. This is the one seen less often.   *BR, Gresley Society Trust*

The LNER was not alone in high speed trials, and in the course of a test run on 29th June, 1937, the LMS achieved what was then to be a 'record' speed of 114 mph down Whitmore bank, before the train was routed unexpectedly into a platform line in Crewe station which was approached by a reverse bend. The rapid deceleration caused consternation, crockery being smashed and officials on board alarmed. Fortunately there were no serious repercussions, and the LNER attempted to better this speed the following day, when during a test run with a 'Coronation' set, 'A4' No. 4489 *Dominion of Canada* could only reach 109 mph down Stoke bank. Nothing more was done that year, but Gresley was determined to see what his locomotives were capable of, and the opportunity offered itself the following July. As it happened, a series of trials were being arranged in conjunction with the Westinghouse Brake Company, in which a newly developed 'QSA' (Quick Service Application) valve was under trial to see if it would lead to reducing braking distance at high speeds. Norman Newsome has described in detail how Gresley asked him to use the trial on 3rd July, 1938 to include a high speed run, with the objective of beating the LMS 'record'. In the event, No. 4468 *Mallard*, one of the last 'A4s' to be built, and enjoying the advantage of double Kylchap blastpipe and chimney, was selected to head a train of six 'Coronation' coaches plus the dynamometer car, weighing 240 tons. A speed of 125 mph was maintained for some 300 yards during the descent of Stoke bank, with a momentary peak of 126 mph.

Unfortunately, *Mallard* had to be taken off the train at Peterborough, white metal having run from the middle big end bearing whilst developing 3,000 cylinder hp, but no serious damage ensued and the 'record' was taken for the LNER. Sir Nigel was not on the run, the senior engineer being D.R. Edge, his personal technical assistant, who telephoned the news to his chief at his home at Watton-at-Stone. The Press were told of the event, and reporters waited at King's Cross for the arrival of the train. Although it was now headed by an Atlantic they appeared not to notice this, and Eric Bannister, one of Gresley's assistants who was on the train, and his colleagues diverted them to the dynamometer car, showing them photographs of *Mallard* and allowing them to examine the chart which recorded the speed.

Plaques on *Mallard's* boiler cladding commemorate the event. Gresley thought that the speed should be claimed as 125 mph, which was probably the more accurate maximum, but posterity has differed, and the plaques state 126 mph. Eric Bannister has said that a higher speed could have been reached, perhaps 130 mph, had there not been an engineering slack through Grantham station, which caused *Mallard* to reduce speed to 25 mph at the beginning of the climb to Stoke. In fact, Gresley had been told that there was 'a dead slow speed restriction at Grantham, so it will not be so easy to get top speed going through Stoke', but nevertheless decided to continue. Bannister adds that Gresley intended to run the test again the following year, to achieve an even higher maximum, but this was frustrated by the circumstances of the period. An investigation into the reason for the 'A4s' higher speed than that of the single chimney LMS Pacific concluded that this was due to *Mallard's* double Kylchap exhaust system, which reduced back pressure and improved steam production. Gresley was greatly impressed by the improvements in performance and speed resulting from this,

As more 'A4s' were built, they were seen on regular non-streamlined services, including the 'Flying Scotsman'. Here is No. 4483 *Kingfisher* at Newcastle Central. Unlike the other named trains, the streamline trains did not carry headboards.   *John Richardson Collection*

One of the 'A4s' allocated to Haymarket, No. 4488 *Union of South Africa*, is seen passing Princes Street Gardens on the approach to Waverley station on 4th August, 1938. This locomotive is one of six 'A4s' preserved.   *L.Hanson, Gresley Society Trust*

and in 1940 he told Col Kenneth Cantlie, the managing director of Associated Locomotive Equipment, the licensees, that he intended to convert all the Pacifics, and the new class 'V2' 2-6-2s, as soon as the patent expired.

Some studies into the commercial side of the streamliners have questioned their overall profit, one factor being the need in some locations for two block sections to be cleared in front of the prestige trains to allow for adequate braking distance. But on the credit side it must be said that their very presence added immensely to the LNER's status, which must have resulted in additional business travel, as well as a gain in morale for every railwayman on the LNER. As a thoughtful detail, a Hornsey 'N1' was specially cleaned to bring in the empty stock and create a good impression whilst standing at the buffer stops at King's Cross.

Other railways in Britain followed suit, but only the LMS made any impact. The GWR made a sad attempt at 'streamlining' by adding a bulbous nose and some fairings to two of their 4-6-0s, but this was hardly worthy of Great Western traditions of excellence. The LMS, however, were not to be left behind, and a new train, the 'Coronation Scot', was introduced on 5th July, 1937, offering a schedule of 6½ hours between Euston and Glasgow, with a stop at Carlisle in each direction. Following the streamline idiom, a number of 'Duchess' class Pacifics were given overall streamlining on the American pattern with 'speed stripes' along the locomotive and coaches, which were originally finished in blue and silver but later in crimson lake and gold to match the normal LMS livery. The locomotives were stripped of their streamlining after the war. However, the 'Coronation Scot' ran at a lower average speed than the 'Coronation', and left at existing departure times, not providing a later afternoon service, so that Glasgow passengers travelled to Edinburgh to connect with the 'Coronation'.

Three other LNER locomotives were streamlined. One was the erstwhile 'Hush-Hush', No. 10000, which in 1937 was rebuilt as a 3-cylinder simple 4-6-4, with a boiler similar to that of 'P2' No. 2006, but with pressure raised to 250 lb./sq. in., a 50 sq. ft firegrate, and the 20 in. x 26 in. cylinders of the original 'A1' class, so becoming the most powerful 6 ft 8 in. passenger locomotive in Britain. The locomotive's appearance was enhanced after dark by electric lighting behind the valances, floodlighting the motion in an impressive way, as well as being an aid to servicing. However, nothing seems to have been attempted scientifically to assess the engine's potential, and it served routine duties alongside the 'A4s', mostly from King's Cross shed, including of course the heavy wartime East Coast main line passenger trains. The other two engines were a pair of 'B17s', provided with streamline cladding in an attempt to give a modernised appearance to a new service introduced between Norwich and Liverpool Street. New teak stock was built and the train named the 'East Anglian' but the GER main line, nominally limited to 80 mph, did not possess the potential for much advantage to be obtained by streamlining of itself. The two locomotives concerned were renamed for this special duty, and were No. 2859 *East Anglian* and No. 2870 *City of London*. In addition to the locomotives which were streamlined, a drawing was made in 1936 of an Ivatt Atlantic with a streamline casing, but this is unlikely to have been the basis of a serious proposal.

After rebuilding on the lines of the 'A4s', No. 10000 was transferred south, working turn and turn about with the Pacifics. It spent most of 1938 allocated to Doncaster, and is seen here north of Potters Bar heading the the 4 pm from King's Cross.

Eric Neve, Gresley Society Collection

No. 2870 was streamlined and renamed *City of London* as one of the two 'B17s' allocated to the 'East Anglian', the new service introduced in 1937 between Liverpool Street and Norwich. Here seen near Shenfield, 10th June, 1938.   *Ken Nunn Collection, LCGB*

The vogue for streamlining was of course seen overseas, indeed a return compliment was paid to Gresley when in 1936 a Pennsylvania 'K4s' Pacific was given an all-over streamlined casing. Elsewhere, the style was generally adopted for appearance rather than enhanced performance. One of the most unusual locomotives of the genre was a 4-6-6T, completely streamlined, which ran the 100 miles between Berlin and Leipzig in the 1930s.

In retrospect, locomotive streamlining offered two benefits, although these were limited by circumstances. There was the impression of modernity, which increased public perception of an up-to-date railway, but this was unquantifiable, although it undoubtedly resulted in increased traffic. The main physical advantage was less resistance to air flow, so enabling more drawbar horsepower to be made available for a given rate of steam production, but this was only worthwhile at speeds over 70 mph. Apart from the additional weight of the casing, the valances were a hindrance to maintenance, as panels had to be removed to gain access to the wheels and running gear. However, during the war, when speed was restricted to 60 mph and streamlining as such had little benefit, the 'A4s' lost the valances over the coupled wheels. Terry Miller, then maintenance foreman at Haymarket shed, and later to rise to become Chief Mechanical and Electrical Engineer of British Railways, believed that this was due to an oversight on his part. One of his 'A4s' had been stripped down for inspection, the side valances having been removed, when it was called into Doncaster for overhaul, and the engine went into Plant without these being refitted. Miller expected a rebuff for allowing this to happen, but to his surprise the opposite was the case, and the locomotive was returned as he had sent it, and the rest of their class also lost their valances in due course. The then CME, Edward Thompson, had seen the engine with its motion exposed and regarded it as an improvement. As it was wartime, the original reasons for the fitting of the valances no longer held, and certainly access for maintenance purposes was improved. They were never replaced, and in any case the streamline trains were not reinstated after the war.

A further important matter was in Gresley's mind in the mid-1930s. This was the question of a medium power express locomotive as a replacement for the pre-Grouping 4-6-0s and Atlantics, which were becoming time expired, as well as for the 'K3s' on the heaviest and fastest vacuum braked freight trains. In 1931 studies were made in some detail of a 2-6-4-4 type, in which the locomotive was to have been articulated to its tender. This was referred to as the 'K3 improved' class, and would have had the 'K3' boiler and 6 ft 2 in. driving wheels. The proposal got as far as inclusion in the 1932 building programme, and a provisional order placed on Darlington for two, for which the running numbers 1339/1399 were allocated. However, the order was cancelled, and instead Gresley decided to develop a much more powerful mixed traffic class, which was in effect a smaller-wheeled 2-6-2 version of his proven 'A3' Pacific. After consideration of a number of proposals, one of which showed a marked similarity to *Cock o' the North,* and another which followed the 'A4' form of streamlining, a more traditional design was evolved. This featured an 'A3' boiler, with its barrel shortened by two feet, 6 ft 2 in. wheels, 18½ in. x 26 in. cylinders, 9 in. diameter piston valves and the large steam pipes and passages

The first of three views of Pacific pairing. Here is one of the final batch of 'A3s', *Singapore*, together with 'A4' *Silver Fox*, at Belle Isle, descending to the terminus.   *Ken Nunn Collection, LCGB*

The two 4 o'clocks from King's Cross emerging from Gasworks tunnel. *Wild Swan* heads the 'Coronation', and *Enterprise* is on the 4 pm to the West Riding and Newcastle.   *Photomatic*

At Grantham, 29th May, 1938, Kylchap-fitted No. 4902 *Seagull* waits the 'right away' with the up 'Junior Scotsman', whilst class 'A1' No. 2545 *Diamond Jubilee* will take the next up train on to King's Cross.   *J.F. Clay, Gresley Society Trust*

A number of locomotives were built overseas using the Gresley 3-cylinder drive and conjugated valve gear. Among these were a class of four built by the Victorian Railways in 1929, at their Newport works in Melbourne. The locomotives were streamlined in the late 1930s, and here we see No. 302 *Edward Henty*, named after the pioneer settler of Victoria. They were built for the 5 ft 3 in. gauge, and their leading dimensions were slightly larger than those of the 'A4s'.   *Public Record Office, Victoria*

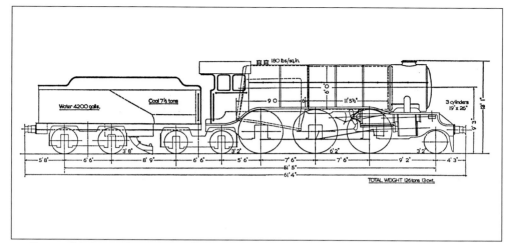

Proposed 2-6-4-4 enlargement of the 'K3' class 2-6-0, for which authority was obtained to build two, but which was abandoned in favour of the more powerful 'V2' 2-6-2.

Five of the 'V2' class were named after infantry regiments. Here is *The Green Howard* in immaculate ex-works condition, posing at Darlington works in September 1938. Note the green cylinder covers.   *BR, Gresley Society Trust*

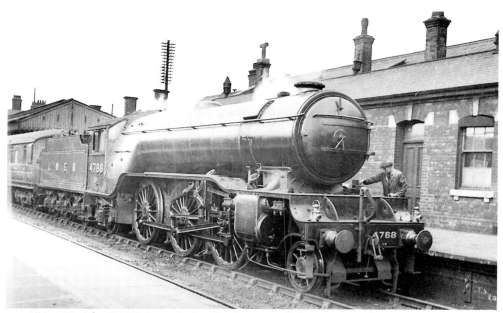

All but 25 of the 184 'V2s' were built at Darlington, including No. 4788, heading an up express at Grantham in August 1938, when shedded at Doncaster.   *J.F. Clay, Gresley Society Trust*

A small number of 'V2s' were allocated to the Great Central section in 1939. Here is an unidentified member of the class passing Bulwell Common golf course with an up express in that year.   *Henry Crooks*

'V2s' were to be seen in Scotland throughout their career as a class. No. 840 (originally No. 4811) was stationed at Dundee when photographed leaving Waverley with a stopping train on 16th August, 1948. Note the early group standard tender, transferred from a 'D49' 4-4-0.

B.W.L. Brooksbank

Due to restrictions, not many action photographs were taken of 'V2s' numbered between 3641 and 3695, which were built during the war. However, here is No. 3679, date and location unknown, except that as the engine was stationed at Gateshead, probably somewhere in the North Eastern Area.

W.B. Yeadon Collection, University of Hull

of the 'A4s'. Classed as 'V2', the new design was powerful and could run as fast in general service as the 'A3s'. Use of the standard 6-wheeled tender enabled the new locomotives to be handled on a 60 ft turntable, which was not possible with the Pacifics, although the axle load of 22 tons precluded them from the Great Eastern main lines. The 'V2' was to turn out to be a splendid locomotive, probably Gresley's most widely successful design, coping effectively with fast and heavy passenger trains, fitted freights, and loose coupled mineral hauls. An initial batch of five was built at Doncaster in 1936, Nos. 4771-75, the first bearing the name *Green Arrow*, the brand name of a new guaranteed delivery goods service.

A batch of 11 'B17' 4-6-0s had been included in a building programme authorised on 9th January, 1936, as part of a total of 43 locomotives of four classes, for which the funding had been provided under a Government New Works Programme. A further 32 'B17s' were authorised in the following October, but at the same time Gresley informed the Board that he contemplated the substitution of an improved type in place of these. This may have been a new design of 4-6-0, details of which were provided by Bert Spencer in his 1947 paper, for use on 'outlying' [sic] routes on which the turntables could not accommodate the 'V2s'. This proposed 4-6-0 would have had a tractive effort of 31,200 lb., somewhat less than that of the 'V2s'. Also, with 6 ft 8 in. coupled wheels, it would have been a less versatile machine, while, with the same axle loading of 22 tons, it would have had similar route restrictions. The submission to the Board stated that it was intended as a replacement for old engines on the Great Central Section and the North Eastern Area. Perhaps it was in mind as an alternative to the 'V2' if this had fallen short of expectations, reservations having been expressed about the use of a pony truck instead of a leading bogie, in a locomotive capable of high speeds. In the event, the installation of longer turntables and construction of new 'A4s' enabled older Pacifics and new 'V2s' to be allocated to the Great Central, and any anxiety about the performance of the pony truck was to be unfounded, for the time being at least. Consequently, for the same expenditure, the 32 proposed 'B17s' were replaced by 28 of the more generally useful 'V2s'.

Quantity orders for the 'V2s' were placed over the next few years, until 184 had been built, mostly at Darlington. They worked interchangeably with the Pacifics on the heaviest East Coast main line passenger expresses, and several outstanding records exist of their performance, including appearances on the streamline expresses. For example, on 14th January, 1938, No. 4789 distinguished itself by standing in for the rostered 'A4' to head the 'West Riding Limited' from King's Cross to Leeds, losing no more than four minutes on schedule. Also, on 9th March of the same year, No. 4782 took over the down 'Coronation' at York, and arrived a minute early at Newcastle, despite several checks *en route*. The 'V2s' were well-known for hauling prodigious loads in the war years, such as No. 4800 with 26 cars, some 850 gross tons, taking 102 minutes for the 76.4 miles from Peterborough to King's Cross in March 1940.

Three of Holden's 4-6-0s known as the '1500' class, LNER B'12', were fitted experimentally with ACFI feedwater heaters, at the end of 1927. Early trials must have been successful, as a further 50 sets of the gear were purchased, and fitted between 1931 and 1934. The apparatus did nothing for the appearance of the locomotives, which as a result were known as 'Hikers', and it was removed by the end of the decade. Over a period of years, a number of the class were transferred to the Great North of Scotland, where their extra power made them very welcome. No. 8536 was one of these, spending the summer of 1933 at Eastfield before transferring to Kittybrewster. The location is on the NBR, but exactly where is uncertain. *Ken Nunn Collection, LCGB*

Edward Thompson was Mechanical Engineer, Stratford, when the first 'B12' was rebuilt on Gresley lines. A later conversion, No. 8555, is seen here to advantage at Liverpool Street in the 1930s. *J.M. Craig, Gresley Society Trust*

Chapter Ten

The Final Years

The CME, his technical assistants, and the drawing offices, must have had their hands full with new design work as the years progressed, but Gresley still pursued his investigations into improving the performance of selected classes. One of these was the Holden 'B12' 4-6-0, but the Lentz valve gear fitted to the 1928 Beyer, Peacock batch (and six others of the class) had not come up to expectations, due to the camshafts becoming distorted and cylinder blocks subject to cracking. Albert English, of the Stratford drawing office, encouraged by the successful rebuilding of the 'N7s' with long lap, long travel valves, suggested that the 'B12s' might be similarly modified. Edward Thompson was then Mechanical Engineer at Stratford, and obtained Gresley's authority to make the improvement, and what was already a good engine was turned into an outstanding one, with a larger round-topped Doncaster type boiler, similar to that of the 'B17s' but with a shorter barrel and a larger but shallower firebox. This had the additional merit that the maximum axle load remained low, no more than 17 tons, so retaining a wide route availability, which was to be of significance during wartime, as the 'B12s' were pressed into ambulance train duty, on which they were to be seen on the Great Western and other parts of the country distant from the LNER. The first of the class to be converted was No. 8579, in May 1932, and in all, 54 out of a total of 80 were rebuilt over the years. Thompson also gave his attention to the Great Eastern 4-4-0s, and from 1933 new round-topped firebox boilers were fitted to most of the 'D15' and 'D16' classes, the second to be dealt with being *Claud Hamilton* itself. The rebuildings transformed the appearance of these two typically Great Eastern locomotive classes into what was recognisably the Gresley style.

Other pre-Grouping classes were also investigated, with a view to improving their performance. John Robinson's large 4-cylinder 4-6-0, LNER class 'B3', were powerful engines, but heavy on coal. At a time when Gresley was experimenting with Lentz poppet valves, it was decided to convert two of the six 'B3s' to the Caprotti rotary cam version, following its successful application to an LMS 'Claughton' 4-6-0. This was in 1929, and once initial problems had been overcome, comparative tests showed that the Caprotti-fitted engines returned a 16 per cent reduction in fuel burned. Such results justified the conversion of a further two, in 1938/39, except that the springs which returned the valves to their seats were replaced by steam. The appearance of the engines was altered by the raised cam boxes above the outside cylinders, but the distinctive paddle box splashers, the Belpaire firebox and Robinson cab, remained. It was Gresley's intention to convert the remaining two 'B3s', as well as the 38 members of the 'B7' class, the 5 ft 7 in. mixed traffic version, but this was frustrated by the war.

The third 4-6-0 to be given attention was the final Raven design of this type, LNER 'B16', a successful mixed traffic class, 70 of which had been built between 1919 and 1924. They had the same coupled wheel diameter and cylinder

Stratford also transformed the Edwardian style of the 'Claud Hamilton' class into a modern outline 4-4-0. Here is the doyen of the 'Clauds', in green livery, at Stratford in July 1933.

Photomatic

Robinson's largest 4-6-0 class was massive in appearance, and the fitting of Caprotti valve gear added a little more to their bulk. No attempt was made to fit them with round-topped boilers, or make other alterations, as was done to the 'B12s'. No 6168 *Lord Stuart of Wortley* is seen on an up slow train from Leicester, at Harrow, 1938.   *C.R.L. Coles, Brian Bell Collection*

dimensions as the 'K3s', and were liked by the NE footplatemen as being better riders, but they suffered in comparison by their short travel, short lap, valve design, inside valve gear, and higher fuel consumption. In 1937 a 'B16' was rebuilt with new cylinders and conjugated gear, and a cab on Doncaster lines to replace the lower window Darlington version. However, the NER chimney was retained and the rebuild did not appear so much in the Gresley style as the Stratford conversions. Only seven were dealt with in this fashion, although a further 17 were rebuilt by Edward Thompson when he was CME, but with three separate sets of Walschaerts valve gear.

Also, in the year before the first 'B16' conversion, one of the celebrated North Eastern 'R' class 4-4-0s, 37 years after it was built at Gateshead, underwent modernisation in which larger diameter, long travel, long lap piston valves were fitted, accompanied by the removal of the large splashers, leaving a raised running plate. This was LNER No. 2020, now class 'D20', and in no way did the locomotive resemble a Gresley rebuild. It is thought that the work was put in hand by Edward Thompson on his own initiative, when he was Mechanical Engineer, Darlington. Gresley was believed to have been displeased at not being informed. Later, three more were similarly converted but retained their original splashers.

Raven's Pacific was another North Eastern class to receive attention. Because no spare boilers had been built for these five locomotives, in 1929 it was decided to adapt an 'A1' 180 lb./sq. in. boiler and fit this to No. 2404 whilst its original was repaired, so that replacement boilers could be made available for the remaining four. This gave an extension of life to the class, but all were withdrawn by the end of 1937.

From 1927 onwards, Gresley strongly advocated the construction in Britain of a comprehensive static locomotive testing plant, where detailed analysis and evaluation of the functioning of the locomotive as a whole, and of its component asemblies, could be carried out in a scientific manner, with the objective of improving design performance and efficiency. He took the opportunities provided by Presidential and other addresses to press the case for a national 'locomotive experimental station', as he termed it. This would offer its facilities not only to the four main line companies, but also to the private locomotive builders and consulting engineers. At the time, in Britain there was only a small installation at Swindon built by Churchward in 1903, plus four dynamometer cars. (The pioneer plant of its kind was opened in 1891 at Purdue University, designed by the eminent American engineer, Professor Goss; this was followed by the much larger installation at Altoona, erected by the Pennsylvania RR in 1903.)

Gresley first expounded his ideas in his 1927 Presidential Address to the Locomotive Engineers, advocating that such a plant should be established under the aegis of the Department of Scientific and Industrial Research. This was taken up by the Government, who appointed a Committee to examine the proposal. The subsequent report, in June 1930, strongly recommended that such a facility should be put in hand, and a dynamometer car included as part of the project. However, due to the economic situation at the time, the report was shelved and nothing done, although in France, suffering similarly from the

Both Gresley and Thompson rebuilt examples of Raven's NER class 'S3' (LNER 'B16') mixed traffic 4-6-0 in their own fashion. The length of the locomotive allowed the drive to be concentrated on the leading axle, and, in the Gresley version, the conjugated valve gear to be placed behind the cylinders. No. 2364 was the first to be modified in this way, in 1937.

BR, Gresley Society Trust

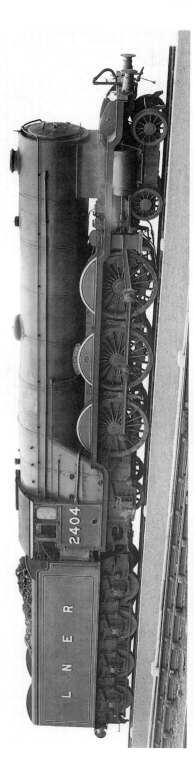

The length of the Raven Pacifics is emphasised in this study of No. 2404 *City of Ripon*, after rebuilding with 'A1' class boiler and cab, and provision of an LNER 8-wheeled high sided tender.

BR, Gresley Society Trust

Ivatt Atlantic No. 3278 was in charge of the first Cambridge buffet car express, leaving King's Cross platform 15 on 2nd May, 1932.   *Gresley Society Trust*

Class 'A3' No. 2501 *Colombo* hauled the up 'Silver Jubilee' throughout its run on 27th September, 1937. Here seen at Peterborough.   *T.G. Hepburn, Gresley Society trust*

'K3' 2-6-0s were to be seen in many parts of the LNER in the 1930s, and were useful for weekend and holiday work. In all, 193 of this class were built, at each of the two main LNER workshops, and by contractors.   No. 1100 (Armstrong, Whitworth, 1931), is nicely turned out for an excursion from the North East to King's Cross.   *F. Moore's Railway Photographs*

On 7th August, 1939, 'K3' class No. 1395 (Doncaster 1929) is leaving Scarborough on express duty.   *R.J. Buckley*

depression, a plant was built in 1933 at Government expense at Vitry, near Paris, which has already been mentioned in connection with the trials of *Cock o' the North*. Gresley amplified the technical case for a testing station in a paper to the Mechanicals in July 1931, but the lack of action by the British Government left the railway companies to act on their own initiative. Sadly there was now even less practical support, despite Gresley's continued pressure, stressing the low overall efficiency of the steam locomotive, and the need to improve it. The Great Western was content to rest on its own limited capability (which in fact was upgraded in 1936), whilst the Southern pointed out that its future lay in electrification and hence declined to participate, although after he had become CME, Oliver Bulleid said that he regretted the Southern Railway had taken that decision. The private locomotive builders and consultants also felt unable to contribute any funding. To their great credit, acting on the advice of their respective CMEs, Nigel Gresley and William Stanier, the LNER and LMS Boards decided to proceed on their own. Agreement was reached on the objectives and design of the plant, and Roland Bond of the LMS was appointed superintending engineer. In his Presidential Address to the Locomotive Engineers in 1939, Stanier paid tribute to Gresley's foresight and perseverance in initiating the Testing Station. He emphasised the need to investigate the questions of thermodynamics, such as combustion, steam flow and front end design, which could not be fully analysed in road testing. 'The large number of variables inherent in locomotive running must be held constant whilst only one is varied at will, and a stationary test facility is essential for the necessary measurements to be taken.'

Originally a site was designated at Cross Gates, near Leeds, but finally it was decided to locate the plant at Rugby, within sight of the West Coast main line. Progress was slow, and work was suspended during the war, but eventually, on 19th October, 1948, the Testing Station was opened, with an LNER test engineer, Dennis Carling, in charge. Gresley did not live to see his ambition fulfilled, but it was appropriate that the first locomotive to be placed on the rollers at the plant was the 'A4' Pacific named after him, then numbered 60007, *Sir Nigel Gresley*.

As the 1930s progressed, in addition to Gresley's advanced new locomotives, older classes such as the 'J39', 'K3' and others continued to be built, as well as, in 1933, a batch of 'O2' 2-8-0s for Great Eastern section mineral trains from Whitemoor to Temple Mills. These were the first heavy freight engines to be built by the LNER since the Mikados of 1925, needs in the meantime having been met by the bought-in ex-WD Robinson 'O4s'. Also, two further locomotive classes were to emerge from Doncaster, each an advance on existing designs. The first was in response to the need for more powerful locomotives to avoid double-heading on the West Highland line, where the enginemen were already familiar with a Gresley class, several 'K2s' having been allocated to Eastfield and Fort William sheds from 1925. An interesting first proposal for a 2-8-0 with 5 ft 2 in. wheels was unacceptable to the civil engineer, and this was replaced by a powerful 3-cylinder 2-6-0 also with 5 ft 2 in. wheels, and the high tractive effort of 36,600 lb., 56 per cent more than the 'K2s', giving greatly improved acceleration and hill climbing. Six of these, class 'K4', were built at Darlington between 1937 and 1939, and were said to be worth another two coaches over

'K2s' were transferred to Scotland from as early as December 1924. No. 4701 is in company with No 9270 *Glen Garry*, heading a southbound meat train at Craigentinny, near Edinburgh, 4th August 1928.   *Ken Nunn Collection, LCGB*

No. 4701 after receiving the name *Loch Laggan* in 1933, at Fort William.   *Gresley Society Trust*

In post-war green and renumbered 1732, it is now 33 years since this 'K2' was built at Doncaster. Here seen passing Retford with a southbound fitted freight in 1947.   *Eric Oldham*

The 'K4' class were welcomed on the West Highland line in the late 1930s. Here is No. 3446 *MacLeod of MacLeod* on an up train near Ardlui.   *G.W. Goslin Collection*

In other times, the two 'V4s' of 1941 would have been the precursors of a large class. Here is No. 3441 *Bantam Cock* which was turned out from Doncaster in immaculate LNER green, despite the war having been in progress for 18 months.   *BR, Gresley Society Trust*

The second of the class was renumbered 1701 in 1946, and appears purposeful in this view, taken at Fort William the following year.   *Photomatic*

their predecessors. They were given splendid names appropriate to the Western Highlands, one, No. 3442 *The Great Marquess*, having been preserved.

The second new class incorporated all Gresley's major design precepts in a medium power general purpose locomotive. After preliminary consideration of a 2-6-2 with a 300 lb. boiler and three 14 in. x 26 in. cylinders, a scaled down version of *Green Arrow* was designed, with 5 ft 8 in. wheels, three 15 in. x 26 in. cylinders and a 250 lb./sq. in. boiler with 1,800 sq. ft heating surface and a short wide firebox. With an axle load of no more than 17 tons, the new 2-6-2, class 'V4', was capable of travelling over 78 per cent of the LNER's route mileage. Two were built early in 1941, the second introducing a development new to Britain in the form of a thermic siphon in the firebox, intended to assist free water circulation, but this was removed in 1945 and replaced by a firebox similar to that of the first of the pair. (It will be recalled that Bulleid's 'Merchant Navy' class Pacifics were provided with thermic siphons, and no doubt the subject had been discussed between Gresley and Bulleid before he moved to the Southern, and each decided to apply the device to one of his own designs.) The 'V4s' were numbered 3401 and 3402, the first being aptly named *Bantam Cock*, so inviting the unofficial appellation *Bantam Hen* for the second of the class. *Bantam Cock* was unveiled only weeks before Gresley's death on 5th April (the 'V4s' would have appeared several months earlier, but the specification called for nickel steel for the boiler plates, and this was not easily procured during this period.) No. 3401 was tested on a number of services, notably the Liverpool Street to Norwich expresses, and gained the approbation of those engaged in these operations. Eventually, the pair settled down in Scotland, where they performed useful work, but did not have the opportunity to display their full capability. During the period when the 'V4s' were under construction, studies were made of a 2-6-4T which would have had a taper boiler and wide firebox, but this project was halted by the war.

From his student days, Gresley had taken a close interest in chemistry and metallurgy, far more than most of his contemporaries. The importance of having a senior staff member who was a specialist in these fields was not lost on the LNER Board, and despite the stringencies of the time, in 1931 the appointment was authorised of T. Henry Turner, as Chief Chemist and Metallurgist. His immediate concern was to recommend to Gresley what steps should be taken to improve the quality of boiler feed water, which varied over the LNER system, with some supplies highly acidic, causing corrosion, and others alkaline, leading to scaling. Feed water if left untreated had seriously adverse effects on boiler repair costs, as on the Great Central section, where locomotives required firebox renewals every five years or so, whilst on the other hand, in Scotland a firebox might last the life of the engine. During his first years in office, Turner made considerable steps in analysing the many sources of feedwater, so that the appropriate corrective treatment plants could be erected. These were first provided along the Great Northern main line, with the result that when *Mallard* made its record run, in Turner's own words, 'It was with water of zero hardness in its boiler'. Gresley's initiative in this field led to the LNER's approach being written into a British Standard Code of Practice for the treatment of water supplies.

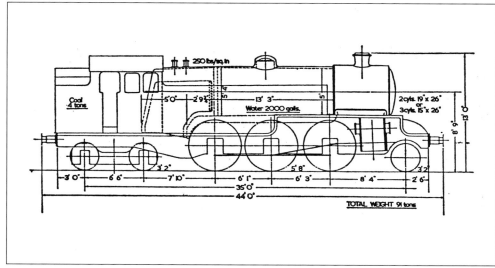

Gresley had given thoughts to a 2-6-4T design, on at least three occasions. This outline was prepared towards the end of the 1930s and incorporated a wide firebox. Two-and three-cylinder alternatives were considered.

Electric Bo+Bo No. 6701, was completed at Doncaster in 1940, with electrical equipment by Metropolitan Vickers. Although he may not have been intimately connected with design detail, the locomotive certainly possessed the clean lines one would expect from Sir Nigel.

Gresley Society Trust

Above: Sir Nigel Gresley and Cecil J. Allen. The occasion is the trial trip of the 'Coronation', 2nd July 1937. *E. Smith, Gresley Society Trust*

Left: In sporting attire, Sir Nigel is on a shooting trip, with his retriever Jock. Even when dressed informally, he was seldom without a handkerchief in his top jacket pocket. *Tim Godfrey*

Right: Bantam Cock and No. 6701 were inspected by members of the LNER Board and chief officers on 19th February, 1941. *Left to right:* Walter K. Whigham, Sir Ronald Matthews, Charles H. Newton, Sir Nigel Gresley, Sir William Gray. This is believed to be the last photograph taken of Sir Nigel, six weeks before his death.
Northern Echo, Gresley Society Trust

A serious collision took place on 7th March, 1950, near Witham, in Essex, which resulted in loss of life, and the destruction of a Thompson 'B1' locomotive, LNER No.1057. Despite the force of the impact, Gresley's insistence on the buckeye type of coupler and well-designed steel underframe gave rigidity to the train, so that the coaches stayed upright and did not telescope. *BR Gresley Society Trust*

Two examples of Gresley's LNER corridor stock. *Above:* No. 1007 was a third class compartment coach, converted to incorporate a hairdressing saloon and ladies retiring room for the 1928 non-stop 'Flying Scotsman' train. *Below:* No. 42463 was an all-steel open third, built in 1927 by Metropolitan C&W Co. *(Both) BR, Gresley Society Trust*

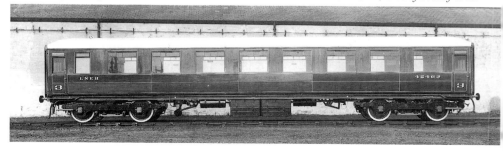

Another of T. Henry Turner's investigations was into the occasional fractures of locomotive driving wheels and tyres, as for example when alarm was caused as pieces of a broken tyre of a Pacific bounced from the roof of Gasworks tunnel on to a train running into King's Cross. In collaboration with Professor Coker of University College, London, and utilising the new technique of photo-elasticity, Turner recommended a modification of the wheel rims, which Gresley adopted.

It is convenient in this chapter to provide a brief review of Gresley's work in the field of carriages and wagons, for the whole LNER period. He had in fact continued with the basic design precepts which had characterised his work on the Great Northern, certain of which he had inherited from Ivatt and Howlden, as described in Chapter Four. His coaches were built on a strong steel underframe, and provided with Pullman type gangways, superior to the 'standard' type. Knuckle type automatic buckeye couplers offered a more rigid and safer coupling than the screw type used elsewhere, except that coaches had to be provided with screw type couplers as well, for coupling to non-buckeye stock. The benefit of this form of coupling was to be found when a serious crash occurred - but the coaches did not telescope. One such occasion was at Castlecary, near Falkirk, in 1937, when many lives must have been saved. Gresley attended the enquiry into the causes of the accident, and robustly defended his design practice. This was a period in which there was media criticism of the continued use of wood in railway carriage construction, but Gresley was emphatic that the traditional Great Northern teak was a hardwood which offered a bodily strength which thin sheet steel did not possess, and did not readily sustain fire. Apart from a small number of all-steel coaches, including the streamline trains, and the plywood sided 'tourist trains', he kept to teak, but, by the end of the 1930s this was becoming difficult to obtain, and subsequent construction was increasingly all-metal, with steel panelled bodies.

An experimental 51 ft non-corridor coach was built in 1933, with proprietary aluminium castings, but this was not repeated. The 'tourist trains' introduced in the same year were built to a low budget, and stimulated a passenger demand which was beginning to grow. External panelling was in plywood, and the coaches were painted a cheerful green and cream, like the railcars. Their low-backed bucket seats were not popular, however, and even less appreciated were the stainless steel chairs provided in another new venture, the buffet cars, new to the LNER, although they had been introduced on the Great Central in 1899. These were included in a number of fast trains between King's Cross and Cambridge. They were an immediate success, despite the seating, and a number of older coaches were converted, but it was not long before purpose built cars were introduced, for Cambridge and other destinations to which the buffet service was extended.

Around 1930, designs changes led towards the provision of end doors only, for much of the new corridor stock, instead of external doors to all compartments. This led to a neater outline and greater passenger safety in that inadvertent opening of compartment doors was avoided, although in the case of emergency, egress of passengers was more restricted. Innovations were introduced on selected trains, such as radio and record entertainment through

Two examples of specially designed wagons. *Above:* No. 204777, built at Dukinfield for the civil engineer's staff, was used for the conveyance of 60 ft rails. *Below:* No. 229080 was one of the first wagons specially constructed for the carriage of alumina powder in bulk; built at Shildon under the 1938 building programme.   *(Both) LNER, Gresley Society Trust*

headphones, film shows, hairdressing saloons and ladies retiring rooms, although these generally did not last very long. Sleeping cars for third class passengers were introduced in 1928 and the first class cars became more luxurious. Two built in 1932 had the benefit of hot showers, whilst Waring & Gillow were responsible for the interior design. New coaches provided in 1928 for the 'Flying Scotsman' had Louis XIV décor in the first class, and the consultants White Allom were retained as interior designers of the streamline coaches. The last trains of coaches built to Gresley design were for the 'Flying Scotsman' and the 'Hook Continental' in 1938, solid and comfortable, with pressure ventilation as an early form of air conditioning. One gains the impression that within a limited budget the LNER was constantly striving to improve the quality of its principal passenger trains, the Passenger Managers in the Areas being in regular debate with Wedgwood and Gresley.

The double bolster bogie developed by Gresley and Spencer Moulton in Great Northern days continued as the basic standard, but with a number of modifications, such as a heavier version where required, and a less costly single bolster where this would suffice. Gresley will of course be remembered for his adoption of the principle of articulation, which he introduced in specific instances where this would be of particular benefit, with the saving of space and weight.   A number of articulated triplet restaurant car sets were constructed, as well as the quintuplet Leeds set. Later, twin articulated sleeping car units were built, which lessened the noise from the bogies, and saved a toilet and an attendant's cabin.   However, it was realised that a set of coaches articulated together did not always meet changing operating needs, and the variety of coach bodies built on to the standard 61 ft 6 in. underframe were mainly individual vehicles.

A drawback to the principle of articulation is that a fault in one coach means the withdrawal of a complete set, but it must be said that the occasions on which coaches had to be hurriedly found to replace a failed articulated set were very few. Good maintenance, particularly of bogies, was the key, especially with the streamline trains. For these, a complete set was kept in reserve, primarily to cover visits to the shops for overhaul, but the occasions on which the substitution of this, or of teak coaches in temporary replacement of, say, a streamlined pair which had developed a fault, again were few. Articulation was of course a help in keeping down the length and weight of non-corridor suburban stock, and twin units were built for several suburban services, including the Tyneside electric stock introduced just before the war. It was generally agreed that Gresley's main line coaches gave the smoothest ride in Britain during the inter-war years, and it is interesting to note the continuation of Gresley practices in early BR days, when buckeye couplers and Pullman gangways were adopted, on account of their ability to hold a train together in case of accident. Although articulation was out of favour for several years after Gresley's death, since 1981 it has been adopted for certain fixed formation sets, notably the French TGV, and more recently, the 'Eurostar'.

As for wagons, the ambitions of Gresley and others to see a standardised high capacity vehicle for conveyance of coal and other minerals were frustrated by the inability of the coal owners to invest in the necessary railside works to accommodate these. The nearest the protagonists of larger wagons could get was the publication by the Railway Clearing House in 1923 of a specification for a standard 12 ton mineral wagon. The LNER version originated in a Doncaster design in 1921 with a 9 ft wheelbase, increased to 10 ft by 1932, wooden underframes later being replaced by steel. The 16 ton all-steel wagon had to wait until 1945, but even then remaining loose-coupled and unbraked.

As an experiment in the utilisation of new materials, the unique aluminium coach had a parallel in the concrete brake van. Again with the interested support of the trade, a concrete 'caboose' (brake van) was built in America in 1924, and the idea was suggested to Gresley. One was constructed and although believed to have been satisfactory for its job, it did not appeal to the goods guards, who claimed it was cold and damp, even when lined with cork and provided with a wooden floor. It was left in a siding at Holloway for some years, and its end is not known. However, it was of sufficient novelty to be reported at the International Railway Conference held in London in 1925.

The Darlington drawing office possessed a capability for designing wagons for special uses, and notable among these were large wagons, some with multiple bogies, for the carriage of loads such as ship propellers and naval guns. The largest had a load capacity of 120 tons. Gresley took a keen interest in this branch of rolling stock construction, particularly in his encouragement of welding, in which Oliver Bulleid did much to develop new techniques.

The mid-1930s were the years of Sir Nigel's greatest triumphs, when he appeared to be in robust health, and taking matters in his stride, visiting Paris from time to time to discuss matters with French engineers, and journeying to South Africa, to inspect the Metropolitan-Vickers electric locomotives at work there. Sadly, towards the end of the decade, his health deteriorated. He showed the classic signs of overwork, and was unable to take time off for the shooting holidays he so enjoyed. Chronic bronchitis set in, he found difficulty in walking, and his heart began to fail. He managed to spend a holiday in Devon, accompanied by his daughter Vi, and was present at the unveiling of his last steam locomotive *Bantam Cock*, and his first electric locomotive, Bo+Bo No. 6701, at York on 19th February, 1941 (*see Chapter Eleven*). Unfortunately he was unable to be among the guests at a similar occasion when Oliver Bullied's new 'Merchant Navy' class Pacific *Channel Packet* was first shown, a month later. Shortly afterwards, on 5th April, 1941, Sir Nigel Gresley died at his home at Watton-at-Stone, in the presence of his son Roger. Four days later he was buried by the side of his beloved Ethel in the family plot beneath the Boscabel Oak at Netherseale, following a service attended by his sons and daughters, and other members of the family. He was the last of the Gresley line to be buried there. On the same day a Memorial Service was held at Chelsea Old Church, at which his professional and business friends were present. This was during the blitz on London, and the following week the church was severely damaged by bombing.

Chapter Eleven

Post-Gresley Developments

Although at the beginning of 1941 Sir Nigel was unwell, he was expected to continue in office - indeed this appears to have been his intention - and it does not seem that the LNER Chairman, Sir Ronald Matthews, regarded it necessary to consider the difficult problem of choosing a successor for the post. (It is believed that Matthews assumed that Gresley would go on until he was 70, when he would be succeeded by Arthur Peppercorn, and then Freddie Harrison.) So, when the question arose, it was a matter of urgency. At the time, none of Gresley's senior staff was recognised as his deputy and hence no one was being groomed as a potential successor. Indeed, the only one who might have been regarded as such had been his erstwhile personal technical assistant, Oliver Bulleid, who had left the LNER in 1937 to join the Southern Railway. He had been followed by D.R. Edge, a competent manager, but who lacked the breadth of experience needed to fill the CME's position. So, the natural successor in 1941 would have been one of the Mechanical Engineers in the Areas, that at Doncaster being regarded as the senior. This position had been occupied by Edward Thompson since 1938, following similar posts at Stratford and Darlington.

Sir Ronald Matthews lived in Doncaster, and was also Chairman of the Sheffield firm of Turton Brothers and Matthews, and had been Master Cutler. Both Gresley and Thompson were his house guests, and evidently close, as Prudence, one of the Matthews daughters, recalls them as 'Uncle Tim' and 'Uncle Ned'. On paper, Thompson should have been the automatic choice to succeed Gresley, but according to Stewart Cox, Sir Ronald made approaches to his opposite number on the Southern, to see if Bulleid could be enticed back, and the LMS, to enquire after the availability of Roland Bond, whom he had interviewed in connection with Bond's appointment to superintend the joint LNER/LMS locomotive testing station. However, Bulleid was engaged in the production of his new 'Merchant Navy' Pacifics, and Bond had just been put in charge of the workshops at Crewe, so neither could be spared. Consequently, there being no other obvious candidates for the post, without further delay, Matthews appointed Edward Thompson as CME of the LNER, the decision being confirmed at the Board Meeting on 24th April, 1941, just 19 days after Gresley's passing.

It is no part of this narrative to dwell on the later career of Edward Thompson. Some of his work has been heavily criticised, notably the controversial rebuilding of the 'P2s' and the unfortunate choice of *Great Northern* as the prototype of his new 'A1' class, but less of a constructive nature has been written about him. He was known to display a brusque manner on occasion, and in his latter years under Gresley the two were obviously at odds. Why this should be is not at all clear, as over the years Gresley gave Thompson successive promotions, but Vi Godfrey told me that her father had said that Thompson had been 'disloyal', so clearly something serious must have

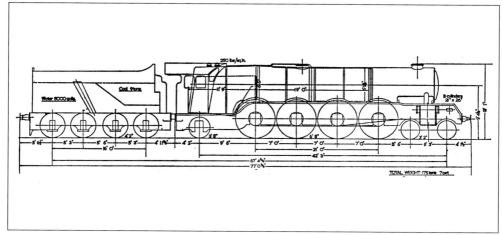

Gresley mentioned his idea for a 4-8-2 enlargement of his basic Pacific on more than one occasion, and this was confirmed by Bert Spencer in 1947, *above*. This is the outline design of the proposed locomotive, whilst (*below*) these post-Gresley drawings are not thought to have been substantative proposals.

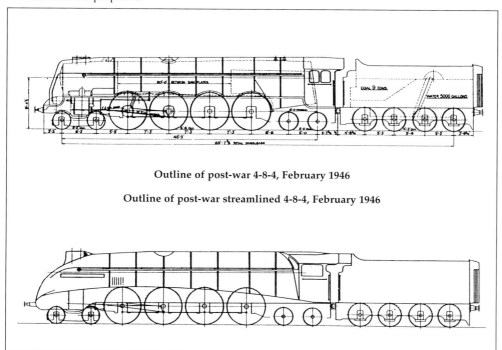

Outline of post-war 4-8-4, February 1946

Outline of post-war streamlined 4-8-4, February 1946

developed between the two men. Possibly it may have been related to the rebuilding of the North Eastern 'D20' without Gresley having been consulted, whilst it has been said that during Gresley's absence in South Africa Thompson promoted two engineers without consulting his chief, and this was not approved on Gresley's return. After his retirement, in an interview with the locomotive engineer and journalist Brian Reed, Thompson complained that Gresley 'had held him back' but it is difficult to pinpoint when this might have been, unless he thought that, following Francis Wintour's retirement in 1927, he should have been given the Mechanical Engineer's position at Doncaster, instead of Robert Thom. When he eventually got the job, it was only after Thom himself retired in 1938. Nevertheless, Thompson was generous in praise of his former chief, telling Reed that Gresley was the greatest British locomotive engineer since Churchward.

To complete the Gresley story, reference will be made in this chapter to what might have been seen had he remained in office beyond 1941, and to the alterations his successors were to make to his Pacific design. Certainly, the 'V4' 2-6-2 would have been multiplied, and put to work all over the LNER system. As for larger engines, Bert Spencer has revealed that in 1939 active consideration was being given to a 4-8-2 with a 250 lb./sq. in. boiler, a 50 sq. ft grate fed by a mechanical stoker and 'P2' size cylinders and valves, resulting in a tractive effort of 45,700 lb. Indeed, Gresley had forecast the need for such a locomotive in remarks he made at the Model Engineer Exhibition of 1937, pointing out that the success of the streamlined trains would result in a demand for the acceleration of existing heavy expresses, which could only be met by faster uphill running requiring more powerful locomotives. There was also to be a more powerful version of the 'A4', with a 275 lb./sq. in. boiler (this seems to have been known about at the time, as in the early war years there were rumours among the lineside observers that one of these, No. 4904 *Hurricane*, had actually been seen!). Anyway, design studies on these two projects were put in hand, and, according to Spencer, there was every prospect of these being proceeded with, when the war intervened. These appear to be the extent of Gresley's plans for the future, and when eventually peace returned, circumstances had altered.

In the event, the leading post-war LNER design was the Peppercorn 'A1' Pacific, which combined some of the best features of the 'A4' and 'P2' classes, but with divided drive and three independent sets of Walchaerts valve gear. Freddie Harrison, who with Bert Spencer and the Doncaster chief draughtsman Teddy Windle, played a leading part in the evolution of the class, claimed that 'These were the engines Gresley would have built had he still been alive, to meet the changing conditions of maintenance'. This may have been the case, but it presumes that Gresley would have departed from his principles of concentrated drive and conjugated motion, and accepted the need for divided drive inherent in the provision of inside valve gear.

Other designs may also have been in mind, as drawings of 4-8-2 and 4-8-4 types came to light in the Doncaster drawing office after the war, but these are likely to have been draughtsman's visions of what might have been, rather than substantive proposals. Harrison's own thoughts extended to a 4-8-2 with 6 ft

Gresley's class 'A3' Pacifics were repainted in LNER green in the immediate post-war years, even in the first months of nationalisation. Here, bearing their post-war numbers, are *(above)* No. 63 *Isinglass* on an up Leeds express at Doncaster, in October 1946, and *(below)* No. E103 *Flying Scotsman* at Grove Road crossing, Retford, before proceeding wrong line with a down semi-fast working, May 1948.   *(Both) Eric Oldham*

4 in. wheels, this being the optimum diameter in relation to the maximum piston speed then thought desirable, to be followed by a Chapelon inspired 4-cylinder compound, with a boiler pressed to 400 lb./sq. in. He confided his ideas to Stewart Cox, whose view was that such a locomotive could not have been built within the British loading gauge, and the problem of getting a reliable crank axle would have been insurmountable. But, for other reasons, it is unlikely that these would have been built, even if the LNER had continued as an independent entity, as the Board were giving active consideration to dieselisation of the East Coast Anglo-Scottish services. In 1947, tenders were invited for the supply of twenty-five 1,600 hp diesel locomotives, to be used in tandem, replacing 32 Pacific locomotives. One of the last acts of Sir Ronald Matthews, the Chairman, was to open the tenders, submitted by six manufacturers, but the project was shelved after Nationalisation.

As has been discussed earlier, of all Gresley's design features, the use of the simple lever conjugated valve gear was the most controversial. More than one locomotive running superintendent has stated that the gear was satisfactory if given reasonable maintenance, but if this was neglected and joints became stiff through lack of lubrication or loose because of wear, then problems arose. A basic component of the gear was the 2 to 1 lever, a casting six feet long, and weighing some 200 lb. which at 90 mph reversed its motion 12 times a second. Its pivot was a robust roller bearing, and provided this was well greased, the gear generally gave no trouble, apart from wear in the pin-joints as mileage between shoppings increased. That it could work well is demonstrated by the excellent daily performance of the 'A4s' on the streamline expresses, and the fact that in pre-war days the Pacifics averaged 75,000 miles between failures on the road. Gresley would have been entitled to assume that these conditions would continue, but in wartime skilled labour became scarce and supervision was sometimes neglected, whilst lack of availability of roller bearings led to their replacement by plain bushes, which wore rapidly. (To reduce the inertia of the 2 to 1 lever, consideration was given to producing a lighter version of box section construction, but this was thought to be too prone to internal corrosion.) Another factor was that, due to lack of information on a drawing, when resetting the valves on the 'K3' and 'V2' classes, Darlington works set them cold, without allowance for expansion of the outside valve spindles. Consequently this led to irregular valve events when running, which contributed to complaints from enginemen, but it took several years before the matter was understood and the drawing rectified. It seems incredible that this unsatisfactory state of affairs should have persisted for so long. Possibly the Doncaster drawing office assumed that Darlington would be aware of the matter, and would make the necessary adjustments.

After he had succeeded Gresley as CME, Edward Thompson took notice of complaints about problems said to be associated with the conjugated gear, although mechanical failures of the gear itself were virtually unknown. He had his own long-standing reservations, anyway, possibly going back to NER days, and sharing Raven's preference of a separate inside valve gear, despite its increase in mechanism and lack of accessibility. It is clear that he considered the conjugated gear to be unsatisfactory, particularly under wartime conditions,

Mallard at the time of the 1948 trials, retaining its LNER stainless steel numerals, but with British Railways lettering and 'E' prefix. *BR, Gresley Society Trust*

The plaque affixed to *Mallard* proclaiming its achievement of 126 mph. *BR, Gresley Society Trust*

and as part of a revision of Gresley practice, he decided to replace it with independent Walschaerts gear for the centre cylinder. To convince the LNER Board that he was justified, he asked William Stanier, as an independent engineer, to look into the subject, and prepare a report. Stanier delegated the task to Stewart Cox, at the time his personal technical assistant, and the outcome gave Thompson the support he was seeking. Cox submitted his report in June 1942, and concluded that the 2 to 1 design, while theoretically correct, was inherently unsound mechanically, with defects in application, leading to irregular steam distribution to the inside cylinder and rapid wear of the pins of the mechanism. He was in fact stressing what was the potential 'worst case' situation, making insufficient allowance for normal maintenance which would have mitigated the effects of wear. His report did not become public knowledge until the 1980s, since when its contents have been the subject of critical discussion on the grounds of over-reacting to perceived drawbacks. He supported his argument by stating that although Gresley's conjugated gear had been widely adopted overseas, it had been abandoned wherever it had been applied. However, this was certainly not the case.

It may be recalled that Harold Holcroft was sufficiently assured of the soundness of his own conjugated design that he made it the subject of a paper to the Locomotive Engineers, without attracting severe adverse comment, whilst Gresley's adviser, Professor Dalby of Imperial College, assured him that the mathematics of his simple lever system were correct.

Undoubtedly, the final Gresley version of conjugated gear is the *simplest* method of operating the piston valves of a 3-cylinder locomotive, and this attracted the attention of other engineers, although its only applications in Britain were on the LNER, and on two Holcroft applications on Maunsell locomotives. As Cox pointed out, it had been adopted overseas, although largely on freight locomotives. It is true that in a few cases the gear was removed, but in several instances the conjugated motion was regarded as successful and examples of these locomotives have been preserved. Among those built were 89 giant 4-12-2s constructed by Alco in the United States, 25 'D57' 4-8-2s in New South Wales, and 97 Pacifics in Japan. In what must have been a unique transformation, three New Zealand Garratts were rebuilt into six Pacifics, retaining their Gresley gear. Moreover, it must be said that 33 more 'V2s' to the original design were turned out from Darlington after the date of the report, as well as a further 25 class 'O2' 2-8-0s, until 782 LNER 3-cylinder locomotives in all had been constructed with the Gresley gear. Are we really to believe that all of these were as fundamentally unsound as Cox suggested? Only seven (the 'P2s' and *Great Northern*) were to be rebuilt with separate inside valve gear, while 13 were converted to 2-cylinder drive, of which 10 were 'B17s', and the others a 'D49', a 'K3', and a 'K4'.

Although not in his remit, the Cox report went on to criticise the detail of the Gresley design of middle big-end, which since the origin of the Pacifics occasionally became overheated, and caused failures on the road. This had been attributed in part to over-running of the conjugated motion at high speed, placing increased loading and stress on the bearing with occasional overheating. Gresley was aware of the matter, and pending further

In BR livery and renumbered 60007, *Sir Nigel Gresley* was the first locomotive on the rollers at the Rugby Locomotive Testing Station. Here seen at the official opening, 19th October, 1948.
BR, Gresley Society Trust

investigation, as an emergency measure, a heat detecting device known as a 'stink bomb' was fitted to the Pacifics. This consisted of a phial containing amyl acetate (later aniseed oil) inserted into the hollow centre crank pin. The phial burst on overheating, giving off a strong smell, warning the driver of potential trouble. This no doubt prevented a number of failures, but was not a long-term solution. The original big-end design was based on marine practice and suffered from a lack of rigidity in the strap, which was thought to be contributory to the failures; in post-war days Doncaster was at work on an improved design with a reinforced strap in harder steel, and steel distance pieces instead of bronze. The matter was finally resolved when Kenneth Cook took over as Chief Mechanical and Electrical Engineer of the Eastern Region of British Railways in 1951, and applied a Swindon continuous form of white metal bearing shell to the redesigned Gresley big-end, machined to a higher degree of accuracy than before. From then on, there were no further problems.

Following the nationalisation of much of the country's public transport on 1st January, 1948, the Railway Executive, the body set up under the British Transport Commission to manage the railways, gave consideration to the question of future motive power. It was decided that for the medium term, the main emphasis would continue to be on steam, and R.A. ('Robin') Riddles, who had been Vice-President of the LMS in charge of engineering, was appointed Member of the Railway Executive with similar responsibilities. He built up a small team of assistants, almost all from the LMS, including Stewart Cox, in charge of locomotive design. With such a heavily LMS-oriented staff, it would have been surprising if that company's policies were not reflected in new construction programmes, but Riddles was anxious to appear to have an open mind in examining and comparing the qualities of the principal locomotive classes of each of the four pre-nationalisation companies. In consequence he set up a small committee to organise a comprehensive series of road tests of locomotives, in three categories - express passenger, mixed traffic, and heavy freight - in which the main aspects of performance, capacity and efficiency would be recorded and compared, and conclusions drawn. Bert Spencer, Gresley's erstwhile locomotive assistant, was appointed chairman of the committee. Unlike the GWR/LNER trials of 1925, those of 1948 were the subject of regulated conditions, and dynamometer cars played an important part.

The locomotives were to be the 'best' of their kind from the four railways, and in the case of the LNER, the class selected in the express passenger category was the Gresley 'A4'. This was reasonable, as although these had been in service for 10 years or more, no other newly built 6 ft 8 in. Pacifics were available apart from *Great Northern*; the Peppercorn 'A1s' had not yet appeared. The final choice fell on those 'A4s' which possesssed the Kylchap exhaust system and double chimney, and the first to be selected was the immortal *Mallard*, no doubt to remind the other railways of its record breaking achievement. This was a political decision, presumably by the Board of the newly formed Eastern Region (Nock refers to 'high authority') overriding the running department who protested that the engine was not the best choice, although this is not easy to understand as it had been through Doncaster Plant for general repairs only a few weeks before (perhaps there had been problems during running-in). These

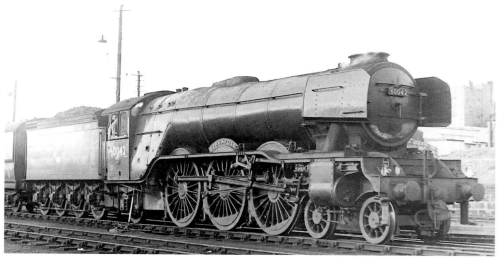

In its final form, with Kylchap exhaust, double chimney and Witte smoke deflectors, No. 60042 *Singapore* is at Kittybrewster, Aberdeen, on 14th September, 1963. Less elegant, but perhaps more purposeful in appearance, than on its first appearance. Named not after an outpost of Empire, but the winner of the 1930 St Leger. *R.F. Orpwood, Gresley Society Trust*

Believed to be the only occasion on which the two locomotives were present alongside one another. *Sir Nigel Gresley* is in company with *Sir William A. Stanier, F.R.S.*, at Carlisle, 1964.
Paul Aston, A4 Locomotive Society

fears were justified when *Mallard* suffered a middle big-end bearing failure on its first preliminary run, at Savernake on the former Great Western main line. It was replaced by *Seagull*, which completed the dynamometer car trials on the Western Region, but also suffered a similar failure as soon as it commenced running on the Southern. By this time *Mallard* had been repaired and took over, but failed again at Salisbury. The third 'A4' to be used was *Lord Faringdon*, renamed earlier in the year from *Peregrine*, and which performed impeccably on the hardest task in the trials, the West Coast main line to Carlisle. This succession of failures could not have come at a worse time, and was attributed to the big-end bolts having been over-tightened, resulting in excessive compression of the bronze distance pieces.

After the results had been analysed, it was found that on a specific fuel consumption basis of pounds of coal burned per horsepower-hour, overall the 'A4s' came out just ahead of the LMS 'Duchess' class (which had generally been worked more easily on rising gradients), and a comfortable 14 per cent better than the GWR 'Kings'. Moreover, specific water consumption of the 'A4s' was 10 per cent less than that of the 'Duchesses' and 15 per cent less than that of the 'Kings', a tribute to the 'A4s' more efficient use of steam. As soon as the data obtained from the trials had been analysed, a very detailed report was published, which makes fascinating reading, although the general conclusion was probably to be expected - that there were no significant reasons why a design policy broadly based on LMS practice should not be adopted. But, to quote Cecil J. Allen, 'The fine record of the 'A4' Pacifics of the late Sir Nigel Gresley was a posthumous triumph', while George Hinchcliffe, when Managing Director of Steamtown Carnforth in the 1980s, told me that 'Sticking my neck out, I believe that the 'A4' is the best passenger steam locomotive ever built in Britain'. Probably the best tribute is from a Western Region chief inspector, who was so impressed by the performance of *Seagull* up Hemerdon Bank with the boiler pressure *rising*, that he stated 'You could not do that with one of ours'.

Gresley's Pacifics enjoyed an Indian Summer in the later 1950s, as successive improvements gave them a new lease of life, not least the earlier ones now 30 or more years old. By then it was well-known that the provision of the double chimney Kylchap exhaust system made a considerable improvement to a locomotive's steaming capability, bearing out Gresley's conversation in 1940 with Col Kenneth Cantlie, that he intended, when circumstances permitted, to fit double Kylchap arrangements to all single chimney Pacifics and 'V2s'. The patent rights expired in 1941, and this enabled Thompson and later Peppercorn to have the option of fitting this improvement to their Pacifics. In the 1950s, a general redraughting of the single chimney Gresley Pacifics was put in hand, although this was not without administrative difficulty, as the ex-LMS staff at BTC Headquarters did not regard the cost of the Kylchap installation to be worthwhile. However, Peter Townend, who had been appointed shedmaster at King's Cross Top Shed in 1956, and who had learned more about operating Gresley's Pacifics than most others in his position, made a convincing case for the alteration, which was finally authorised by C.K. Bird, the Eastern Region General Manager, at a cost of no more than £153 for an 'A3' and £203 for an 'A4', whilst the locomotives were in works for general repair.

Flying Scotsman, after renovation at Derby Locomotive Works, following its visit to Canada and the United States. Seen in 1973, it was then owned by the Hon. William McAlpine.

BR, Gresley Society Trust

Resplendent in LNER blue, in preservation, *Sir Nigel Gresley* stops for a photo-call on the Forth Bridge.

John Hunt

However, a visibility problem arose from the Kylchap fitting of the non-streamlined 'A3s', as the softer exhaust could lead to smoke drifting and obscuring the driver's vision, so lending emphasis to the need for an effective smoke clearing device. The earlier attempts to deal with this on *Humorist* were not satisfactory, so Townend determined to resolve the matter once and for all, and consequently was responsible for the final modification to the 'A3' Pacifics. On holiday in Germany, he noticed the effectiveness of the Witte deflector plates fitted to DB locomotives, and on his return arranged for a pair to be made and fitted as a trial. These were immediately successful, and although the Pacifics were approaching the end of their lives, most had these side shields before the end finally came. They did nothing for the gracefulness of the original Pacific outline, but certainly the combination of Kylchap double exhaust and Witte shields gave the increased performance capability which Gresley himself had intended once the Kylchap patent rights had expired. One other refinement introduced by Kenneth Cook was the Swindon method of optical lining-up of frame components, when being reassembled at Doncaster after repairs. At first, over-tight tolerances resulted in a higher than normal incidence of hot axlebox bearings, due to the greater degree of frame flexure in the ex-LNER locomotives, compared with those of the Great Western. However, once these had been eased and the fitters had become accustomed to using the equipment, it proved to be a considerable improvement over the usual less scientific sighting methods of alignment. By this time the 'A4s' had received the double Kylchap exhaust, and the middle big-end problem had been finally overcome, so they were in the prime of their condition. They were the first choice for the 'Elizabethan', non-stop between King's Cross and Waverley, at an average speed of 60 mph, and with a substantial train weight, the successor of the pre-war summer 'Flying Scotsman', which had taken 30 minutes longer, and which had been their responsibility 20 years before.

Twice Gresley reminded the Institution of Locomotive Engineers that 'We are not the Institution of Steam Locomotive Engineers . . . we must turn our attention to electric locomotives if the steam locomotive is to be superseded . . . but I think there will be a great field for steam and oil locomotives'. He first disclosed a broad interest in electrification in 1922, when, in a discussion at the Institution of Electrical Engineers on the electrification of the Midi Railway in France, he observed that it was important from a railway company's point of view that it should possess a co-operative interest in the electricity supply system, to avoid placing itself in the hands of a supply company - although he would have revised his views in later years as the national grid improved reliability and reduced costs. In any case, electrical supplies were needed for other purposes than traction. For example, because of the local limitations of the public electricity supply, a small generating station was built at Whitemoor to provide electricity for lighting and operating the retarders of the new hump yard. Some years later, his thoughts on electrification were expressed in the discussion following a comprehensive but little publicised paper comparing steam, electric and diesel-electric traction, which was presented by the LNER electrical engineer, H.W.H. Richards, to the Civil Engineers.

On 1st May, 1968, 40 years after the inauguration of the non-stop 'Flying Scotsman' train, *Flying Scotsman*, now owned by Alan Pegler, headed a specially organised celebratory non-stop. Here seen at Belle Isle, side by side with a 'Deltic' hauling the regular 'Flying Scotsman'. A once in a lifetime photograph.
Patrick Russell

Nevertheless, on more than one occasion, Gresley put up a robust defence of the steam locomotive. In 1934 at a meeting of the Batti-Wallahs Club, a society of naval electrical engineers, he said that he objected to electrical men comparing the results of the latest electrical systems with the average results of old steam systems, and remarked on 'the wonderful efficiency of the steam locomotive', adding that electrification was 'further off now than it was twenty years ago, except for suburban lines'. Again, on the occasion of the Institution of Mechanical Engineers Annual Dinner in 1935, he was emphatic in saying that

> We must do all we can to further the steam locomotive . . . coal is our national product . . . obviously it is better to develop to the utmost the possibilities of the steam locomotive and burn our own coal rather than use an engine which burns fuel which we have not got, and must purchase from abroad.

He was clearly referring to diesel oil, but ignored the use of coal for generating electricity. But, of course, his attitude to electrification was also necessarily limited by the economics of the period: primarily, the capital for extensive conversion was not available within the LNER's resources.

Certainly, studies had been made of the possible electrification of the Great Northern and Great Eastern suburban lines, but little was done in practice, due to economic stringency. Exceptions were the Altrincham route conversion in 1931, jointly with the LMS, and the 1938 extension of the Tyneside system to South Shields. New coaches were built by Metro-Cammell in 1937 for the north Tyneside services, which showed a Gresley influence in their articulated construction, but later designs for suburban services to Glossop and Shenfield, built after the war, reverted to individual coaches.

However, a change was on the way, as in the mid-1930s a Government loan enabled the electrification of the Great Central route over the Pennines between Sheffield and Manchester to be put in hand. This carried a very heavy coal traffic from the Yorkshire pits, and had been planned many years before, but was beyond the ability of the LNER to finance. Work was suspended soon after the outbreak of war, by which time the overhead gantries were under construction. However, decisions had been taken on the locomotives to be used, and two types were postulated, one a mixed traffic Bo+Bo, the other a Co-Co for passenger duties. Gresley was impressed by the Metropolitan Vickers Bo+Bo which had been built for service in South Africa, and took the opportunity to visit the Union to observe the locomotives at work. An order was placed, and Sir Nigel had the satisfaction, only weeks before his death, to see the prototype, No. 6701, unveiled. The story of the Bo+Bos, class 'EM1', lies outside the scope of this volume, but 58 were eventually built, the first spending the early post-war years on the Netherlands Railways, where it received the name *Tommy*, and several detail improvements were suggested. The 'EM1s' can be regarded as successful on mineral and freight hauls, but they rode roughly at higher speeds, a result of the drawgear being fitted directly to the interconnected bogies, and occasionally damage was caused to the king-pins following a heavy shunt. At one time it had been thought that 27 locomotives of the larger Co-Co type (class 'EM2') would be needed to handle the passenger traffic, but in the event only seven were built, the first entering service in 1953.

The Prince of Wales, accompanied by Nigel Gresley and the Mayor of Doncaster, acknowledges the crowd outside the boiler shop at Doncaster Plant, in November 1926.

Topical Press, Gresley Society Trust

Nigel Gresley in conversation with Queen Mary, at a formal visit to Stratford Works in 1928. Between them can be seen William Galloway, for many years the conductor at concerts given by the Great Eastern Railway Musical Society. To the right of the Queen are King George V and William Whitelaw, the LNER Chairman.

Gresley Society Trust

Chapter Twelve

Sir Nigel Gresley:
An Appreciation

Gresley had been appointed CBE for services to the Government in the Great War (arising from the contribution to the 1914-1918 war effort made by the manufacture of armaments at Doncaster Plant), but his greatest distinction came in 1936 when he was awarded a knighthood. This is generally regarded as being in recognition of his work in mechanical engineering, and it would have been a just reward for his outstanding contribution in this field. However, in those days there was a form of hierarchical distinction on the railways, in that while a General Manager might achieve this status, as Ralph Wedgwood had on the LNER, similarly to honour a Chief Mechanical Engineer would create a precedent. It is true that at the Grouping Sir Vincent Raven was CME of the North Eastern Railway, but his knighthood had been conferred for his wartime work as Chief Superintendent of the Woolwich Arsenal, and so he was already knighted when he returned to the NER. William Stanier was similarly honoured in World War II, for his work in production engineering, but he did not return to the LMS as CME.

In August 1935, Gresley, as an eminent engineer unconnected with the subject in question, was appointed to chair a Board of Trade committee of investigation into the loss of two small merchant ships, the *Usworth* and the *Blairgowrie*, which was attributed to defects in their steering mechanism. The committee's report was to the effect that the conventional rod and chain type of steering gear of these two ships was reliable when properly designed and fitted, provided it was kept in thorough repair and efficiently maintained. Thus, there was no blanket condemnation of the system itself. It was often the case in those days for public service of this nature to be recognised by inclusion in the Honours List, and Gresley was heard to say that his knighthood came about as a result of his chairing this committee; indeed, his daughter Vi was emphatic about the truth of this account. But this does not seem to have been the official reason at all, as the wording of the recommendation by the Prime Minister of the day, Stanley Baldwin, to Edward VIII, referred simply to his work on the LNER - and so apparently setting a precedent, although by now this was probably of less importance (*see Appendix Four*). However, for whichever reason the title was awarded, it was thoroughly merited, and brought distinction to Sir Nigel, his family, his profession, his staff, and his employers, the London & North Eastern Railway, as it gave him the status his railway work deserved. A further recognition came in 1936, when he was awarded the degree of Doctor of Science, *Honoris Causa*, by the University of Manchester. At the presentation ceremony, he was in the company of Sir Thomas Beecham, the eminent musician. He was also tremendously pleased when the hundredth Pacific built to his designs, LNER No. 4498, was named *Sir Nigel Gresley* at a ceremony at Marylebone, presided over by his Chairman for so many years, William Whitelaw. The idea had not come from within the LNER, but from K. Risdon Prentice, a member of the Railway Correspondence and Travel Society, who wrote to Sir Ralph Wedgwood making the suggestion, which was acted on, Prentice receiving an invitation to the naming ceremony. The proposal had the full support of William Whitelaw (*see Appendix Five*).

Above: The International Railway Congress at Cairo in 1933 offered the opportunity for relaxation. Nigel Gresley is seen astride a mule, and equestrians will note his skill as a rider, with his feet in the 'heels down' position. *Tim Godfrey*

Right: Sir Nigel in his robes at his investment as a Doctor of Science of the University of Manchester, 1937.   *Tim Godfrey*

Gresley also took part in other Government committees, notably on Automatic Train Control and Railway Electrification. He played an active part in the work of the International Railway Congress Association, becoming a delegate to the Permanent Commission, and attending meetings in such places as Cairo, Madrid and Paris, where he gave papers reviewing international steam locomotive practice. At home, he was elected to the General Council of the British Standards Institution, and also to the Association of Railway Locomotive Engineers, of which he became a member as soon as he was promoted to be Locomotive Superintendent of the Great Northern Railway. He soon began to take a leading part in the Association, and was elected President in 1926 and 1936. It is interesting to note that in 1918 he was responsible for obtaining general agreement to the use of 85 per cent boiler pressure in the calculation of tractive effort, in place of the variety of coefficients which had been the case before. In view of his earlier collaboration with Harold Holcroft in connection with the design of the simple lever conjugated valve gear, it was a nice touch for Gresley to nominate Holcroft to membership of the ARLE, in 1939. Moreover, to paraphrase Holcroft's words, 'Sir Nigel performed the ceremony of induction, adopting a very paternal attitude towards me, a fitting sequel to our first meeting 21 years ago'.

Perhaps because of his own chosen lack of an academic engineering education, Gresley did not take any leading part in technical education. Indeed, in his application for membership of the Institution of Mechanical Engineers in 1907, he claimed that 'I learned my engineering at Crewe, I did not go to any of the Engineering Colleges, nor have I entered for any technical examinations'. He obviously was a good learner, with mainly 'on the job' training to supplement his natural aptitude for absorbing mechanical engineering principles, and for producing clear drawings. His notebooks from his time at Horwich fortunately have been preserved, and are models of their kind. In later years he used his ability to draw freehand outlines, which, as Norman Newsome found, could be taken away and reproduced by a draughtsman with only minimum correction. The story is probably true that the manager of the Great Northern Hotel was instructed that, after Gresley had had a meal there with other engineers, the white damask tablecloths should not be laundered, but sent over to the CME's office so that his staff could reproduce the sketches which had been drawn on them. Barney Symes, a senior draughtsman at Doncaster, recalled that the final outline of the 'V1' tank locomotive was drawn on a sheet of blotting paper.

Probably more than any of his predecessors or contemporaries, Gresley contributed regularly to the proceedings of professional bodies. He was a Member of the Institutions of Civil, Mechanical, Electrical and Locomotive Engineers, and in addition to giving papers, took part in discussions. He was President of the Mechanical Engineers in 1936/37, and of the Locomotive Engineers in 1927 and 1934. In his presidential year at the Mechanicals, a nice gesture on his part was to acknowledge the debt he owed to Sir John Aspinall, when on behalf of the Institution he made the first award of the James Watt Gold Medal to his mentor. Aspinall was clearly moved by the occasion, but was unwell at the time. He passed away the following year, aged 85. One of Gresley's ambitions was achieved in 1932, when he was elected to membership of the Smeatonian Society. This prestigious body was founded in 1771 when seven leading engineers of the day met in the King's Head Tavern, High Holborn, 'to share experiences and get to know each other better'. In Gresley's day, membership was limited to 48 of the engineering elite.

As described in Chapter Two, Gresley in effect planned his own personal training programme. But the railway companies had their own systems of formal education of young engineers, and both the Great Northern and the LNER offered two programmes, pupillage and premium apprenticeship, to young men who were keen to become engineers. The pupils, restricted to six a year, held privileged status in that they could select what they did and where they went in Doncaster Plant, and were not subject to the usual employee working hours. For this, the CME received a fee of £150 a year, but the pupils received no wages. The 'premiums' paid an initial £50 to the CME, and received the normal wage of a craft apprentice, working in most departments at Doncaster Plant (it is reliably reported that Gresley donated his income from these fees to educational and charitable organisations in Doncaster). Unfortunately, there were only a very limited number of job vacancies on the LNER for pupils and premiums when they had completed their training, and most had to follow their careers elsewhere. But some of the best were retained, perhaps held as supernumaries until a vacancy occurred, whilst a few who left the railway - W.O. Bentley, of motor car fame was one - attributed their engineering success to the quality of training provided by Doncaster. All apprentices were encouraged to enrol at Doncaster Technical College to further their theoretical studies, whilst for a short period pupils and premiums were eligible for a course at Sheffield University, specially drawn up for their needs.

For many years a Doncaster Pupils and Premium Apprentices Association was in existence, Gresley, as might be expected, being their President. He was always invited to their annual dinner, and, despite the many pressures on his time, often managed to attend. Cecil Elliot, a pupil in early LNER days, recalled that to be interviewed by Gresley was a memorable experience.

> He was a big man with an impressive head and a rather stern face that could turn its expression into something very paternal and encouraging. You were asked a few conventional questions, then perhaps a couple of very searching ones, followed by a nutshell of crisp advice and the interview would be over.

In this context of training, it is also worth mentioning that on the operating side the LNER offered a traffic apprenticeship scheme, giving a young man experience in all forms of traffic management and which might take him from assistant yardmaster at a marshalling yard to working as a junior in one of the business offices. This LNER scheme, originated in North Eastern days by Sir George Gibb, was acknowledged as one of the best of its kind.

Before the Grouping, the Great Eastern Railway had supported an engineering programme at the East London College, later Queen Mary College, and this was continued by the LNER, Gresley being appointed to the Board of Governors in 1928. Clifford Rose, who was secretary of the students association there, invited him to address one of their meetings, and to his surprise and pleasure, they were given a paper previously read to the Locomotive Engineers.

On a similar occasion Gresley read his paper on 3-cylinder locomotives to the Royal Technical College, Glasgow (now the University of Strathclyde), and answered questions. In 1937, he travelled to Scotland again to deliver the James Watt lecture to the Greenock Philosophical Society, which dealt with the development of high speed running on railways. This was the last of his addresses on engineering subjects, and was an appropriate finale to his 20 years of active participation in the work of the professional institutions, probably more than any other in his position. Moreover, Gresley encouraged members of his staff to take up membership of their appropriate professional institution, and to read papers on subjects in which they specialised. Bulleid, Windle and others, often relatively junior, were among them.

A little known aspect of the work of senior railway managers and engineers was membership of the Engineer and Railway Staff Corps, a branch of the Royal Engineers. The duty of this body was to furnish the Government with advice on matters concerned with railway transportation. It was remarkable that its members were given the rank of major, lieutenant colonel, or colonel, according to their civilian status, but they received no pay, nor did they normally wear uniform. Gresley was commissioned as a major in 1920, promoted to lieutenant colonel in 1925, and continued as a member of the Corps throughout the remainder of his life. It was fascinating, when researching Ministry of Defence records, to find Sir Nigel's military service history documented together with those of his sons, Nigel and Roger.

As might be expected, Gresley had a number of meetings with Royalty. The first of these was probably on one of the occasions when Edward VII travelled in the Royal Train for his annual visit to the St Leger meeting. A later, well-reported occasion, was at the Prince of Wales' visit to Doncaster Plant, in November 1926, when, to commemorate the event, the Pacific *Manna* was renamed by Royal consent *Prince of Wales*. The following year, King George V and Queen Mary visited Stratford works, and Gresley was photographed in conversation with the Queen. He met the Duke of York at the Centenary exhibition in Darlington in 1925, and two years later, at the Romney, Hythe and Dymchurch Railway, as well as in 1937, when his knighthood was conferred by King George VI, the Duke having then succeeded his brother Edward as King. Their Majesties made a practice of rewarding members of the LNER staff who had been involved in running the Royal trains, and each Christmas Gresley, among others, received a brace of pheasants from the Sandringham estate.

Reference has been made earlier to the plaque for Sir Nigel in the chapel at Marlborough College. Another, an English Heritage Blue Plaque, can be seen at King's Cross, on the wall beneath his office window, and a further memorial has been placed in the travel centre at Waverley station, Edinburgh. At Netherseale, the Parish Council have erected an information board by the Church, and in nearby Swadlincote there is a hostelry called the 'Sir Nigel Gresley'. Plaques to earlier members of the family are to be found in Bath Abbey, and in the parish churches in Netherseale, Overseale, Castle Gresley and Ledbury - and no fewer than 10 in Lichfield Cathedral. In addition, the Gresley name is commemorated in a dozen or so roads in such diverse locations as Crewe and Hastings, the strangest being the highway simply named 'Gresleys', in Ross-on-Wye, the origin of which is not known. Several firms in the town of Castle Gresley incorporate

Above: Sir Nigel at the controls of a small scale *Flying Scotsman*, with Jack Somers, later to be a member of the LNER locomotive running department, peering over the smokebox, at the Model Engineer Exhibition 1937.   *Gresley Society Trust*

Right: Sir Nigel Gresley, daughter Vi and sister Beatrice after his investiture at Buckingham Palace, 1937.   *Tim Godfrey*

Below: English Heritage Blue Plaque beneath Sir Nigel's office window at King's Cross Station.   Unveiled by Tim Godfrey, September 1997.
    Geoffrey Hughes, Gresley Society Trust

ENGLISH HERITAGE
SIR
NIGEL
GRESLEY
1876-1941
Locomotive Engineer
had his office
in this station
1923-1941

'Gresley' in their title, and the name is carried throughout the country on away fixtures by the local football club, Gresley Rovers. A plaque in an out-of-town industrial site commemorating Ivatt and Gresley is the only record of his presence in Doncaster, where he lived and worked for so many years, apart from the Gresley Cup, awarded to the winners of a cricket competition held at the railway sports ground. And, over 150 years after Gresley's mother Joanna Wilson was born there, Barton Under Needwood is now the home of a new train maintenance depot, built by Bombardier Transportation.

In the 1930s, when Sir Nigel Gresley was at the height of his prowess, I was a teenager. I have often wondered whether, if I had had the effrontery to approach him, he would have granted me an interview. He was known sometimes to agree to informal contacts, but generally to organisations such as student societies. One occasion was at the Model Engineer Exhibition in 1937, when he was photographed at the controls of a small gauge Pacific. Also seen in the photograph is Jack Somers, then a young member of the LNER staff, who in later years was to become Assistant District Locomotive Superintendent at Peterborough. But Jack was then too nervous to approach the great man, who was accompanied by his friend William Stanier, and his hosts, notably the well-known model engineer Percival Marshall. Except for Charles S. Lake of the *Railway Gazette*, Gresley does not seem to have had many off-the-record chats with technical journalists, in which some of the reasons for his principles might have been debated. True, Cecil J.Allen, himself an LNER employee (he was inspector of materials, including steel rails, purchased by the LNER and consequently able to travel throughout the country on visits to suppliers), must have had at least a limited access to Gresley. He was often invited to act as recorder of the times of special trains, and runs behind LNER locomotives were featured in his monthly articles in the *Railway Magazine*.

In the absence of contacts with Gresley himself, I have been fortunate in having been on friendly terms with his daughter Vi, who dearly loved her father and would hear nothing to his detraction. In addition I have met people who worked in close contact with him, and who had the opportunity to assess him personally. Eric Trask was the most senior in years, having been taken on as a pupil by Henry Ivatt, and often drawn into discussions with Gresley about matters affecting the design and performance of his engines. Freddie Harrison, a pupil in 1922, rose to become Chief Mechanical and Electrical Engineer of British Railways, a broader scope then even Gresley had achieved, although in these days of decision by committee, not perhaps with the same individual influence. Alec Emerson, an assistant in the Electrical Engineer's office in the 1930s, was in charge of the West Coast electrification 30 years later. Norman Newsome was the closest to his chief, having been recruited from the Doncaster drawing office in 1927 to join the CME's small personal team at King's Cross, where he spent 14 years on carriage & wagon design. All held Gresley in the highest respect, both as a man and as their chief. A special mention must be made of André Chapelon's regard for his friend Gresley. Chapelon, who has been described as the man who gave a new life to the steam locomotive, greatly admired Gresley, both as an engineer and a man, especially his determination to investigate thoroughly all developments in design likely to improve the

Two cab appearances by Sir Nigel Gresley, at naming ceremonies. *Above:* At King's Cross, with the Canadian High Commissioner, the Hon. Vincent Massey, 15th June, 1937, the engine being No. 4489 *Dominion of Canada. Below:* A White Rose occasion at Doncaster Plant on 20th May, 1939, with Lady Deedes, the wife of the colonel of the regiment, when 'V2' No. 4843 was named *King's Own Yorkshire Light Infantry.* *(Both) Gresley Society Trust*

performance and efficiency of his locomotives. And, finally, at the conclusion of these comments, it is fitting to record that whatever criticisms he may have made in his report to Edward Thompson, Stewart Cox, in his book *Speaking of Steam*, clearly stated that he too regarded Gresley as a great engineer.

It is unfortunate that no personal record of Sir Nigel seems to exist, other than the two portraits by William Brealey, one in the lecture theatre of the Institution of Mechanical Engineers, and one in the possession of the family, plus of course numerous still photographs and documents. He does not appear to have recorded for radio, or film, except that he appears briefly in a cine film taken during the Royal tour of the Centenary exhibition in 1925. So, we have to rely on personal memories. Norman Newsome, who lived well into his nineties, still clearly recalled Gresley the Chief Mechanical Engineer. 'He had a very receptive mind and would listen to anyone from whom he could learn anything. He was never too busy, nor too big a man, to go to any trouble to explain his point of view. He never avoided contact with the staff who made and operated his engines.' Two maxims were fixed in Newsome's mind: 'Never be afraid to tell Gresley if you didn't know. And certainly never attempt to mislead him.' Freddie Harrison, another nonagenarian, said 'He was admired and very greatly respected, having the natural ability to inspire confidence and enthusiasm. A visit from him was an inspiration'. This is echoed by Eric Bannister, a premium apprentice who for a time was a junior technical assistant in the CME's office, where Gresley was regarded - although not in his hearing - as 'The Great White Chief '. 'The main emphasis of Gresley's training of his staff was always to show by example rather than preach methods. He was unfailingly courteous and prepared to listen to other points of view' (however, Bannister added, he did not appreciate criticism of his conjugated valve gear, or of his marine type inside big-end). Barney Symes, who was responsible for detailed work on the original design of *Cock o' the North*, recalled that in those days Gresley would enter the drawing office unannounced, and discuss with individual draughtsmen the work on which they were engaged. In particular, he recalls the occasion on which the contour of the 'A4' footplate was decided. 'This is how I want it done' said Gresley, drawing a line in pencil on the wooden model which had been used for the wind tunnel experiments.

Those further removed from the CME than his personal staff, sometimes perceived a slightly different personality, no doubt depending on the occasion. 'He liked to live in the style of a country gentleman . . . Bluff, gregarious, fond of food and drink . . . A delightful man, easy to get to know'. He was reputed by his many manufacturer friends to be a hard bargainer, perhaps pressing a point to extremes, as in the 1929 negotiations with Beyer, Peacock over the extra to be paid for fitting the new 'B12s' with Lentz valves (*see Appendix Two*). Others who had a customer/supplier relationship with him found that Gresley had to be approached cautiously, and was very sure of himself, but always kept his word. 'A peppery old gentleman who didn't want to listen to a lot of excuses' sounds like a contractor being late on delivery.

So, the recollection of Sir Nigel Gresley is of a tall, well built man, often with a twinkle in his eye, and who enjoyed smoking his pipe, and an occasional glass of whisky. I think that I can do no better to summarise his personality by quoting from a letter written by Robert Bell, the LNER Assistant General Manager:

Sir Nigel was a great man, forceful at times, but always kind at heart. He hated shirkers, but always put in a good word for those who put their backs into their work. He had a real affection for many of his people in all grades and positions. If only our CME could have restrained his expenditure of energy he might have lived longer, but it is some consolation to know that he didn't outlive his powers.

Sir Nigel Gresley developed a unique style of steam locomotive. He was resourceful and highly skilled. His contribution to his profession was of the highest order. He was a man's man, a truly great engineer.

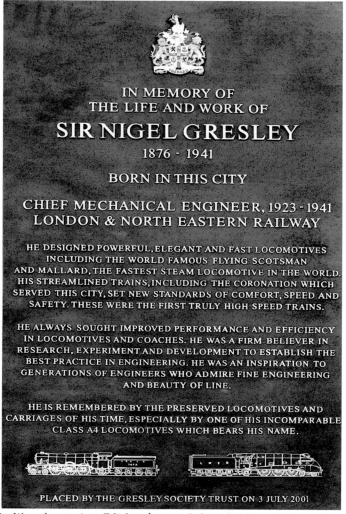

Plaque in Waverley station, Edinburgh, unveiled on 3rd July, 2001, by Tony Roche, President of the Institution of Mechanical Engineers, 65 years after Nigel Gresley's Presidential year.   *Fastline, York, Gresley Society Trust*

Appendix One

Memorandum to the LNER Locomotive Committee from H.N. Gresley, 3rd June, 1925

The trials extending over the week ending May 2nd between the Great Western Castle class engine and the London and North Eastern Pacific engine, which have caused a great amount of public interest, have shown that each engine was able to undertake the work of the other, and maintain the time schedules with ease. On every run made by the Great Western Railway engine on the L.N.E.R. system and the L.N.E.R. engine on the Great Western system, time was made up, and in no case was time lost by the Engine.

The coal consumption of the engines when working over the Great Western system was as follows:

Great Western engine ....42 lbs per mile
L.N.E.R. 48   ditto

Difference   6 lbs

When working over the L.N.E.R system
Great Western engine ....53.4 lbs per mile
L.N.E.R. ....57.1   ditto

Difference   3.7 lbs

The characteristics of the two engines are dissimilar, as the following table shows:

	Great Western Engine	L.N.E.R. Engine
Type	4-6-0	4-6-2
Cylinders	4	3
Tractive Power	31,625 lbs	29,825 lbs
Cylinder H.P.	2,030	1,946
Boiler H.P.	1,440	1,815
Boiler Pressure	225	180
Weight of Engine	79 tons 17 cwts	92 tons 9 cwts
Weight of Tender	40 tons	56 tons 6 cwts
Total weight	119 tons 17 cwts	148 tons 15 cwts
Capacity of Tender - coal	6 tons	8 tons

The narrow type firebox of the G.W. engine is more suitable for Welsh coal than the wide shallow firebox of the L.N.E. engine. When burning Yorkshire coal a thin fire is necessary; therefore the firebox of the L.N.E. engine should be the most suitable. I anticipated that on Welsh coal the G.W. engine would probably be the more economical, but expected that with Yorkshire coal the L.N.E. engine would give the better results.

Conclusive results, however, cannot be obtained from such a short trial, and so far as burning Yorkshire coal is concerned, I am confident that if the trial had been extended, the position would have been reversed.

The average coal consumption of all Pacific engines over the whole of last year running on the L.N.E. system was 54 lbs per mile, the lowest on the G.N. section being 47 lbs per mile, the weight of the trains hauled running up to 550 tons.

The high boiler pressure of the G.W. engine tends to economy in coal, but involves higher cost in boiler maintenance. Although the tractive effort of the G.W. engine is higher than that of the L.N.E. engine, the boiler power is considerably less. Fast running was therefore made by the G.W. engine on short rising gradients, such as London to Finsbury Park, but on the long hill grades of the G.W. system, the Pacific engine ran faster. As to high speed running on the flat and down grades, there is nothing to choose between the two engines, which are both very free running and capable of running at high speeds.

The trials show that the road bed of the L.N.E. is superior to that of the Great Western. The Pacific engine could not be safely run at such high speeds on falling grades on the Great Western road as their own engines, probably due to the greater length, weight and height of the Pacific engine. Strict observation had therefore to be observed on the speed limits on the curves and crossings by the Pacific engine, and consequently higher speeds were required on the up grades to mantain the schedules. The higher coal consumption is partially consequent upon this.

It was arranged, before the trials were started, between Mr Collett, the Chief Mechanical Engineer and myself, that no results should be published without our mutual concurrence; this agreement has not been kept. The Great Western Publicity Department have obtained all the data and furnished them to the Press for advertising purposes.

When it is remembered that the trials over the Great Western system consisted of only three trips - London to Plymouth and back - by the L.N.E. engine, it will be realised that no conclusive results could be arrived at.

(signed)   H.N. Gresley

Author's Note
I think that the wording of this Memorandum illustrates that Gresley did not initiate the trials. However, he might have furnished the Directors with a little more information emphasising the greater haulage capability of the Pacifics. Moreover, no reason is given for the short period of the trials. One gets the impression that Gresley was not best pleased to have had the trials foisted on him at the time, but he is careful not to criticise his Chief General Manager, if indeed it was he who was party to agreeing them with Sir Felix Pole.

Letter to H.N. Gresley from Sir Sam Fay, Chairman of Beyer, Peacock & Co. Ltd, 10th October, 1929

Dear Gresley,

Adverting to our conversation upon the loss sustained by Beyer, Peacock and Co in the building of 10 engines for your Company, the subject has again been before my Board which is composed of men all of whom have had experience in contracts. They expressed surprise at the view taken by you of the claim made for a portion of the loss, which was not due in any way to the fault of Beyer, Peacock & Co.

The fact that other manufacturers gave in tenders somewhat similar in price to that of Beyer, Peacock & Co does not mean that a claim would not have been made by them if they had not secured the contract.

I may mention that the diagram accompanying your invitation to tender is very different to the photograph you showed me. The former is dated 1913.

Under the circumstances I am sorry to say that we cannot let the matter rest.

No manufacturer could possibly live under such conditions and I must ask you to please go into the question again with a view to the meeting of our claim.

Yours faithfully,

(signed) Sam Fay

Author's Note
As explained in Chapter Eight, this refers to an order for ten 'B12' locomotives, the price for which had been fixed. However, whilst the engines were under construction, Gresley requested that they should be fitted with Lentz poppet valves, but no price was agreed in advance. Beyer, Peacock asked for an additional £3,000, which Gresley thought was far too much. Sir Sam began to lose patience, and threatened court action. In the end the matter was settled for £1,500. Here, obviously, were a couple of hard bargainers. There was more to the CME's job in those days than just designing locomotives.

Appendix Three

New CPR 2-10-4 Engines

(Edited version of Article by H.N. Gresley in the *Railway Gazette* 29th November, 1929.)

During my recent visit to Canada I saw some of these new 2-10-4 engines under construction in the Angus shops at Montreal, and the officials of the CPR were kind enough to make the necessary arrangements to enable me to travel on the footplate of one of these engines over the Rocky Mountains (*see photograph on page 36*). The first two engines of the class, 5900 and 5901, are fitted with boosters. The remaining 18 engines are not so fitted, but the trailing truck is so designed that the boosters can be readily applied.

While staying at Banff during the first week of September I travelled on the footplate, accompanied by my daughter, from Field to Golden - a distance of 35 miles - which is all down grade, with some very sharp curves. The engine ran very easily and appeared to negotiate the curves very smoothly without any lurching. The speed, of course, was not fast - during the whole trip it did not exceed 30 miles per hour. West of Golden the line was practically level, so I travelled in the train as far as Beavermouth, which is at the foot of the long incline leading over the Selkirk Range of mountains, where we rejoined the engine.

The gradient is about 20 miles at 1 in 45; the load behind the engine was 950 tons. After a few miles a slight drizzle started, causing the rails to be greasy, and the engine began to slip to such an extent that it seemed as though the train would come to a stand. When the speed had got down to about 4 miles per hour the driver put in the booster and speed was regained up to about 12 miles per hour, when the booster was taken out. This performance had to be repeated five times before reaching the eastern end of the Connaught tunnel. This is five miles long and dead straight, and being perfectly clear, it was possible to see the exit when we entered it. There are two tracks through the tunnel, and it is interesting to note that through this tunnel the English rule of the road is followed, in that the train is on the left hand line, the reason being that as the driver's seat is on the right side of the engine, he has more air and a better view on the side away from the wall of the tunnel.

We took about 13½ minutes to get through the tunnel, and on arrival at Glacier on the other side, I joined an east bound train. It was extremely interesting travelling on the footplate of this great engine during the night and being able to see about half a mile ahead on the straight with the assistance of the powerful headlight. The cut-off was kept at about 50%; the engine is oil fired, and there was no difficulty in maintaining steam. The boiler pressure varied only between 250 and 275 lb. per sq in.

I was told the tender carried 4,000 gallons of oil, and that on the 126 miles between Field to Revelstoke the consumption works out generally at 1,400 gallons for the trip, equivalent to about 11 gallons per mile, with trains of an average weight of 1,000 tons.

Appendix Four

Memorandum from Stanley Baldwin to King Edward VIII

Mr Baldwin, with his humble duty to the King, has the honour to submit for Your Majesty's gracious approval the attached list of names for inclusion in Your Majesty's Birthday Honours List.

18th June, 1936

(signed) Stanley Baldwin   (initialled) Approved ERI [*Eduardus Rex Imperator*]

Herbert Nigel Gresley, C.B.E., M.Inst.C.E., M.I.Mech.E., M.I.E.E.
Chief Mechanical Engineer, London and North Eastern Railway since 1923.

Mr Gresley was for a number of years Locomotive Superintendent of the Great Northern Railway Company and since 1923 has been Chief Mechanical Engineer of the London North Eastern Railway [*sic*].

His work as mechanical engineer has been outstanding in the advanced design of both locomotive and rolling stock. He has played a prominent part in the International Railway Congresses at Madrid and Cairo and has served on departmental committees on automatic train control and electrification rules.

He is a past President of the Institution of Locomotive Engineers and a Member of the Council of Mechanical Engineers.

Author's Note
Despite what Gresley himself claimed and has been quoted elsewhere, his knighthood clearly was awarded to him for his work as Chief Mechanical Engineer of the LNER, so creating a precedent concerning the award of Honours to senior railway staff (*Chapter Twelve*).

Tributes

In a letter from his daughter Vi Godfrey to T. Henry Turner, after her father's death.

After my dear mother's death in 1929 I became virtually my father's hostess and confidant, resulting in a great love and complete understanding for one another, and involving much travelling abroad with him and meeting many interesting people. I remember in Brussels on one occasion meeting Dr Dortmüller, who was head of all transport in Germany, and he told me that in Germany my father was recognised as the most outstanding engineer in Europe.

In spite of his brilliant brain, he loved a simple life in the country best, with his grandchildren and his dogs and shooting and fishing. He was a most understanding man, and very kind, with a ridiculous sense of humour and full of enjoying life. He was much loved by a large circle of friends and was the life and fun of any party. I can remember when we were living in Hertfordshire he would often say to me after dinner 'Let's go and watch the night express go by' and we would drive off to an open stretch near Hatfield and wait until we heard it coming, always the exact time my father expected from King's Cross, and after it had flashed by on its long journey to Edinburgh, we would drive home again.

Note by Toram Beg (Norman McKillop) a Haymarket driver, in his book 'The Lighted Flame'

The first time I clapped eyes on on his Pacifics I could not believe my eyes . . . it was an almost complete liaison between the designer and the Engineman.

Letter from an LMS fireman signing himself 'J.M.', Lanark

This letter concerns the running and working of N.E. and L.M.S. engines, as I am an L.M.S. fireman , and have recently experienced a run of some 60 miles on one of Gresley's A3 Pacifics on an express train.

I would like some of our drivers and firemen to read this, as I think it would interest them.

During the run on the A3, I thought I was sitting inside a first-class coach, compared with our 'Black 5s', as during a revolution of our 5's wheels you get lifted off the seat about four times. Comparing the two firemen, the N.E. man has a gentleman's life, as the L.M.S. men are always shovelling coal, and fighting for steam, which we don't always get. From my point of view, I think that the L.N.E.R. has the best foot-plate, as the driver and fireman can sit back and enjoy a good seat with a leather back.

I could write a book about the two engines, but space forbids, so here's hoping the National engine will be one of Sir Nigel Gresley's.

Author's note
This letter was discovered in an LNER file; its origin its not known. It appears to have been written soon after Nationalisation. But surely the anonymous fireman must have had more than one 60 mile run, before coming to this conclusion?

Letter from Sir Nigel Gresley to Driver A.J. Taylor, following his award of the OBE

May 26th, 1937

My dear Taylor,

I was delighted when I read in the papers of the great honour which has been conferred on you, and I am writing to send you my warmest congratulations. The honour is one in which your colleagues can feel that they have a share. But in view of your memorable achievement on that first record breaking run with the Silver Jubilee, you have I feel thoroughly deserved the honour - you were the first to show what one of my engines can really do.

I expect you have been inundated with letters of congratulation, and mine though late is nevertheless sincere.

 With kind regards,
    Yours sincerely
       H. Nigel Gresley

Letter from William Whitelaw to Nigel Gresley, 9th September, 1937

My dear Gresley,

I think that *Golden Fleece* and *Flying Shuttle* are both good names for the Leeds engines. Bye the bye I had better let you know that Thom has my instructions to name the 100th Pacific *Sir Nigel Gresley*, so that's that.

 Yours sincerely
    Wm Whitelaw

Editor's Note
This shows that the Directors were at least conversant with naming policy. *Flying Shuttle* should of course have been *Golden Shuttle*.

Letter from William Stanier to Sir Nigel Gresley, 4th July, 1938

My dear Gresley,

What a magnificent effort. Sincerest congratulations on the fine performance of 'The Mallard' yesterday.

I shall be very interested in seeing the details of the run and particulars of the engine working at some future time.

 Yrs very sincerely,
    W.A. Stanier

Greetings Telegram from Lady Wedgwood to Sir Nigel Gresley, 4th July, 1938

 Three cheers for the Mallard. LMS out for a duck. Iris.

Sir Nigel feeds his mallards in the garden at Salisbury Hall, *c.*1937 *Tim Godfrey*

Memory of Sir Nigel Gresley, by H.Harper, his personal clerk

At the outbreak of the war, Gresley's personal staff moved out to Watton-at-Stone. I lived at Enfield and travelled home each evening by a car lift to Welwyn station, thence train to New Barnet and bus to Enfield. By autumn of 1940 I was feeling the strain of this extra travelling, and also of ARP (*Air Raid Precautions*) duties in Enfield. As a result, for the first time in my life, I must have displayed irritability in the presence of Sir Nigel. He leaned back in his chair, stared at me, and said 'Harper, you need a break. Take a fortnight's holiday at Torquay with your wife'. He produced from his desk a book of Great Western Railway first class free passes and wrote out one for each of us. He signed them without reference to the GWR.

Recollection by T. Henry Turner, of the last occasions on which he saw his chief, Sir Nigel Gresley

On September 10th, 1940, I was on a routine visit to my laboratory at Stratford. There were three air raids that day, and the staff went to their shelters. I went down to the office of the Mechanical Engineer, Mr Carr, and found him and Sir Nigel standing at the entrance to the big arch through which locomotives could enter. I was carrying the normal tin hat and gas mask, but Sir Nigel had none. I offered him mine but he did not want to wear it, so neither did I. After a while a bomb went off a long way in front of us, and then the all clear went. Sir Nigel and I were driven by road to King's Cross passing roped off craters with unexploded bombs, and a crashed German fighter plane. That night I stayed in our King's Cross Hotel, and there were eight hours of air raid warning. I next saw Sir Nigel in his office at 10 am on 20th December, and stayed in the hotel for two nights. Three weeks later, the Stratford laboratory was burned out by an incendiary bomb, but most of the apparatus and furniture had been moved to Doncaster on Sir Nigel's instructions. I did not see him again, as he died on April 5th at his home.

Locomotive Classes designed by Sir Nigel Gresley

Date First Introduced	Type	LNER class	Driving wheels ft in.		Cylinders dia. x stroke inches	Boiler pressure lb./sq. in.	Remarks
1912	2-6-0	K1	5	8	20 x 26	180	Rebuilt to class K2
1912	0-6-0	J6	5	2	19 x 26	170	Modification of Ivatt design built 1911
1913	2-8-0	O1	4	8	21 x 28	180	
1913	0-6-0T	J50	4	8	18½ x 26	170	Original with smaller boiler, class J51
1914	2-6-0	K2	5	8	20 x 26	180	
1918	2-8-0	O2	4	8	18 x 26	180	3-cylinder with original valve gear
1920	2-6-0	K3	5	8	18½ x 26	180	3-cylinder with 6 ft boiler
1920	0-6-2T	N2	5	8	19 x 26	170	Improved Ivatt N1
1921	2-8-0	O2	4	8	18½ x 26	180	Standard 3-cylinder with simple valve gear
1922	4-6-2	A1	6	8	20 x 26	180	All but the first one rebuilt to A3 class
1925	2-8-2	P1	5	2	20 x 26	180	
1925	2-8-0+0-8-2T	U1	4	8	18½ x 26	180	Unique Garratt
1926	0-6-0	J38	4	8	20 x 26	180	
1926	0-6-0	J39	5	2	20 x 26	180	
1927	4-6-2	A3	6	8	19 x 26	220	'Super-Pacifics'
1927	4-4-0	D49	6	8	17 x 26	180	'Shire' and 'Hunt' classes
1928	4-6-0	B17	6	8	17½ x 26	200	'Sandringham' and 'Footballer' classes
1929	4-6-4	W1	6	8	12 x 26 hp 20 x 26 lp	450	Water tube boiler 4-cylinder compound
1930	2-6-2T	V1	5	8	16 x 26	180	Some reboilered to V3
1934	2-8-2	P2	6	2	21 x 26	220	Cock o 'the North
1935	4-6-2	A4	6	8	18½ x 26	250	Streamlined Pacifics
1936	2-6-2	V2	6	2	18½ x 26	220	'Green Arrow' class
1937	2-6-0	K4	5	2	18½ x 26	200	
1937	4-6-4	W1	6	8	20 x 26	250	Rebuilt from experimental high-pressure locomotive
1939	2-6-2T	V3	5	8	16 x 26	200	Higher pressure V1 locomotive
1941	2-6-2	V4	5	8	15 x 26	250	Bantam Cock
1941	Bo+Bo	EM1			electric		Prototype for MSW electrification

Acknowledgements

In preparing the Gresley story, I have been at pains to investigate as many sources as possible, published and unpublished, the more important of which are listed in the bibliography. I have been greatly helped by access to material held in the Public Record Office, Kew; the libraries of the Institutions of Civil, Mechanical and Electrical Engineers; the National Railway Museum, York; and the British Library of Political and Economic Science. But a great deal has come from individual recollection, from friends and relatives, and from many railwaymen who knew or worked for Sir Nigel, sadly no longer with us. Among these are the Chief Mechanical Engineers, Freddie Harrison and Terry Miller, as well as Alec Emerson and Norman Newsome, who were on Gresley's staff at King's Cross, and Eric Trask, for many years a senior engineer in the locomotive running department.

The book could not have been completed without the substantial technical help and guidance readily offered by George Carpenter, who transformed the text from a first draft into the comprehensive volume we now have. He has also given special assistance in providing his own historical and personal recollections, notably of the eminent French engineer, André Chapelon, whose advice was greatly valued by Gresley. Ian Gardiner, sometime Director of Engineering of the British Railways Board, has offered information from a later generation of railway engineers. Peter Townend has provided a unique contribution from his first hand acquaintance with Gresley locomotives, and Peter Coster, Allan Garraway, Richard Hardy and Jack Somers, have all come forward with their reminiscences. I have been fortunate in being presented with the work of T. Henry Turner, a great admirer of his onetime chief, and who had undertaken original research into the family. Fellow members of the Gresley Society, *Sir Nigel Gresley* Locomotive Preservation Trust, and the LNER Study Group whom I have consulted have been most supportive: in particular John Aylard, Bert Collins, Andrew Dow, Geoff Goslin, Peter Hall, Bernard Harding, Peter Holmes, Doug Landau, Julian Riddick, Peter Rodgers, and Willie Yeadon. I count myself fortunate to have been able to discuss topics with them over the 20 years this project has been coming to fruition. If in this list of acknowledgements, I have unwittingly omitted any name or source, I can only apologise for the oversight. So many have been involved. Of course, any factual errors are my responsibility.

I must make special mention of Sir Nigel's family, especially his daughters Vi and Marjorie, who in the period during which I made their acquaintance were generous in providing recollections of their beloved father. Vi's husband, Geoffrey Godfrey - himself the son of an illustrious father, the musician Sir Dan Godfrey - gave me access to family records and other treasures, and I continue to be indebted to Tim Godfrey, who can claim that both of his eminent grandfathers received knighthoods. Other descendants of the Gresleys, including Penelope Rigby-Hall and Peter Aldridge, must be mentioned as well as those who helped me with the Fullagars, John and Winifred Fullagar, Jennifer Atkins, and Yvonne Fullagar-Watterson, of Sydney, Australia.

Special thanks are due to Tony Roche, President of the Institution of Mechanical Engineers, for contributing the Foreword, and Sir Michael Moore, Director-General, for his support. Permission was readily given for the reproduction of the portrait of Sir Nigel, painted in his Presidential year, 1936, which hangs in the Institution's Lecture Theatre. Keith Moore, the Institution's Librarian, has been most helpful in opening the archives for me.

Lastly, as always, I acknowledge the help and support of my wife, Rose Mary, not least for taking part in many of the interviews and asking the kind of questions which I tend to overlook, but also for percipient reading of countless drafts, until the final version emerged.

Bibliography

For those wishing to read more about the Gresley dynasty, Falconer Madan's *The Gresleys of Drakelowe,* (Oxford, printed for private subscription, 1899) is the main source. He was related to the family, a Fellow of Brasenose College, and Librarian of the Bodleian. A number of copies remain in private collections, and several have been acquired by County Libraries and Record Offices. The narrative is surprisingly readable, and is full of interest. Where there is a conflict of source information, I have generally followed Madan. Other studies include L.G. Pine, *They came with the Conqueror* (1954) and unpublished manuscripts by V.A. Shaw, *A Brief History of the Gresley Family,* and Joanna Gresley, *Netherseale Past and Present.* Information on the history of Drakelowe has been published by the Central Electricity Generating Board, and there have been various articles in the *Burton Daily Mail, Derbyshire Life,* and similar journals, by Robin Innes-Smith and others.

Much more has been written about the career and work of Sir Nigel, although there are a number of books which are no more than superficial. Among those which deserve to be more widely known are the trilogy of biographies of Great Northern Railway locomotive engineers by F.A.S. Brown. (He had hoped to become a Doncaster apprentice, but failed on account of his lack of height.) Inspired by Bert Spencer's paper *The Development of LNER Locomotive Design,* read before the Institution of Locomotive Engineers in 1947, Brown made friends with staff at Doncaster, and took note of their recollections. Two of his books are *Nigel Gresley: Locomotive Engineer* (Ian Allan 1961), and *From Stirling to Gresley* (OPC 1974). I met him shortly before his death in 1981, and subsequently acquired a number of his photographs, which are now in the archives of the Great Northern Railway Society.

For a detailed commentary on the design and performance of Sir Nigel's most famous locomotives, by far the best is by Peter Townend, writing with the authority of several years as shedmaster at King's Cross, *East Coast Pacifics at Work* (Ian Allan 1982); his *Top Shed* (Ian Allan 1975) and an album of colour photographs, *The A4 Pacifics,* (Ian Allan 1989) are also recommended. O.S. Nock's *The Locomotives of Sir Nigel Gresley* (Railway Publishing Co. 1945) is an early summary of Gresley's work, whilst the same author's *The Gresley Pacifics* (David and Charles 1982) contains much detail on these locomotives. For information on classes and individual engines, essential reading is contained in the Railway Correspondence and Travel Society's multi-part series *Locomotives of the LNER,* edited by Eric Fry, supplemented by Norman Groves' *Great Northern Railway Locomotive History* (vols 3a and 3b) from the same Society. Willie Yeadon's multi-volume *Register of LNER Locomotives,* currently published by Book Law, contains photographs and histories of individual locomotives. George Carpenter's translation of André Chapelon's volume *La Locomotive a Vapeur* (Camden 2000) provides a comprehensive account of the work of this eminent French engineer, who was a close friend of Gresley.   Other books containing relevant information are *Master Builders of Steam* by H.A.V. Bulleid (Ian Allan 1963), *Gresley and Stanier* by John Bellwood and David Jenkinson (National Railway Museum 1976), *The LNER 2-8-2 and 2-6-2 Classes* by J.F. Clay and J. Cliffe (Ian Allan 1973), *Great Northern Steam* by W.A. Tuplin (Ian Allan 1971).   Sandy Mullay's *Non-Stop!* (Alan Sutton 1989) and *Streamlined Steam* (David and Charles 1994) offer useful commentary on the LNER and LMS services between London and Scotland.   A history of the Association of Railway Locomotive Engineers, in which Gresley played a leading part, may be found in the *Minutes of the ARLE*, which I have compiled and published privately.   Two short books worth reading are Eric Bannister's *Trained by Sir Nigel Gresley* (Dalesman 1984), and notes prepared by Derrick Hasted for the Centenary Commemoration Excursion of the A4 Locomotive Society, 30th April, 1977.

Gresley's many contributions to carriage design are well described and tabulated in books by Michael Harris, notably *GNR and ECJS Carriages* (Oakwood, 1995), *LNER Carriages* (Atlantic 1996) and *LNER Standard Gresley Coaches* (Mallard Books, 1999).   *East Coast Joint Stock* by Ken Hoole (OPC 1993) offers another specialised study.   David Jenkinson's *British Railway Carriages of the 20th Century* (Patrick Stephens, two vols 1988/90) also contains much of interest.   For Gresley's work in wagon design see *A Pictorial Record of LNER Wagons,* by Peter Tatlow (Pendragon 1998).   Norman Newsome's account of *The Development of LNER Carriage and Wagon Design* springs from his period as Gresley's assistant in this area, and was given as a Paper to the Locomotive Engineers in 1948, complementing Spencer's paper on locomotives.

Histories of the LNER, containing information on the work of Sir Nigel, include *The London & North Eastern Railway* by Cecil J. Allen (Ian Allan, 1966), *A History of the LNER* by Michael Bonavia (George Allen & Unwin, 3 vols, 1982) and my own *LNER* (Ian Allan, 1986, now in its third printing.)

Many railway periodicals feature articles on Gresley's work, and in particular his memory is kept alive by a number of specialist societies, notably the Gresley Society Trust, *Sir Nigel Gresley* Locomotive Preservation Trust (owners of *Sir Nigel Gresley*), the LNER Study Group, the Stephenson Locomotive Society, and the Great Northern Railway Society, each of which publishes its own journal. Finally, the A1 Steam Locomotive Trust is engaged in the construction of a brand new 'A1' 4-6-2, the linear descendent of Gresley's Pacifics, the progress of which is reported in their journal *Pioneer.*

The illustrations are of course an integral part of the story. Where possible, new photographs are included, but where specific details require emphasis, as in locomotive profiles, a few more familiar views are seen. The Gresley Society possesses a substantial photograph collection, many acquired originally from LNER or early BR sources, while others have been supplied by individual photographers or societies, for which I am grateful.   However, despite serious efforts, it has not been possible to identify the sources of all photographs. Diagrams have mainly been redrawn from the originals in Bert Spencer's paper of 1947.

Index

References to illustrations are shown in **Bold**